D1544056

BIBLICAL NATURAL LAW

Biblical Natural Law

A Theocentric and Teleological Approach

MATTHEW LEVERING

OXFORD
UNIVERSITY PRESS

OXFORD

UNIVERSITY PRESS

Great Clarendon Street, Oxford OX2 6DP

Oxford University Press is a department of the University of Oxford.
It furthers the University's objective of excellence in research, scholarship,
and education by publishing worldwide in

Oxford New York

Auckland Cape Town Dar es Salaam Hong Kong Karachi
Kuala Lumpur Madrid Melbourne Mexico City Nairobi
New Delhi Shanghai Taipei Toronto

With offices in

Argentina Austria Brazil Chile Czech Republic France Greece
Guatemala Hungary Italy Japan Poland Portugal Singapore
South Korea Switzerland Thailand Turkey Ukraine Vietnam

Oxford is a registered trade mark of Oxford University Press
in the UK and in certain other countries

Published in the United States
by Oxford University Press Inc., New York

© Matthew Levering 2008

The moral rights of the authors have been asserted
Database right Oxford University Press (maker)

First published 2008

British Library Cataloguing in Publication Data

Data available

Library of Congress Cataloging in Publication Data
Levering, Matthew, 1971-
Biblical natural law : a theocentric and teleological approach / Matthew Levering.
p. cm.
Includes index.
ISBN 978-0-19-953529-3 (alk. paper)
1. Natural law–Biblical teaching. 2. Law (Theology)–Biblical teaching.
3. Christianity and law. 4. Natural law. I. Title.
BS680.L33L48 2008
241'.2–dc22 2007043999

Typeset by SPI Publisher Services, Pondicherry, India
Printed in Great Britain
on acid-free paper by
Biddles Ltd., King's Lynn, Norfolk

ISBN 978-0-19-953529-3

1 3 5 7 9 10 8 6 4 2

Acknowledgements

This book began under the tutelage of my colleagues Marc Guerra and Steven Long in the summer of 2005. Marc met with me on a weekly basis to discuss key books and articles in the field of natural law doctrine, and Steve patiently answered my questions at a theology faculty retreat. Much of what is good in this book is owed to them.

Joseph Good, a librarian at Ave Maria University, and Andrew Mullally helped me to obtain important secondary literature on the topic of natural law; many thanks to them. Other friends generously assisted the development of the manuscript. Jörgen Vijgen, to whom I am once again indebted, read and critiqued an early draft. Andrew Hofer, OP, and Guy Mansini, OSB, offered highly valuable criticisms on later drafts. Graham McAleer helped me with the chapter that engages his work, and Cyril O'Regan kindly read the section on Hegel. Steve Long greatly improved the Introduction and the final chapter. Romanus Cessario, OP, generously read the penultimate draft. Thanks also for the excellent suggestions made by Christopher Kaczor and an anonymous reviewer for Oxford University Press.

I completed the book under the auspices of the Myser Fellowship at the Center for Ethics and Culture at the University of Notre Dame. For encouraging me to pursue the Fellowship, I am grateful to my dean, Michael Dauphinais, and my department chair, Father Matthew Lamb. David Solomon gave me the Fellowship at his Center, and his larger-than-life personality, intelligence, and wit are a joy to behold. I have also had the privilege of getting to know his collaborators, among them Dan McInerny, Ralph McInerny, Alasdair MacIntyre, John O'Callaghan, and Elizabeth Kirk, as well as the Center's Senior Fellow for 2006–2007, Kevin Flannery, SJ. Special thanks are owed to Thomas Hibbs, Michael Sherwin, OP, and Russell Hittinger for recommending me for the Fellowship. Thanks also to Joseph Torchia, OP, and Gregory LaNave for publishing an earlier version of Chapter 3 in *The Thomist*. Tom Perridge skilfully guided the manuscript through Oxford University Press, and Louise Mitchell graciously prepared the bibliography.

I wish to thank all the other friends who continue to do so much to encourage me in the theological vocation, as well as my parents, in-laws, and brother for their love. My children David, Andrew, Irene, John, and Daniel are a delight: may God bless them! This book is dedicated to my greatest friend, my wife Joy: I 'give thanks to God always for you' (2 Thess. 1:3).

Contents

Introduction

This study proposes that the full scope of natural law doctrine is learned best by means of a dialogue between biblical exegesis, theology, and philosophy, where each enriches the other. Whereas Enlightenment thinkers generally assumed that the 'book of Scripture' would only mystify and distort the reading of the 'book of nature', more recently both 'books', separated from each other, have been deemed unreliable. On this view, the appeal in ethics either to natural law or to Scripture is no longer viable. As the biblical scholar John J. Collins, a Catholic, approvingly remarks, 'The Bible can no more provide us with objective, transcendent moral certainties than can natural law'.[1]

Pace this view, this study seeks to uncover once again the fruitfulness for moral theology of reuniting the two 'books'. Most biblical scholars today who treat the topic of ethics in the Bible, especially as regards the New Testament, do so without reference to 'natural law'. Natural law seems for such scholars to be a foreign philosophical concept that can be ignored in ethics rooted in the Bible, and that indeed may pose a threat to such ethics, since 'natural law' often has been used in Protestant and Catholic liberalism to advance a public ethics grounded solely in the exercise of reason apart from any relation to God. Chapter 1 therefore explores contemporary ethics and exegesis, specifically through the work of the Protestant

---

[1] John J. Collins, 'The Biblical Vision of the Common Good', in his *Encounters with Biblical Theology* (Minneapolis, MN: Fortress Press, 2005), 78. On this view neither the 'book of nature' nor the 'book of Scripture' is intelligible in a unified fashion. Collins affirms nonetheless that the Bible remains relevant to contemporary ethics, both because of its influence upon Western culture, and because it is the 'foundational document' of the Christian tradition.

scholars Richard B. Hays, Allen Verhey, and John Barton and the Jewish scholar David Novak. Hays and Barton are biblical scholars with particular expertise in the New Testament and Old Testament respectively. Verhey is a moral theologian, and Novak a theologian and philosopher. Other than Novak, these scholars work entirely outside the guild of natural law thinkers. The chapter engages their work so as to explore three questions: whether there are biblical warrants for natural law doctrine, what kind of natural law doctrine biblical texts support, and what happens when natural law doctrine is left out of constructive ethics arising from the Bible. The chapter proposes that biblical revelation supports a theocentric and teleological understanding of natural law, and also that the oppositions that some find between natural law and the life of grace as well as between divine commandments and natural law are unwarranted.

Chapter 2 then sets forth the modern philosophical movement away from the theocentric and teleological natural law doctrine that we identified in the Bible. The chapter contrasts teleological (Cicero) and theocentric (Augustine) natural law accounts with the anthropocentric philosophical accounts of René Descartes, Thomas Hobbes, John Locke, David Hume, Jean-Jacques Rousseau, Immanuel Kant, Georg W. F. Hegel, and Friedrich Nietzsche. By narrowing human teleologies to self-interest or self-construction, the anthropocentric shift inverts the biblically revealed human teleology of self-giving imitation of the divine *ecstasis*.

When modern thinkers bracket the biblical Creator and his ordering wisdom from their natural law reflection, they replace this viewpoint variously with natural inclinations (self-interest) and human rationality (self-construction). For the Christian, the question then becomes how natural inclinations relate to the rational freedom that is the life of grace witnessed to in Scripture and the lives of the saints. Chapter 3 engages these questions by means of a substantial dialogue with the views of three scholars: Martin Rhonheimer, Servais Pinckaers, and Graham McAleer. This chapter argues that the natural inclinations are the building-blocks of natural law in the human person because they express the 'ecstatic' body–soul dynamism of the person, an ecstatic dynamism that fits with the biblical promise of interpersonal communion of God.[2]

Lastly, Chapter 4 investigates the relationship between law and love, so as to understand further the place of natural law in the biblical ethics of Christ's New Law. The chapter first sets forth the standard contrast between 'law' as constricting the natural inclinations and 'love' as transcending the limitations of both law and natural inclinations. Suggesting that this contrast is not adequate to the reality of either law or love, the chapter turns to Aquinas's detailed account of the character of natural law in relation to God's 'law' or ordering wisdom for creation's attainment of its end. Aquinas's analysis suggests how the intelligent receptivity and free body–soul *ecstasis* that characterize natural law as a participation in God's eternal law, also characterize the graced fulfilment of natural law in supernatural charity witnessed to by biblical revelation.[3] The synthesis of nature and grace exists in the eternal law.

Joseph Ratzinger, while still a Cardinal, summed up the perspective that governs this book in a recent dialogue with the president of the Italian Senate: 'The Christian is convinced that his or her faith opens up new dimensions of understanding, and above all that it helps reason to be itself. There is the true heritage of faith (the Trinity, the divinity of Christ, the sacraments, and so on), but there is also the knowledge for which faith provides evidence, knowledge that is later recognized as rational and pertaining to reason as such'.[4] The natural law is 'rational and pertaining to reason as such', but it is

---

[2] 'Inclination' here must not be understood as one passion or sensual drive among others, but as a more fundamental ordering inscribed in the body–soul constitution of human beings. See in this regard, e.g. Henry B. Veatch, 'Telos and Teleology in Aristotelian Ethics', in Veatch, *Swimming Against the Current in Contemporary Philosophy* (Washington, DC: Catholic University of America Press, 1990), 99–116.

[3] In *A Preserving Grace: Protestants, Catholics, and Natural Law*, ed. Michael Cromartie (Grand Rapids, MI: Eerdmans, 1997), Carl E. Braaten offers a 'Response' (31–40) to Russell Hittinger's essay in the same volume. From a Lutheran perspective, Braaten argues that Hittinger is saying nearly the same thing as Protestant theologians have been saying since the Reformation. In the conversation that follows, Hittinger replies that it is indeed unthinkable to 'posit man-without-God as a normative fact for Catholic moral discourse' (41).

[4] Joseph Ratzinger and Marcello Pera, *Without Roots: The West, Relativism, Christianity, Islam*, trans. Michael F. Moore (New York: Basic Books, 2006), 130.

also 'knowledge for which faith provides evidence'. While all human beings know the natural law at least to some degree, explanations of the character and content of the natural law are greatly assisted by faith, and thus also by biblical revelation.[5]

NATURE AND GRACE

Before entering into the chapters of our study, we should examine a bit more closely the meaning, as regards natural law, of Ratzinger's claim that faith (and thus biblical revelation) helps 'reason to be itself'. At its deepest level, this claim has to do with the relationship of nature and grace. In order to examine this relationship in the context of natural law doctrine, John Courtney Murray's famous study of natural law and American political life, *We Hold These Truths: Catholic Reflections on the American Proposition*, offers a helpful starting point.

Murray remarks that '[i]t would not, of course, be difficult to show that the doctrine [of natural law] is, in germinal fashion, scriptural'.[6] He goes on to observe that natural law, while pointing the way to 'manhood' rather than 'sainthood', is hardly opposed to the latter:

the law of nature, which prescribes humanity, still exists at the interior of the Gospel invitation, which summons to perfection. What the follower of Christ chooses to perfect is, and can only be, a humanity. And the lines of human

---

[5] The distinction between natural law and explanations of natural law is important. As Ralph McInerny writes, 'It would be odd for anyone to say that everyone's grasp of fundamental guides for moral action involves explicit recognition of the existence of God. But it is not odd to say that any adequate account or theory of such fundamental guides must make appeal to God's existence' (McInerny, 'Foreword' to Fulvio Di Blasi's excellent *God and the Natural Law: A Rereading of Thomas Aquinas*, trans. David Thunder (South Bend, IN: St Augustine's Press, 2006), xi–xii, at xii). For further discussion of the distinction between natural law and explanations of natural law, see also McInerny's eloquent essay *Implicit Moral Knowledge*, ed. Fulvio Di Blasi (Rubbettino: Soveria Mannelli, 2006).

[6] John Courtney Murray, SJ, *We Hold These Truths: Catholic Reflections on the American Proposition* (1960; Lanham, MA: Sheed & Ward, 1988), 296–7. Mention should also be made here of Murray's contemporary Yves R. Simon, whose *The Tradition of Natural Law: A Philosopher's Reflections* (1965; New York: Fordham University Press, 1992) was put together from 1958 course lectures by Simon and, after Simon's death, by his student Vukan Kuic.

perfection are already laid down in the structure of man's nature. Where else could they be found? The Christian call is to transcend nature, notably to transcend what is noblest in nature, the faculty of reason. But it is not a call to escape from nature, or to dismantle nature's own structure, and least of all to deny that man is intelligent, that nature is intelligible, and that nature's intelligibilities are laws for the mind that grasps them. In so far as they touch the moral life, the energies of grace, which are the action of the Holy Spirit, quicken to new and fuller life the dynamisms of nature, which are resident in reason.[7]

Writing in the midst of the struggle for civil rights and little more than a decade after the Holocaust (as well as the Nazis' practice of abortion and euthanasia of those deemed undesirable), Murray recognized the need for society's positive law to be informed by sound natural law doctrine, as a support to the interior experience of knowing, however vaguely, natural law principles.[8] With this goal in view, Murray denies that classical natural law doctrine has any uniquely 'Roman Catholic presuppositions'[9] that would incapacitate it for application in a pluralist society such as the United States. On the contrary, its presuppositions, which can be verified by rational enquiry, are 'that man is intelligent; that reality is intelligible; and that reality, as grasped by intelligence, imposes on the will the obligation that it be obeyed in its demands for action or abstention'.[10] These claims in turn require also belief in an orderer who has an 'end' in mind, a provident Creator.[11]

---

[7] Murray, *We Hold These Truths*, 298. For an introduction to the account of human 'nature' that Murray presumes, one might see Jan Aertsen, *Nature and Creature: Thomas Aquinas's Way of Thought* (New York: E. J. Brill, 1988). Compare this view to the modern understanding of nature as a mechanism: Steven Vogel, *Against Nature: The Concept of Nature in Critical Theory* (Albany, NY: State University of New York Press, 1996).

[8] As Russell Hittinger observes, 'positive laws, both divine and human, are crucial to the way we come to learn about the natural law' (Hittinger, 'Theology and Natural Law Theory', *Communio* 17 (1990): 402–8, at 408). Cf. 407 where Hittinger points out that 'Aquinas's account of the *lex vetus* and the *lex nova* contains an historical analysis of what becomes of natural law reasoning in the absence of the covenantal context of law'.

[9] Murray, *We Hold These Truths*, 109.   [10] Ibid.

[11] In an admirable passage, Murray states that natural law requires four key theses: 'Natural law supposes a realist epistemology, that asserts the real to be the measure of knowledge, and also asserts the possibility of intelligence reaching the real, *i.e.*, the nature of things—in the case, the nature of man as a unitary and constant concept beneath all individual differences. Secondly, it supposes a metaphysic of nature,

Thus while affirming natural law's metaphysical presuppositions, including God's eternal law and natural teleology, Murray holds out hope that such natural law doctrine will be embraced by contemporary legal scholars, jurists, and politicians so as to become 'the dynamic of a new "age of order" '.[12] Taken as a whole, Murray thinks, the claims of natural law, including belief in the Creator God, fit with 'the tradition of reason as emergent in developing form in the special circumstances of American political-economic life' as of 1960.[13] If Lockean individualism and even Marxist socialism have exerted profound influence in American political theory, why not a theocentric and teleological natural law doctrine? Such an account of natural law, he argues, would greatly assist the ongoing formation of just political order in the United States.[14]

David L. Schindler, however, challenges *We Hold These Truths* on the grounds that Murray's understanding of 'nature' is representative of the extrinsicism of nature and grace that Henri de Lubac worked so hard to overcome. Schindler argues,

> For Murray, grace's influence on nature takes the form of assisting nature to realize its own finality; the ends proper to grace and nature otherwise remain each in its own sphere. For de Lubac, on the contrary, grace's influence takes the form of directing nature from within to serve the end given in grace; the ends proper to grace and nature remain distinct, even as the natural end is placed *within*, internally subordinated to, the supernatural end. For Murray, then, the result is an insistence on a dualism between eternal (ultimate) end

especially the idea that nature is a teleological concept, that the "form" of the thing is its "final cause," the goal of its becoming; in the case, that there is a natural inclination in man to become what in nature and destination he is—to achieve the fullness of his own being. Thirdly, it supposes a natural theology, asserting that there is a God, Who is eternal Reason, *Nous*, at the summit of the order of being, Who is the author of all nature, and Who wills that the order of nature be fulfilled in all its purposes, as these are inherent in the natures found in the order. Finally, it supposes a morality, especially the principle that for man, a rational being, the order of nature is not an order of necessity, to be fulfilled blindly, but an order of reason and therefore of freedom. The order of being that confronts his intelligence is an order of "oughtness" for his will; the moral order is a prolongation of the metaphysical order into the dimensions of human freedom' (ibid., 327–8).

[12] Ibid., 334–5.   [13] Ibid.

[14] No one since Murray has made this case better than Hadley Arkes. See Arkes, *First Things: An Inquiry into the First Principles of Morals and Justice* (Princeton: Princeton University Press, 1986).

and temporal (penultimate) ends. . . . Again, neither theologian denies the distinctness of the goals proper to citizenship and to temporal existence. The difference lies rather in the way each respectively conceives this distinctness: whether sanctity and citizenship, the temporal and the eternal, are understood as first within or as first outside or juxtaposed to each other; whether any resulting unity between them therefore comes about by way of 'integration' or, contrarily, by way of addition.[15]

Schindler proposes that Murray's accounting of the 'natural', including natural law, leads inevitably to a mere juxtaposition of 'secular' and 'sacred', rather than a deeper integration of 'secular' ends within the ultimate end identified by grace—a false juxtaposition that allows for the privatization of religion. Schindler is not denying the distinction between nature and grace: 'To be sure, there is a distinction between the orders of creation and redemption: no responsible Catholicism would deny this'.[16] But the distinction, he

[15] David L. Schindler, 'Religious Freedom, Truth, and American Liberalism: Another Look at John Courtney Murray', *Communio* 21 (1994): 696–741, at 732–3. A greatly different reading of de Lubac's *Surnaturel* is offered by John Milbank, *The Suspended Middle: Henri de Lubac and the Debate concerning the Supernatural* (Grand Rapids, MI: Eerdmans, 2005). Milbank argues that de Lubac provided 'an ontology between the field of pure immanent being proper to philosophy on the one hand, and the field of the revelatory event proper to theology on the other. This new ontological discourse concerned the paradoxical definition of human nature as intrinsically raised above itself to the "super-nature" of divinity. Since, as we shall see, for de Lubac all created nature was in some sense orientated to human nature, this paradoxical structure even extended to the constitution of all finite beings as such' (5). Suggesting that desire, not 'power' or 'capacity', should be the lens through which to view human nature, Milbank observes, 'For von Balthasar the issue is sometimes one of "how much" to grant to grace and "how much" to nature. But for de Lubac of course there can be no such question. Indeed that is the whole point' (67). The phrase 'the suspended middle' means that there can be no neat division of 'nature' and 'grace': rather, with Bulgakov and other Orthodox thinkers, one can hold 'grace' to be 'gratuitous' simply because 'a gift can be a gift without contrast to gift' (88). Even if one could then distinguish the 'two' gifts, I wonder whether one can successfully replace created 'powers' or 'capacities' with 'desires'. One certainly need not speak of created 'powers' or 'capacities' in a non-teleological, mechanistic sense. For criticism of Milbank's view, see Reinhard Hütter, '*Desiderium Naturale Visionis Dei—Est autem duplex hominis beatitudo sive felicitas*: Some Observations about Lawrence Feingold's and John Milbank's Recent Interventions in the Debate over the Natural Desire to See God', *Nova et Vetera* 5 (2007): 81–131, especially his summary of his position on 131. For similar concerns, treating Milbank's earlier studies, see Hans Boersma, 'On the Rejection of Boundaries: Radical Orthodoxy's Appropriation of St. Augustine', *Pro Ecclesia* 15 (2006): 418–47, especially 424–5.

[16] Schindler, 'Religious Freedom, Truth, and American Liberalism', 731.

suggests, needs to be worked out in a way that does not encourage, in a dualistic fashion, the privatization of faith. He explains, '[E]ver distinct from the sacred, the secular, for de Lubac, everywhere and always retains an ordering that is first *from within*, toward the end which is God in Jesus Christ'.[17]

As described by Schindler, Murray's view is that grace assists 'nature to realize its own finality'; but it should be noted Murray would also hold that graced capacities work through, by elevating, natural capacities, in order to attain the ultimate end of communion with the Trinity. It might also be observed that for Murray, too, 'the ends proper to grace and nature remain distinct' with the natural end being 'subordinated to the supernatural end'. If as Schindler says the two ends 'remain distinct', then what he terms the 'apparently subtle difference between de Lubac and Murray'[18] comes down for him largely to what it means for the natural end—metaphysically distinguishable—to be 'placed *within*' the supernatural end.

As we have seen, Schindler holds that it means that 'the secular, for de Lubac, everywhere and always retains an ordering that is first *from within*, toward the end which is God in Jesus Christ'. Human nature from within itself possesses an 'ordering' to the supernatural end. But if the 'ordering' implies that the natural capacities of human nature naturally ('*from within*') have Trinitarian communion as their 'end', then difficulties arise.[19] Since finite capacities are not on the same metaphysical level as Trinitarian communion, any 'ordering' intrinsic to the resources that belong to finite capacities as such, remains metaphysically on the level of creatures. No matter how far the movement of human intelligence and love extends, by its own resources,

---

[17] Ibid.   [18] Ibid., 733.

[19] This concern has been expressed by Steven A. Long, 'On the Possibility of a Purely Natural End for Man', *The Thomist* 64 (2000): 211–37. See also Long's 'On the Loss, and Recovery, of Nature as a Theonomic Principle: Reflections on the Nature/Grace Controversy', *Nova et Vetera* 5 (2007): 133–83, especially Long's point that 'the first impulse of de Lubac—the prime resort to teleology—is condign, but this resort must be to genuinely *natural teleology* as conditioning our reception of Revelation. For this natural conditioning... is part of the divine economy itself and not something alien or extrinsic to the divine governance' (178). For further insight into how Aquinas's treatment of the possibility of a natural end arises from a keen sense of the difference between the infinite Trinity and finite creatures, see Jean-Pierre Torrell, OP, 'Nature et grace chez Thomas d'Aquin', *Revue Thomiste* 101 (2001): 167–202.

it cannot extend to the entirely other, transcendent realm of Trinitarian communion—unless one holds that the distinction between human and divine has been blurred in creation. Schindler himself does not grant such a blurring: to repeat, he observes that for de Lubac 'the ends proper to grace and nature remain distinct' and that 'there is a distinction between the orders of creation and redemption'.

Schindler's fundamental concern is to avoid an understanding of the nature–grace relationship that, as he puts it, 'effectively replaces an understanding of the human act as constitutively oriented to God with an understanding of the human act as not constitutively oriented to God: "indifference" to God is placed (logically) before positive relation to God'.[20] Such 'positive relation' or constitutive orientation to God must be built into 'the *first meaning*' of the human act.[21] As Steven Long notes, however, 'Schindler suggests that distinguishing the natural and supernatural orderings of the person to God leaves us with a nature that is neutral with respect to God. But this is not the case. That nature is ordered to God in ways sublunary to those of grace does not make this ordering "neutral," nor the structuring of this order dispensable'.[22]

We can identify here, then, two foundational questions for natural law doctrine. First, can we legitimately speak of 'human nature' distinguished metaphysically from the action of (or the wound of the absence of) the grace of the Holy Spirit? Second, if we attempt to speak of human nature in this way, how do we avoid falling into a disjunction, rather than a distinction, between 'manhood' and 'sainthood' (in Murray's terms)? Schindler's later work provides further insight into these questions. On the one hand, he writes that 'God's invitation in Jesus Christ to share in his life, rooted in the

[20] Schindler, 'Religious Freedom, Truth, and American Liberalism', 721. See in the same vein Schindler, 'Charity, Justice, and the Church's Activity in the World', *Communio* 33 (2006): 346–67, at 362; idem, 'Christology and the *Imago Dei*: Interpreting *Gaudium et Spes*', *Communio* 23 (1996): 156–84, at 162.

[21] Schindler, 'Religious Freedom, Truth, and American Liberalism', 721. Schindler states here, 'All of this must be carefully understood: certainly Murray wants to affirm, and indeed in an important sense does affirm, that the human act is positively related to God, or at least must finally be so related for its full integrity. He nonetheless does not build this positive relation into the *first meaning* he accords the human act in his proposals for public order.'

[22] Steven A. Long, review of *Heart of the World, Center of the Church* by David L. Schindler, *Crisis* (June 1997): 50.

heart of man's moral consciousness, establishes an openness and restlessness anterior to all human decisions and actions....Moral norms, therefore, in their original nature as such in the one concrete order of history, cannot but be "formed" by this inner openness to and restlessness for the divine life embodied in Christ'.[23] Here the movement toward the divine good seems to be *established* by God's invitation in Christ (the grace of the Holy Spirit), and philosophical reflection on the capacities of human nature would seem to be trumped by theology.

Yet, a few sentences later, Schindler remarks, 'The movement proper to freedom from its beginning comes filled with "in-*form*-ation" given through the call of God, through the attractiveness of God as good. This always-in*form*ed desire is what may be termed love: human freedom is by nature love—a natural love, if you will'.[24] Here Schindler's position moves back toward that of Murray and Long: God creates human nature with a natural (not due to grace) body–soul *motio* toward God. In other words, God establishes, *in human nature itself*, an 'ecstatic' teleological grammar toward the good (ultimately God who draws). This natural ordering—for example 'natural love' in distinction from supernatural charity—is taken up and elevated in the call of God in Christ.[25] Displaying philosophically the *natural* ordering, precisely in its non-neutrality as described by Long, would on this view possess a significant role in formulating moral norms.

This point, interestingly, corresponds to a number of Schindler's recent comments regarding moral theology. Thus he observes with regard to *Veritatis Splendor*, 'If we are to recover the foundations of morality as conceived by *VS*, we must, as an anterior condition of this recovery, (re-)awaken the sense in which the cosmos and culture, each in its own way and in its original structure as such, bears the

---

[23] David L. Schindler, 'The Significance of World and Culture for Moral Theology: *Veritatis Splendor* and the "Nuptial-Sacramental" Nature of the Body', *Communio* 31 (2004): 111–42, at 116.

[24] Ibid.

[25] See Pope Benedict XVI, *Deus Caritas Est*; for discussion of the encyclical's presentation of the relationship of natural love and charity, see Serge-Thomas Bonino, OP, ' "Nature et grace" dans l'encyclique *Deus caritas est*', *Revue Thomiste* 105 (2005): 531–49.

"anticipatory signs, the expression and promise of the gift of self" '.[26] Or as he puts it earlier with respect to human bodiliness, 'The body, in its physiology as such, is not "pre-moral" but "moral": it bears an order characterized by "the anticipatory signs, the expression and promise of the gift of self, in conformity with the wise plan of the Creator" ([*Veritatis Splendor*] n. 48)'.[27] For his part, Long speaks of a hylomorphic 'teleological grammar' that belongs to moral action.[28] This 'teleological grammar' flows not simply from 'God's invitation in Jesus Christ to share in his life', but also from human natural capacities' created ordering toward the goods proper to human nature as such.

In answer to the two foundational questions raised above, therefore, we can say that the task of discerning the scope of the graced 'ecstatic' ordering of human nature cannot do without a properly philosophical analysis of human nature. Lacking such analysis of human nature's teleological ordering, one falls inevitably, no matter how nuanced one's theological appeals, into the historicism that Norbert Rigali has expressed through the distinction between a 'historical consciousness' and a 'classicist consciousness'. Rigali proposes that 'historical consciousness understands the intrinsic finality of human sexuality not as an abstract, seemingly self-contained purpose or set of purposes, but as the sexual finality of persons-in-time-and-history'.[29] As Rigali states, 'For historical consciousness, then, Christian moral reflection begins by asking: What is the Christian

---

[26] Schindler, 'The Significance of World and Culture for Moral Theology', 113. See also his 'Religion and Secularity in a Culture of Abstraction: On the Integrity of Space, Time, Matter, and Motion', in *The Strange New World of the Gospel: Re-Evangelizing in the Postmodern World*, ed. Carl E. Braaten and Robert W. Jenson (Grand Rapids, MI: Eerdmans, 2002), 32–54.

[27] Schindler, 'The Significance of World and Culture for Moral Theology', 112–13.

[28] See Steven A. Long, *The Teleological Grammar of the Moral Act* (Naples, FL: Sapientia Press, 2007), especially chapter 1. Jean Porter describes the resurgence of natural teleology among some scientists and philosophers of science in her *Nature as Reason: A Thomistic Theory of the Natural Law* (Grand Rapids, MI: Eerdmans, 2005), chapter 2. On natural teleology, see also Daniel McInerny, *The Difficult Good: A Thomistic Approach to Moral Conflict and Human Happiness* (New York: Fordham University Press, 2006), 55–71, 74–6.

[29] Norbert J. Rigali, SJ, 'Artificial Birth Control: An Impasse Revisited', *Theological Studies* 47 (1986): 681–90, at 690. Recent years have witnessed an outpouring of such argumentation in *Theological Studies* and elsewhere.

life and what can it authentically become in our time?'[30] In Rigali's hands, this distinction between 'historical' and 'classicist' consciousness comes to mean that no order of creation or natural teleology is discernible as a ground for the ethics of grace, as so the ongoing graced transformation can have no more than fluid moral norms. What Rigali calls the 'classicist view' is no more than a commitment to the intelligibility of the created order, a presumption that nature expresses the wisdom and goodness of God the Creator.[31]

How then does natural law rightly relate to the truth that 'manhood' always already has, by grace, an interior orientation toward fulfilment in 'sainthood'? The grace of the Holy Spirit brings about a personal communion with the Holy Trinity in supernatural charity, and yet this unfathomable elevation both heals and *perfects* the natural capacities of human nature. Put another way, the glorious 'discontinuity' of the grace of the Holy Spirit builds upon, due to the first gift of creation, a 'continuity' with respect to the *ecstatic* (self-giving rather than self-cleaving) dynamism of human nature toward its fulfilment, that is to say its 'teleological grammar' toward the good that attracts. This understanding of human nature, as Hittinger has remarked, grounds natural law in the Trinitarian creative act and thus upholds a 'theological view of nature as divine mission'.[32] When turned 'inward' toward the creature rather than 'outward' toward the divine source and goal, natural law is deformed. As the Orthodox

[30] Ibid., 688. On 'historical consciousness' see John Finnis, *'Historical Consciousness' and Theological Foundations* (Toronto: Pontifical Institute of Mediaeval Studies, 1992).

[31] Cf. Matthew L. Lamb, 'Nature Is Normative for Culture', *Nova et Vetera* 3 (2005): 153–62, at 161: 'Natural law is not constituted by human cultures or human traditions; it is constituted by the Eternal Law who is God, who alone can create.' A quite different set of claims is made by Larry Arnhart in *Darwinian Natural Right: The Biological Ethics of Human Nature* (Albany, NY: State University of New York Press, 1998), which equates Darwinian teleology (survival of the fittest) with the teleology of natural inclinations.

[32] Hittinger, 'Theology and Natural Law Theory', 405. Hittinger goes on to remark, 'Aquinas argued that the end of man is not man; nor is his end, *secundum naturam*, any finite thing or aggregate of finite things, including himself. Insofar as ethics concerns human *dirigere*, ordering actions toward ends, there cannot be, as von Balthasar rightly contends, a "self-evident intramundane ethics". Given the immanent powers and capacities of the human subject, the *telos* cannot be achieved simply through intramundane action ... Any effort to deduce categorical imperatives from the formal necessities of man's nature apart from friendship with God is to misunderstand Aquinas's natural law theory' (406).

moral theologian Vigen Guroian, citing Basil the Great, depicts the 'outward' or 'ecstatic' dynamism that natural law inscribes within the human person:

The natural law is counted as an image in human beings of the divine love which draws them toward the fulfillment of their nature, i.e., deification and union with the Godhead. Basil expressed this point of view in the following fashion: 'Instruction in divine law is not from without, but simultaneously with the formation of the creature—man, I mean—a kind of rational force was implanted in us like a seed, which, by an inherent tendency, impels us toward love.'[33]

A true appreciation of natural law comes about when human beings affirm natural law as God's wisdom for human *ecstasis* toward the goods connatural to human perfection. By means of this 'ecstatic' dynamism inscribed in human natural ordering toward ends, a dynamism healed and elevated by grace, God draws human beings to himself. Natural law thus forms an important part of the history of human beings' return to God. As Hittinger says, 'the basic story is this: God wants his bride back. Adam and Eve are created to be, eventually, married to God, not just to each other.'[34]

NATURAL LAW AS A SHARED HUMAN POSSESSION

If one is not careful, however, it might seem at this stage that knowledge of biblical revelation, or at least the gift of grace, is *necessary* for

[33] Vigen Guroian, *Incarnate Love: Essays in Orthodox Ethics* (Notre Dame, IN: University of Notre Dame Press, 1987), 21. As Guroian rightly observes, 'The person in whom Christ abides experiences the Law not as externally imposed rules and commandments but as an inner call to theanthropic life' (22). Guroian's point is echoed by Marc Ouellet in 'The Foundations of Ethics According to Hans Urs von Balthasar', *Communio* 17 (1990): 379–401. Ouellet writes in conclusion, 'It is only the proclamation of the true God that can decenter man from his unhealthy anthropocentrism and recenter him on Jesus, the one and only, who opens for him an infinite horizon of liberty, in love' (401). Revelation and grace do not constitute natural law, but they enable us to see more deeply into what is already inclinationally present within human nature, heal this nature of the effects of sin, and elevate human nature to a higher participation in the eternal law—the New Law.

[34] Russell Hittinger, in his comment during the conversation on Calvin transcribed in *A Preserving Grace: Protestants, Catholics, and Natural Law*, ed. Michael Cromartie (Grand Rapids, MI: Eerdmans, 1997), 102.

the discernment of natural law. On the contrary, natural law is operative, though impaired by sin and thus known in varying degrees, in all human beings who possess the use of reason. As Ralph McInerny observes, 'The natural law, as St. Paul remarks, is inscribed in our hearts. But knowing natural law does not entail knowing St. Paul.'[35] Although natural law mandates worship of God, it is not necessary to know even God's existence and Providence to know some natural law principles.[36] This is so because neither grace nor the wound of its absence, but rather the created order explains what David Novak calls the 'overlappings' in morality across cultures, for instance the prohibition of murder. Such overlappings belong to the natural capacity of the human person, due to the divine imprint bestowed in creation, to apprehend somewhat the eternal law, God's wisdom for human fulfilment.[37] Again, human beings are ordered to their supernatural good (personal communion with the Trinity) in a way that exploits, rather than sets aside, the natural capacities of the human person.

Yet, as Schindler is keenly aware, claims about 'overlappings' in morality across cultures originally made plausible the modern anthropocentric project of grounding a universal morality in the human nature (or the human mind), rather than in God. As we will

[35] Ralph McInerny, 'Thomistic Natural Law and Aristotelian Philosophy', in *St. Thomas Aquinas and the Natural Law Tradition: Contemporary Perspectives*, ed. John Goyette, Mark S. Latkovic, and Richard S. Myers (Washington, DC: Catholic University of America Press, 2004), 25–39, at 38. Hittinger points similarly to the distinction between 'knowing something because of a connatural avidity for an end, in contrast to enjoying a term of knowledge by virtue of reasoning it out' (Hittinger, 'Yves R. Simon on Law, Nature, and Practical Reason', in *Acquaintance with the Absolute*, ed. Anthony O. Simon (New York: Fordham University Press, 1998), 114).

[36] Thomas Aquinas recognizes the difficulty of coming to know God philosophically: 'the science to whose province it belongs to prove the existence of God, is the last of all to offer itself to human research, since it presupposes many other sciences: so that it would not be until late in life that man would arrive at the knowledge of God' (*Summa Theologiae* II–II, q. 2, a. 4; cf. ad 1). Similarly he observes regarding knowledge of God's Providence, accessible in theory to natural reason, 'By faith we hold many truths about God, which the philosophers were unable to discover by natural reason, for instance His providence and omnipotence, and that He alone is to be worshipped, all of which are contained in the one article of the unity of God' (II–II, q. 1, a. 8, ad 1).

[37] See David Novak, *Natural Law in Judaism* (Cambridge: Cambridge University Press, 1998); although see Hadley Arkes, *First Things*, 130 for the difficulty of evaluating the significance of such 'overlappings'. Cf. C. S. Lewis's description of what he calls the '*Tao*' in *The Abolition of Man: How Education Develops Man's Sense of Morality* (New York: Macmillan, 1955), 26–30, 56f.

see in Chapter 2, this anthropocentric project cut itself off from what makes 'nature' and 'law' plausible as concepts, and ended by turning 'natural law' on its head. The lesson that I draw from this history is that when natural law theory tries to distance itself from the God who has inscribed teleological ends in human beings—a God whose plan, given the disorder wrought by sin and death, becomes infinitely more plausible in Christ—then natural law theory, despite the cross-cultural 'overlappings', itself becomes distorted.

In other words: if, as Daniel McInerny remarks, 'even our most rudimentary grasp of the natural law precepts is a grasp of something that is an extrinsic cause of human acts, which binds the powers of our nature to some good',[38] how can one account for such an 'extrinsic cause' able to *bind* our 'nature' to its 'good'? This question plagues modern anthropocentric doctrines of natural law. Although 'knowing natural law does not entail knowing St. Paul', explaining natural law adequately is greatly assisted by knowing St Paul. And better explanations of natural law strengthen our ability to live in accord with God's wisdom for our fulfilment.

For his part, it should be noted, John Courtney Murray hoped to reclaim a theocentric understanding of 'natural law' for the public discourse of the United States with a full recognition of the teleological order of God's providence. Responding to an essay by John Rawls during a 1963 symposium, Murray—sounding much like Schindler—warns that Rawls evinces 'the will to remove from human law all manner of transcendental reference, and indeed any note of heteronomy, in the name of a morality of perfect personal autonomy'.[39] Murray affirms that he, Murray, stands 'within the older

---

[38] McInerny, *The Difficult Good*, 60. McInerny rightly notes, 'The notion of a providential God who promulgates his rule of reason through the inclinations of human nature presupposes much knowledge of God that is contestable—not the least of which being the very notion of God's existence. But here we must underscore that *quoadnos*, from the point of view of our cognition, it is not necessary to grasp the existence of a providential God who promulgates his rules of reason through the inclinations of human nature in order to grasp the non-gainsayability of the first precepts of the natural law' (60). This is true as regards our practical reasoning. Defending the doctrine of natural law requires further resources.

[39] Murray, 'The Problem of Mr. Rawls's Problem', in *Law and Philosophy: A Symposium*, ed. Sidney Hook (New York: New York University Press, 1964), 29–34, at 33. Murray is responding to John Rawls's 'Legal Obligation and the Duty of Fair Play' in the same volume, 3–18.

tradition, derivative from the Old and New Testaments and developed by the schools in the wake of Augustine' which seeks to bring 'about, in theory and in practice, that in society a man should, in the end, obey only God'[40]—motivated ultimately by 'the fear of the Lord, the desire to sojourn in his tent, to dwell on his holy hill'.[41]

Admittedly, in his attempt to present this viewpoint to a widely religious American public and to defend the Constitution's separation of church and state, Murray may have at least rhetorically underestimated the impact that original sin has upon human ability to affirm God's existence and wise ordering, and the corresponding need for the revelation of the divine law to support and sustain a natural law doctrine adequate to the divine Good that draws and fulfils the human creature. Hittinger describes the impact of sin: 'While the created order continues to move men, the effect of that law (in the creature) is bent by sin—not so bent that God fails to move the finite mind, for the fallen man is still a spiritual creature, possessed of the God-given light of moral understanding, but bent enough that this movement requires the remediation of divine positive law and a new law of grace.'[42] According to Thomas Aquinas, for fallen human beings to be left entirely under natural law, without the illuminative aid of divine revelation, is a condition of punishment.

In this light, one can fully agree with Schindler and others that natural law loses much (though certainly not all) of its effective power when dissociated from the matrix of grace and revelation, which efficaciously teaches God's existence and providential ordering of all things to their fulfilment.[43] As Oscar Brown observes, 'Wherever he

---

[40] Murray, 'The Problem of Mr. Rawls's Problem', 33.

[41] Ibid., 34. While emphasizing Murray's pursuit of a 'rational faith' consisting solely of natural law principles, Peter Augustine Lawler also remarks, 'Political life, for Murray, is really not all that autonomous; it points beyond itself, and its character and limits are to a great extent determined by the trans-political dimension of every human life' (Lawler, 'Natural Law and the American Regime: Murray's *We Hold These Truths*', *Communio* 9 (1982): 368–88, at 387).

[42] Russell Hittinger, 'Natural Law and Catholic Moral Theology', in *A Preserving Grace: Protestants, Catholics, and Natural Law*, ed. Michael Cromartie (Grand Rapids, MI: Eerdmans, 1997), 1–30, at 7–8.

[43] Cf. Michael Buckley, SJ's well-known thesis that, as he summarizes it, 'the strategies of theism or religious apologetics in early modernity had led theologians to bracket whatever was of specific religious character or warrant and to rely upon the new and prospering sciences for "the first foundations of religion." The implicit

treats the subject of law Aquinas sets the issues at least implicitly in the overall context of divine providence.'[44] That Aquinas does so indicates how biblical revelation assists the mind in defending the existence and truth of eternal law and natural law. In this vein Fergus Kerr notes that because Aquinas holds that the natural law is a participation in the eternal law, 'it is plain that he would not endorse the idea of a natural law ethics which is autonomous and independent of theological considerations'.[45] Simply put, absent a belief in a provident Creator and in created human teleology—absent eternal law (made manifest by divine law)—it is difficult to defend persuasively the existence of a 'law' that human beings are morally obliged to follow for the fulfilment of their 'nature'.

As Murray well knew, the prima facie difficulty of this task has not stopped modern thinkers from attempting it by means of a variety of anthropocentric accounts of natural law. But no matter how nuanced the schemes for exhibiting the basic requirements of human flourishing (Hobbes, Hume, Rousseau, and so forth) or however much one attempts to provide an autonomous role for human practical reason apart from natural teleologies (Descartes, Kant, and so forth), such answers, when located within the anthropocentric framework, encounter what seem to me to be insuperable difficulties. The 'human flourishing' answers reduce to sophisticated pragmatism rather than real 'law'; the 'practical reason' answers appear to be a premature restriction of the possibilities of human freedom in ever-evolving history. Thus among those who have consciously rejected or agnostically bracketed the biblical revelation of a provident Creator, acknowledgement of a natural 'law' is almost always viewed as a threat to human freedom—no matter that by natural law human beings

but unrecognized premise in such a strategy, building upon the new mechanics, was that the uniquely religious—in all of its experiential, traditional, institutional, and social forms—was cognitively empty' (Buckley, *Denying and Disclosing God: The Ambiguous Progress of Modern Atheism* (New Haven, CT: Yale University Press, 2004), xi, summarizing his *At the Origins of Modern Atheism* (New Haven, CT: Yale University Press, 1987)).

[44] Oscar J. Brown, *Natural Rectitude and Divine Law in Aquinas: An Approach to an Integral Interpretation of the Thomistic Doctrine of Law* (Toronto: Pontifical Institute of Mediaeval Studies, 1981), 1.

[45] Fergus Kerr, OP, *After Aquinas: Versions of Thomism* (Oxford: Blackwell, 2002), chapter 6, 'Natural Law: Incommensurable Readings', 107.

can and do 'grasp the reasonableness of some practical rule without understanding the cause of that rule'.[46] Those who have rejected the biblical witness to the provident Creator are not oblivious to the fact that, as Steven Long remarks, 'the natural law implies that the human agent is naturally subject to the author and promulgator of the law'.[47] This subjection (which in fact belongs to the order of love) appears as subjugation solely by power, and is firmly repulsed as such.

BIBLICAL REVELATION AND NATURAL LAW DOCTRINE

Biblical revelation has thus been excluded from many contemporary discussions of natural law doctrine on mistaken grounds: natural law doctrine does not become significantly more persuasive or effective once pluralism dictates the exclusion of biblical revelation. Yet, if biblical revelation provides significant assistance in affirming and defending eternal law and natural law, does this fact undercut appeals to natural law in response to unjust laws promulgated by avowedly secular states, and turn natural law doctrine into a faith-based discourse that has no claim on the realm of secular public philosophy? If secular versions of natural law, which proceed without God, do not work, will we then have to do without natural law doctrine altogether when addressing secular individuals and societies? Were Christian ethics to follow my proposal to exploit the resources of biblical revelation in natural law reflection, would such ethics thereby fall even further into what Vincent Twomey has described as its 'increasing irrelevance' as 'a peripheral activity within an increasingly secular society'?[48]

[46] Daniel McInerny, *The Difficult Good*, 60.

[47] Steven A. Long, 'Natural Law or Autonomous Practical Reason: Problems for the New Natural Law Theory', in *St. Thomas Aquinas and the Natural Law Tradition*, ed. John Goyette, Mark S. Latkovic, and Richard S. Myers (Washington, DC: Catholic University of America Press, 2004), 165–93, at 177.

[48] D. Vincent Twomey, 'Moral Renewal Through Renewed Moral Reasoning', *Josephinum Journal of Theology* 10 (2003): 210–29, at 210.

In response, one might recall Pius XI's appeal to natural law, citing Romans 2:15 and Cicero's *De officiis*, against the Nazis in his 1937 encyclical *Mit Brennender Sorge*:

It is part of the trend of the day to sever more and more not only morality but also the foundation of law and jurisprudence, from true belief in God and from His revealed commandments. Here We have in mind particularly the so-called natural law that is written by the Finger of the Creator Himself in the tables of the hearts of men and which can be read on these tables by sound reason not darkened by sin and passion. Every positive law, from whatever lawgiver it may come, can be examined as to its moral implications, and consequently as to its moral authority to bind in conscience, in the light of the commandments of the natural law. The laws of man that are in direct contradiction with the natural law bear an initial defect that no violent means, no outward display of power can remedy.[49]

In dealing with the Nazis, the Pope does not grant that his insistence upon the importance of 'true belief in God' and in God's 'revealed commandments' is at odds with the further claims that the natural law is present in every human being and that every human being whose reason is 'not darkened by sin and passion' has access to natural law. Rather, the point for our purposes is that precisely by affirming the former, the Pope strengthens his grounds for affirming the latter.[50] An explicitly theocentric natural law is arguably a stronger, not a weaker, basis for ongoing public discourse about the goods that human nature, precisely as created, requires.

Indeed, the view that connecting natural law and biblical revelation makes natural law more intelligible and persuasive—and more *inviting* as a path to the joy of holiness—undergirds John Paul II's

---

[49] Pius XI, *Mit Brennender Sorge*, in *Principles for Peace: Selections from Papal Documents, Leo XIII to Pius XII*, ed. Harry C. Koenig (Washington, DC: National Catholic Welfare Conference, 1943), 505–6. On Pius XI's political thought, see Russell Hittinger, 'Introduction to Modern Catholicism', in *The Teachings of Modern Christianity on Law, Politics, and Human Nature*, vol. 1, eds. John Witte Jr. and Frank S. Alexander (New York: Columbia University Press, 2006), 3–38, at 17.

[50] As Hittinger puts it in the conversation that follows his essay, 'Natural Law and Catholic Moral Theology', and Braaten's 'Response' in *A Preserving Grace*: 'We don't need theology to explain how people know that murder is wrong... You need a theology to *explain*, maybe, but not to know, the rudiments of natural law. I am an old-fashioned natural law theorist in the sense that I believe that God is the cause of the natural law. Human minds are a proximate cause of the *knowing* of it; but God is the cause *of the law*' (49).

encyclicals on moral theology.[51] Hittinger observes that epistemology or how we know the natural law is not the root of the contemporary problem: 'The problem is not whether the gentiles are moral agents, but rather the meanings they assign to the rudiments they possess by virtue of the natural law'.[52] Unmoored from the biblical doctrines of creation and providence, from God's wise ordering, natural law doctrine has become an anthropocentric discourse of individual rights grounded upon a false sense of human autonomy. Hittinger recalls that Genesis 2 'is the patristic common place for the discussion of natural law', and that John Paul II's *Veritatis Splendor* and *Evangelium Vitae* contain substantial sections devoted to this section of Genesis.[53] As Hittinger points out, by highlighting this biblical context for natural law doctrine, John Paul envisions the place of natural law argumentation in a manner similar to Thomas Aquinas's discussion of natural law within the context of eternal law, the Old Law, and the New Law.[54]

---

[51] On divine revelation of the natural law, cf. Lawrence J. Welch, 'Christ, the Moral Law, and the Teaching Authority of the Magisterium', *Irish Theological Quarterly* 64 (1999): 16–28; idem, 'Faith and Reason: The Unity of the Moral Law in Christ', *Irish Theological Quarterly* 66 (2001): 249–58.

[52] Hittinger, *The First Grace*, 35; cf. G. J. McAleer, *Ecstatic Morality and Sexual Politics: A Catholic and Antitotalitarian Theory of the Body* (New York: Fordham University Press, 2005). For further valuable discussion of natural law in theological context, see Romanus Cessario, OP, *Introduction to Moral Theology* (Washington, DC: Catholic University of America Press, 2001), chapter 2.

[53] Hittinger, *The First Grace*, 29. See also Vigen Guroian's strong warning (not without its misunderstandings of Catholic theology) that Western human rights doctrines 'reflect a legacy of secular humanism and rationalism that flirts with or even affirms the idea of autonomous human existence, whereas Orthodoxy starts from the premise that everything human is in "need" of, is dependent upon, God...[O]ur *humanum* is grounded in the being and act of God. Human existence is by origin and nature theonomous' (Guroian, 'Human Rights and Modern Western Faith: An Orthodox Christian Assessment', in *Does Human Rights Need God?*, ed. Elizabeth M. Bucar and Barbra Barnett (Grand Rapids, MI: Eerdmans, 2005), 41–7, at 47).

[54] Hittinger, *The First Grace*, 21. Hittinger comments that 'the phrase "natural law" is inherited from a tradition that asked the question about law(s) in the economy of divine providence... When Catholic moral theologians, however, evacuate the theological premises allowing morals to be placed under the genus of law, a different problem emerges. Once divine providence is stripped of the predicates of law (a command of reason, on the part of a proper authority, moving a multitude toward a common good), moral theology is reduced, at best, to deism (which posits a creating but not a commanding God). In that case, moral theology has but two options: (1) Law as exclusively the work of human practical reason; (2) Law as the positive law of the Church' (62).

It is from this Thomistic perspective, attentive both to biblical revelation and to metaphysical precisions, that the present book locates its efforts to articulate the reality, witnessed to by the Bible, that is natural law: not a rationalistic rulebook, but the eternal law imprinted in the spiritual–bodily human person, who participates rationally in God's teleological ordering of the human beings to their fulfilment.

1

The Bible and Natural Law

We might begin with a question: Does natural law reflection in fact rightly belong to moral reflection that is grounded in biblical revelation? In *Veritatis Splendor* John Paul II answers strongly in the affirmative:

The Church has often made reference to the Thomistic doctrine of natural law, including it in her own teaching on morality.... Even if moral-theological reflection usually distinguishes between the positive or revealed law of God and the natural law, and, within the economy of salvation, between the 'old' and the 'new' law, it must not be forgotten that these and other useful distinctions always refer to that law whose author is the one and the same God and which is always meant for man. The different ways in which God, acting in history, cares for the world and for mankind are not mutually exclusive; on the contrary, they support each other and intersect.[1]

Most contemporary Catholic thinkers have agreed, though not without some cautionary notes. Hans Urs von Balthasar, for instance, sees the law given to Israel as belonging to the period of 'waiting' for the fulfilment of the promise, a faithful 'waiting' upon God that 'no doubt corresponds to the constitutive structure of human nature ("natural law"), because God is not only Creator but the continual

---

[1] John Paul II, *Veritatis Splendor* (1993), §§ 44–5. For further discussion of natural law and Scripture, see also (in addition to works cited above) Thomas L. Pangle, *Political Philosophy and the God of Abraham* (Baltimore, MD: Johns Hopkins University Press, 2003); Pamela M. Hall, *Narrative and the Natural Law: An Interpretation of Thomistic Ethics* (Notre Dame, IN: University of Notre Dame Press, 1994); Brian L. Dunkle, SJ, 'A Development in Origen's View of the Natural Law', *Pro Ecclesia* 13 (2004): 337–51.

Giver of blessing'.[2] Von Balthasar emphasizes that the natural law must be understood as relational, as 'ecstatic'. In this vein he cautions that 'natural law' must not be allowed to overshadow the personal 'I–Thou' call of God at the heart of biblical ethics. According to von Balthasar, natural law, when properly understood, serves rather than overshadows the 'I–Thou' call.[3]

Describing the natural inclinations as the matrix of natural law, he observes, 'Man's whole constitution is unconditionally (*necessitate naturalis inclinationis*: de Ver 22, 5) predisposed toward goodness as it reveals itself in a light of transcendence (*synderesis*, primal conscience). He tends toward it in some way even in the sensual parts of his spirit-directed nature.'[4] Natural law expresses the call for human 'self-expropriation in favor of the divine good and the good of one's fellow man', and in this way points, as a 'signpost', toward the deeper personal response to Christ.[5] Natural law is perfected and fulfilled by the ecstatic movement of response to Christ's love. Rejecting Christ's call turns natural law anthropocentrically inward: 'If this freedom [of the human person as *imago dei*] will not render thanks to the God of grace in the Christian understanding, it will logically seek its source in itself. It will understand ethical action as self-legislation, initially, perhaps, recapitulating earlier patterns of cosmology (cf. Spinoza, Goethe, Hegel) and ultimately jettisoning

[2] Hans Urs von Balthasar, 'Nine Propositions on Christian Ethics', in Heinz Schürmann, Joseph Cardinal Ratzinger, and Hans Urs von Balthasar, *Principles of Christian Morality*, trans. Graham Harrison (German 1975; San Francisco: Ignatius Press, 1986), 92. See also Hans Urs von Balthasar, *The Christian State of Life*, trans. Sr. Mary Frances McCarthy (San Francisco: Ignatius Press, 1983), 105–19.

[3] See for this emphasis on the 'I–Thou' call, Martin Buber, 'What Are We to Do About the Ten Commandments?', in Buber, *On the Bible: Eighteen Studies*, ed. Nahum N. Glatzer (New York: Syracuse University Press, 2000), 118–21.

[4] Von Balthasar, 'Nine Propositions on Christian Ethics', 96. Russell Hittinger identifies a key point of convergence between von Balthasar and Aquinas with respect to moral theology: 'for both Aquinas and Balthasar the activity of moral theorizing is meant to serve the goal of moral perfection. That is to say, moral theorizing is not just a matter of describing human potential for various ranges of goods, according to which we might then infer schemes of duties and rights ... Their theories represent a different sort of perfectionism. The perfection of human agency consists, for them, in the participation in a mission that originates in the divine persons, and which takes concrete shape in the person of Christ. The other sub-themes of ethics (political, legal, personal) are not dissolved, but rather are keyed to a theological drama' (Hittinger, 'Theology and Natural Law Theory', *Communio* 17 (1990): 402–8, at 403).

[5] Von Balthasar, 'Nine Propositions on Christian Ethics', 100.

this preliminary stage (cf. Feuerbach, Nietzsche).'[6] Von Balthasar differentiates natural law understood in this way from natural law in 'prebiblical ethics' that fails to recognize the transcendence, vis-à-vis nature, of the human person as the *imago dei* and thereby imagines natural law as an enclosed this-worldly system of happiness.[7]

The question of the place of natural law in Christian ethics thus leads back, for both von Balthasar and John Paul II, to the question of how natural law relates to the biblical order of the Old and New Covenants, the question of God's wise ordering of the human person to 'self-expropriation'. But does natural law in fact have significant biblical warrants? Almost all recent studies of New Testament ethics—including the works by Richard B. Hays and Allen Verhey that I will discuss in this chapter—suggest, by avoiding the subject of natural law altogether, that the answer is 'no'.[8] As Markus Bockmuehl

---

[6] Ibid., 101–2. As Hittinger points out, 'In the "Nine Propositions", Balthasar stresses that law is not just teleological (as if it were simply so many rules for the unfolding of human potential). Scripturally, the theme is covenantal; as he points out, "not man himself, but the deeper unveiling of God's holiness in his covenant faithfulness." In this respect, law norms action in the context of a relation which is at once historical and eschatological. Balthasar notes that while this "no doubt corresponds to the constitutive structure of human nature ('natural law')", the correspondence is apt to convey the impression that we can prescind from the covenantal picture and derive norms simply from the constitutive structure of human nature. Hence, once abstracted from the covenant, natural law theory quickly moves to an ethic of autonomy—the very antipode of covenantal ethics' (Hittinger, 'Theology and Natural Law', 407).

[7] Von Balthasar, 'Nine Propositions on Christian Ethics', 101. Here von Balthasar may have Aquinas in mind. Whereas both the Stoics and the Fathers considered common ownership to belong to the natural law, von Balthasar remarks that this changes in Alexander of Hales and even more in Aquinas, leading in von Balthasar's view to a self-enclosed view of 'nature'. See von Balthasar, *The Christian State of Life*, 105–19. Elsewhere, however, von Balthasar is more positive toward Aquinas: 'Thomas never fails to remember the way in which being points critically to the eternal, hidden God nor the way in which reason points noetically to the possible revelation of that God, and consequently he wants all metaphysics to be seen as orientated towards "theology"' (von Balthasar, *The Glory of the Lord: A Theological Aesthetics*, vol. 4: *The Realm of Metaphysics in Antiquity*, trans. Brian McNeil, CRV, Andrew Louth, John Saward, Rowan Williams, and Oliver Davies (German 1967; San Francisco: Ignatius Press, 1989), 396).

[8] Richard B. Hays, *The Moral Vision of the New Testament: A Contemporary Introduction to New Testament Ethics* (San Francisco: HarperSanFrancisco, 1996); Allen Verhey, *Remembering Jesus: Christian Community, Scripture, and the Moral Life* (Grand Rapids, MI: Eerdmans, 2002). A similar study by a Catholic New Testament scholar, Frank J. Matera, devotes a bit more attention to the Old Testament law but strives to stay strictly within the letter of the New Testament texts, thereby excluding

observes, the general neglect of natural law in New Testament studies arises both from the influence of Barth's concerns and from 'the widespread academic suspicion besetting any study of universal or "natural" law' that has resulted from postmodern scepticism about our ability to discern, rather than construct, human nature.[9] Recent work in Old Testament ethics, by contrast, exhibits a significant interest in natural law. Thus, for instance, the Old Testament scholar John Barton, drawing upon his earlier work on the prophets, offers a chapter on 'Divine Commands or Natural Law?' in his *Ethics and the Old Testament*, and the Jewish theologian David Novak, drawing upon biblical and rabbinic sources, makes a significant case for natural law's biblical warrants in his *Natural Law and Judaism*.[10]

Before proceeding, a comment on Bockmuehl's *Jewish Law in Gentile Churches: Halakhah and the Beginning of Christian Public Ethics* is in order. Influenced by John Barton's writings, Bockmuehl's work provides an exception to the general neglect of natural law in New Testament scholarship.[11] Bockmuehl successfully shows that the interest in natural law in the period of late antiquity influenced the content of the biblical writings composed in Second Temple Judaism and in early Christianity. By 'natural law', however, Bockmuehl means 'moral principles that correspond to "the way things are", rather than being derived from a specific positive command of God'.[12] This definition of natural law makes it difficult both to differentiate moral

discussion of 'natural law'. See Matera, *New Testament Ethics: The Legacies of Jesus and Paul* (Louisville, KY: Westminster John Knox Press, 1996).

[9] Markus Bockmuehl, *Jewish Law in Gentile Churches: Halakhah and the Beginning of Christian Public Ethics* (Edinburgh: T. & T. Clark, 2000), 147. With regard to the massive field of Pauline studies, for instance, Bockmuehl finds only two studies on 'Paul's use of "natural law" reasoning', both published before 1970, in the past half-century (127): Robert J. Austgen, *Natural Motivation in the Pauline Epistles*, 2nd edn. (Notre Dame, IN: University of Notre Dame Press, 1969); and C. H. Dodd, 'Natural Law in the New Testament', in idem, *New Testament Studies* (Manchester: Manchester University Press, 1953), 129–43. On the influence of Barth, see Stephen J. Grabill, *Rediscovering the Natural Law in Reformed Theological Ethics* (Grand Rapids, MI: Eerdmans, 2006), chapter 1.

[10] John Barton, *Ethics and the Old Testament* (Harrisburg, PA: Trinity Press International, 1998); David Novak, *Natural Law in Judaism* (Cambridge: Cambridge University Press, 1998).

[11] As does, from a different perspective, James Barr's *Biblical Faith and Natural Theology* (Oxford: Clarendon Press, 1993).

[12] Bockmuehl, *Jewish Law in Gentile Churches*, 90.

principles from social conventions, and to recognize the order of creation in God's positive commands. Indeed, as a result of this definition, Bockmuehl has to concede that his effort to find 'natural law' in the Old Testament has failed: 'Strictly speaking, there is no "natural" law in Second Temple Judaism. That is to say, we have seen that neither the Hebrew Bible nor post-biblical Jewish literature allows for a moral authority in nature that is somehow distinct from that of God himself. Law inasmuch as it carries any real authority, is never "natural" in the sense of being anything other than divine in origin.'[13] But in fact this last sentence describes natural law far more adequately, as Bockmuehl seems at times to recognize. The literature of Second Temple Judaism, he points out, holds that 'by rightly observing the regular *patterns* of creation one can discern both order and purpose as intended by the Creator', and also affirms that '[t]he unity of the Creator demands that his voice in positive, special law does not contradict his voice in the order of creation'.[14] Although Bockmuehl does not draw this conclusion, it seems clear that the Bible itself suggests that natural law can only be properly understood in light of natural law's divine origin.

Despite these insights, however, Bockmuehl's definition of 'natural law' also limits his ability to find natural law in the New Testament. For example, he writes that Jesus' teaching on divorce 'grounds the prohibition of divorce in the created order, and yet it does so on the strength of a direct scriptural quotation (Gen 2.24). This is "natural law" only in a highly contingent sense, if it all....'[15] The appeal to

[13] Ibid., 110–11.

[14] Ibid., 111. As he says earlier, 'For the ancients, nature is by no means inanimate or dumb, as much of Western civilization has supposed ever since the Renaissance. Instead, it speaks with a voice that makes powerful claims of allegiance not only in regard to human self-understanding, but also in the area of practical conduct. In Old Testament and Jewish thought, more specifically, God and his creation never ultimately speak with two distinct voices. Although of course it is true that ancient Israel had no abstract concept of 'nature' or of the 'cosmos', God's voice is clearly heard both in creation and in the Torah, and the two are fundamentally related. And while there is thus, significantly, no 'law of nature' terminology as describing a reality distinct from the law of God, the Hebrew world view does operate on the assumption that all creation expresses God's law and moral purpose, and all of God's law is law according to nature. This is clear as early as the account of Gen 1–11, where (after the initial state of *tohu wabohu*, 1.2) there is really never any ἄνομα, any "lawless moment": everything proceeds according to God's command' (89).

[15] Ibid., 120.

Genesis seems, to him, to rule out its 'natural' character. Similarly he suggests that Romans 2:14–15 does not exemplify 'natural law' because it too has the Torah in view: 'What is in view is the possibility that some of the Torah's stipulations (τὰ τοῦ νόμου) might be kept instinctively by Gentiles who do not actually know them. Paul's concern, in other words, is not some sort of separate "natural law", but rather a "natural" or common-sense *knowledge* of the one Law of God, subjectively mediated by the individual's moral consciousness.'[16] But why would the 'natural law' need to be *separate* from 'some of the Torah's stipulations' in order to preserve its character as 'natural'? Lastly, Bockmuehl finds that in some of Jesus' teachings, such as his teachings on marriage and the family, 'a harsher clash between obligations to the order of creation and to the Kingdom of God seems difficult to imagine.... Endorsements of the perceived order of creation stand side by side with cases of profound subversion or subordination of that same order.'[17] But Bockmuehl does not make the differentiations—necessarily philosophical—within the order of creation (as opposed to 'the way things are', too often merely the conventions of a fallen world) that would show why such actions as celibacy and commitment to Jesus over certain family duties do not violate the order of creation toward the common good. He therefore concludes that while the New Testament affirms 'a shared awareness of an underlying "hierarchy of goods" that transcends the complex specificities of time, place and custom', nonetheless 'Paul and the Gospel tradition show a deeply subversive attitude to "natural" morality, shaped largely by considerations of soteriology, eschatology and resultant moral implications'.[18] The question is what counts as ' "natural" morality.'

---

[16] Ibid., 131. Bockmuehl states, 'In the past, scholars frequently considered Romans 2.14–15 to be the key New Testament passage on natural law. Paul seems here at first sight to allow for the possibility of a "natural" law observance by Gentiles. Upon closer examination, however, the passage turns out to have remarkably little to say about our subject.'

[17] Ibid., 125.

[18] Ibid., 142. ' "Natural" morality' here means 'creational givens' that include, for instance, such 'conventional obligations and expectations' as the thriving of 'the fittest and strongest' (142–3). Thus the 'creational givens' must be 'relativized' and 'redeemed', as severely lacking, even while also being 'embraced' (143). What is missing in Bockmuehl's account is adequate philosophical reflection upon what constitutes 'creational givens' that have moral significance.

The problems raised by Bockmuehl regarding the relationship of Scripture and 'natural' law and the relationship of nature and grace, the order of creation and the order of redemption, will recur throughout the present book. By the end of the book, I hope to have offered some initial answers, or at least promising paths toward answers. As a means to this goal, this chapter will present and evaluate the perspectives of Hays, Verhey, Barton, and Novak. Their positions on biblical ethics shed light on why discussing 'natural law' in the context of biblical revelation is important, both with respect to the Bible's warrants for such discussion, and with respect to the problems that arise when informed discussion of natural law is lacking as regards ethics in the Bible. After comparing their positions, I offer a preliminary constructive account of 'natural law' in biblical context. This account provides a first step toward reclaiming natural law doctrine as an exegetical, and not solely philosophical, project—that is, 'natural law' as understood by the Christian tradition prior to the modern reconfiguration of natural law.

BIBLICAL ETHICS: HAYS, VERHEY, BARTON, NOVAK

Richard B. Hays

Richard Hays's account of law in the Bible takes its starting points from the contrasting positions of Karl Barth and Reinhard Niebuhr. Barth organized his ethics in the *Church Dogmatics* around divine command. Hays quotes a programmatic passage from Barth: 'Barth's argument proceeds in two stages: "(1) that the divine law in the Bible is always a concrete command; and (2) that the concrete commanding to be found in the Bible must be understood as a divine command relevant to ourselves who are not directly addressed by it." '[19] For Hays the main problem with Barth's approach is that it requires asserting

[19] Hays, *The Moral Vision of the New Testament*, 229, citing Barth, *Church Dogmatics* II/2, 672. For placement of divine command within the broader context of Barth's ethics, see Nigel Biggar, 'Barth's Trinitarian Ethic', in *The Cambridge Companion to Karl Barth*, ed. John Webster (Cambridge: Cambridge University Press, 2000), 212–27. See also David Novak, 'Karl Barth on Divine Command: A Jewish Response', in Novak, *Talking with Christians: Musings of a Jewish Theologian* (Grand Rapids, MI: Eerdmans,

the perspicuity of the divine positive law for concrete situations today. With Calvin, Barth affirms such perspicuity because he fears that otherwise the human interpreter will, as in liberal Protestantism, take centre stage rather than God, and the theocentric character of Christianity will be lost.[20] Hays suggests that this is exactly what has happened in Reinhold Niebuhr's ethics. Hays writes,

Niebuhr finds in Scripture ideals and principles that must be approximated by human choices, informed by a sober estimate of likely consequences. Barth emphatically rejects all appeal to principles and consequentialist reckoning, while finding God's command in Scripture's explicit rules and in its paradigmatic narratives—elements that play no direct role in Niebuhr's ethics. While both theologians see the symbolic world of the New Testament as determinative for Christian ethics, their readings of that world stand in dramatic counterpoint. Niebuhr reads the symbolic world of the New Testament as an illuminating account of the tragic and transcendent *human* condition (*The Nature and Destiny of Man*), while Barth reads the symbolic world of the New Testament as a powerful account of the identity and action of *God*, who claims us through Jesus Christ for covenant partnership. Niebuhr insists that human reason and experience must be determinative for our interpretation of the New Testament and that inattention to 'the facts of experience' is a sign of heresy; Barth insists that human reason and experience must bow in obedience before the Word of God and that deference to human experience is a sign of idolatry.[21]

Hays agrees with Barth's theocentricity and with the secondary place for human reason that Barth upholds, even while refusing to go as far as Barth as regards the complete perspicuity of Scripture's divine commands for concrete situations today.

In turning away from this claim of complete perspicuity, Hays appeals instead to another key element of Barth's approach. Namely, Barth emphasizes the narrative particularity of biblical ethics. Barth,

---

2005), 127–45. Novak agrees with Barth about the importance of divine command, without granting that thereby 'natural law' is excluded.

[20] In this tradition John Webster affirms that the biblical 'text is self-interpreting and perspicuous' (Webster, *Word and Church: Essays in Christian Dogmatics* (Edinburgh: T. & T. Clark, 2001), 75). He explains that 'both the character of the Bible as self-interpreting and its perspicuity are confessions, faith's depictions of the activity of God discerned in the Church's activity of reading the Bible' (76).

[21] Hays, *The Moral Vision of the New Testament*, 238–9. Cf. 295 for Hays's agreement with Barth over Niebuhr.

followed by Hays, denies that one can extract abstract principles from the divine commands; God's commands, God's positive law, belong within the narrative frame. The story—covenantal election—cannot be separated from the ethics. Efforts to lift out an abstract, speculative moral theology from the Bible's concrete stories or *'paradigms'* are fundamentally flawed, because they lose the particularity of God's work in history.[22] Jesus Christ is *the* story who, in his obedience and freedom, serves as the 'template' for us.[23]

Here Hays argues that the 'contemporaneousness' of the biblical stories, above all Christ's, cannot be simply claimed: there must be some work of 'analogical imagination in reading the texts'.[24] This analogical imagination brings in human interpretation but, because of its secondary place to the divine commands as embodied in the biblical stories, it does not result, Hays thinks, in the mistake of Niebuhrian anthropocentrism. Furthermore, for Hays analogical imagination allows room for other categories of biblical or narrative ethics, such as 'principle, paradigm, and symbolic world',[25] even if Hays agrees that Niebuhrian 'timeless moral principles'—as opposed to rules and principles that recognize their embeddedness in the paradigm and symbolic world of the story—deviate mistakenly from biblical particularity.[26]

Once analogical imagination is allowed, Hays emphasizes his strong agreement with Barth's focus on concrete biblical hermeneutics and the paradigmatic story of Christ. For Hays, Christian ethics that moves away from the particularity of the biblical narrative thereby *fails* to be Christian ethics. In this regard Hays issues a stern criticism against attempts—inevitably, he thinks, through 'hermeneutical gerrymandering'—'to annex New Testament texts to foreign modes of ethical discourse'.[27] This corruption began, he observes, at least by the late second century with the doubtful exegesis and ethics of St Clement of Alexandria. These 'foreign modes of ethical discourse' inevitably, Hays suggests, change the character of Christian ethics by causing it to lose its regulative biblical particularity. He therefore concludes that 'a Christian ethic that seeks to be faithfully responsive to the New Testament texts will not move abstractly away

---

22 Ibid., 237.   23 Ibid. Cf. 295 for Hays's agreement with Barth.
24 Ibid., 237.   25 Ibid., 310.   26 See ibid., 294.   27 Ibid.

from the form in which the texts present themselves to us'.[28] So long as the 'form' of the biblical texts stands at the centre of all Christian ethical reflection, Hays grants the inevitability of some role for 'other sources', specifically '*tradition, reason,* and *experience*',[29] in shaping the 'analogical imagination' with which we engage Scripture. These other sources should always be critically governed and normed by the biblical texts.[30]

Hays does not specify to what degree the injunction against deviating from the concrete form of the biblical texts rules out speculative ethical thinking. Certainly for Hays the loss of the 'narrative particularity' of biblical texts always opens up onto rationalism, as in Niebuhr. Perhaps Hays does not intend his 'analogical imagination' to be free of metaphysical anthropology. Yet, he would appear to reject the speculative investigation into the moral life that integrates biblical texts and metaphysical anthropology. Instead, he considers metaphor and 'imaginative integration' to be more suitable than speculative intellectual integration for the work of biblically grounded ethical teaching, since the biblical stories, in his view, are, as stories, largely metaphorical and imaginative.[31]

---

[28] Ibid.   [29] Ibid., 295.

[30] See ibid., 296: 'This guideline by no means excludes exceedingly serious consideration of other sources of wisdom, but it assigns those sources an explicitly subordinate role in normative judgments. They [any extrabiblical sources] function instrumentally to help us interpret and apply Scripture. They must not, however, be allowed to stand as competing sources for theological norms.'

[31] As Hays states, 'our hermeneutic must value rather than denigrate the particularity of the New Testament texts: the storied, culturally specific forms of the apostolic testimony are to be received and heeded just as they present themselves to us. But this leads back to my proposal that New Testament ethics is necessarily an exercise in metaphor-making. If we seek to honor the particular form of texts that are predominantly narrative and occasional, without subjecting them to analytic procedures that abstract general principles from them, we will find that the most promising hermeneutical strategy is one of metaphorical juxtaposition between the world of the text and our world' (300). Or as Hays summarizes his point somewhat later: 'The use of the New Testament in normative ethics requires an integrative act of the imagination; thus, whenever we appeal to the authority of the New Testament, we are necessarily engaged in metaphor-making' (310). Patristic and medieval exegetes, in contrast, supposed that since the texts give access to existing realities, metaphysical and not merely metaphorical judgements would be required to interpret the texts adequately.

Barth also values biblical 'particularity' for sustaining God's freedom. As Hays summarizes Barth's position: 'Barth's approach to ethics as "the command of God" is conducive to an emphasis on the *rules* in the Bible as directly normative, always with the twin provisos that the rules must be understood in their narrative context as belonging to the story of God's covenant election of a people, and that God is always free to decree particular exceptions to the rules.'[32] In commanding human beings, God does not tie himself down. Since the divine commands function simply as positive law, God can make exceptions and even change the commands. It follows that Jesus' teachings, and not only the Old Testament commands (e.g. the Decalogue[33]), retain this aspect of contingent particularity for Barth. Hays observes that for Barth 'the New Testament rules, such as those given in the Sermon on the Mount, are to be taken literally and obeyed "until further notice".'[34]

How does Hays treat this second aspect of biblical particularity in his own thinking on New Testament ethics? Like many others influenced by Barth, he turns to the community of the Church. In this regard Hays's approach bears the imprint especially of George Lindbeck, Hans Frei, and Stanley Hauerwas.[35] The community consists in those human beings called into communal participation in Jesus'

---

[32] Ibid., 236.

[33] For discussion of the Decalogue in contemporary Christian ethics one might see Servais Pinckaers, OP, 'Scripture and the Renewal of Moral Theology', in Pinckaers, *The Pinckaers Reader: Renewing Thomistic Moral Theology*, ed. John Berkman and Craig Steven Titus (Washington, DC: Catholic University of America Press, 2005), 46–63, at 50–2. Pinckaers argues that in *Veritatis Splendor* (and in the *Catechism of the Catholic Church*), 'The Decalogue is being reestablished on the foundation of charity and put in direct contact once more with the New Law' (51). See also the essays in *I Am the Lord Your God: Christian Reflections on the Ten Commandments*, ed. Carl E. Braaten and Christopher R. Seitz (Grand Rapids, MI: Eerdmans, 2005).

[34] Hays, *The Moral Vision of the New Testament*, 236.

[35] Hays includes 'community' within his three keys to New Testament ethics: 'the New Testament calls the covenant *community* of God's people into participation in the *cross* of Christ in such a way that the death and resurrection of Jesus becomes a paradigm for their common life as harbingers of God's *new creation*' (292). He explains the order of these three keys earlier in his book: 'By placing *community* first, we are constantly reminded that God's design of forming a covenant people long precedes the New Testament writings themselves, that the church stands in fundamental continuity with Israel. By placing *cross* in the middle, we are reminded that the death of Jesus is the climax and pivot-point of the eschatological drama. By placing *new creation* last, we are reminded that the church lives in expectation of God's future redemption of

paradigmatic story, understood as radical 'self-giving love',[36] and thus into the firstfruits of resurrected life (the 'new creation') with all that this entails as regards living out Jesus' paradigmatic story in the world. In other words, the community participates in the biblical story, and absorbs the world into the biblical story. The community thus has a crucially important role in Hays's New Testament ethics as the corporate embodiment of 'an alternative order that stands as a sign of God's redemptive purposes in the world'.[37] Christian ethics primarily has to do with the obedience of Christ's whole body, not primarily to do with individuals.

Yet, the community too experiences the contingent particularity that marks the biblical texts and paradigmatic stories, in which context ethics must be understood. Like Barth, then, Hays emphasizes that God has not limited his freedom. God may command an entirely new thing that impels Christian ethics in a new and different direction. Hays describes the grounds upon which he rests the claim that the biblical commands do not limit God in God's ethical instruction of his people:

Are there cases, however, where the church as a whole might acknowledge some new experience as revelatory even against the apparent witness of Scripture? The paradigm case for such a possibility is found in the story of Peter's preaching to the household of the Gentile Cornelius in Acts 10 and 11, and the church's subsequent acknowledgment that God had given the Holy Spirit even to those who were 'unclean' according to biblical norms.[38]

For Hays, such cases are possible but should be discerned with grave caution, and should be granted 'only after sustained and agonizing scrutiny by a consensus of the faithful'.[39]

This freedom differs of course from the Holy Spirit's freedom to renew the Church along biblical lines. Such renewal, Hays affirms, is necessary when communal traditions, as in Jesus' time, stifle Scripture. As he says, 'When tradition comes into conflict with the New Testament's portrayal of the life and vocation of the Christian community, the time is at hand for judgment, repentance, and

---

creation. In other words, the images are to be understood within a plot; they figure forth the story of God's saving action in the world' (199).

[36] Ibid., 197.   [37] Ibid., 196.   [38] Ibid., 297.   [39] Ibid., 298.

reformation.'[40] Although he does not capitalize 'reformation', his earlier comments about the corruption from Clement of Alexandria
onward suggest that he has in view perhaps especially *the* Reformation with its opening up of the evangelical forms of Christianity
to which he adheres as, in his view, biblically grounded. The Holy
Spirit's work of renewal need not, however, take the radical form that
it took during the sixteenth century. It may come about simply in
communities that learn to 'perform' the Scriptures better.[41]

Despite his significant agreement with Barth, however, Hays parts
ways with the important place of 'law', as divine positive law, in
Barth's ethics. Hays does not include a significant discussion of the
Decalogue or the other laws of Israel, including 'law' as descriptive
in the Wisdom literature of the wise ordering of creation toward
its teleological end, in his *The Moral Vision of the New Testament*.
How then does the Old Testament relate to what Hays calls New
Testament ethics? Affirming that the New Testament has a 'privileged
hermeneutical function', Hays notes that the Old Testament, by itself,
could be used to justify armed violence and other actions that, in
his view, the New Testament prohibits.[42] The Old Testament instead
functions within the New by providing the *framework* of the biblical
story of salvation, whose 'continuation and climax' is found in the
New. In the particularity of the New Testament stories, and especially in the paradigmatic story of Jesus Christ, Hays assumes that
the divinely willed ethical meaning of the Old Testament stories will
become manifest—as well as God's ability to change his commands
as the story progresses.

Interestingly, however, Hays finds that since 'we have no command of the Lord' (one might think of the commandment 'You
shall not kill', but Hays is referring to Jesus Christ), the community
may approve the abortion of infants in their mothers' wombs in
certain difficult cases.[43] Hays states, 'Surely if the New Testament
writers could dare to formulate exceptions to Jesus' explicit teaching
against divorce, the church can also act—in fear and trembling under
the guidance of the Spirit—to identify exceptions to the traditional

---

[40] Ibid., 297.
[41] Cf. ibid., 305; also Richard B. Hays, 'The Future of *Christian* Biblical
Scholarship,' *Nova et Vetera* 4 (2006): 95–120.
[42] Hays, *The Moral Vision of the New Testament*, 309.   [43] Ibid., 456.

prohibition of abortion.'[44] He names two kinds of exceptions as 'justifiable options for Christians': the abortion of the infant when the mother's life is at stake and the abortion of an infant conceived by rape or incest.[45]

Other kinds of exceptions regarding the 'traditional prohibition of abortion', he adds, can also be prayerfully considered by Christian couples in the context of their communities. As an example, he takes up the case of an 'unplanned Down's syndrome child'. Their parents, he argues, should not simply decide on their own; rather the 'decision ought to be addressed corporately by the local church community' of the parents. The local church community should, if it encourages the parents not to kill the handicapped infant in the womb, assist with the undeniably 'heavy personal costs of bringing such a child to birth'.[46] How should the community undertake its discernment? Hays suggests reading biblical texts and absorbing their 'metaphorical paradigms'. But if 'the community does not find these metaphorical readings illuminating, or if the cost of assuming responsibility for such a child is reckoned to be too great, then the church will assent to their decision to proceed with an abortion, all the while praying for God's mercy on all concerned: mother, father, child, doctor, and church'.[47] In response to this particular case Hays identifies himself rather strongly as against the abortion of Down's syndrome infants in the womb, given what Christian communities are called to be, although he grants that '[i]n a case where the New Testament offers us no clear instruction, it is perhaps inevitable that Christians will in good conscience reach different conclusions'.[48]

---

[44] Ibid.

[45] Ibid. See, from a Lutheran perspective, arguments against this kind of exception-making in Bernd Wannenwetsch, 'Intrinsically Evil Acts; or: Why Euthanasia and Abortion Cannot Be Justified', in *Ecumenical Ventures in Ethics: Protestants Engage Pope John Paul II's Moral Encyclicals*, ed. Reinhard Hütter and Theodor Dieter (Grand Rapids, MI: Eerdmans, 1998), 185–215; idem, 'You Shall Not Kill—What Does It Take? Why We Need the Other Commandments if We Are to Abstain from Killing', in Braaten and Seitz, *I Am the Lord Your God*, 148–74; Oswald Bayer, 'Self-Creation? On the Dignity of Human Beings', *Modern Theology* 20 (2004): 275–90.

[46] Hays, *The Moral Vision of the New Testament*, 456.   [47] Ibid., 457.

[48] Ibid. Cf. for some of the anti-abortion arguments in Hays's treatment of the topic, Stanley Hauerwas, 'Abortion Theologically Understood', in *Virtues and Practices in the Christian Tradition: Christian Ethics after MacIntyre*, ed. Nancy Murphy, Brad

Thus, while generally standing against the killing of human life in the womb, Hays recognizes cases where Christians may rightly kill human life in the womb. In addition to the cases where the human life in the womb endangers the life of the mother or where the human life in the womb has been conceived by rape, he holds that some selective killing of deformed human life in the womb may be acceptable for Christians depending upon personal and communal circumstances, prayer, and prudence. Yet one might ask whether, absent a direct 'command of the Lord', Hays's reliance on the story-shaped community suffices. On what grounds can we kill this defective human life in the womb, and not that less defective one? Should children pay in blood for the sins of their fathers? Can 'self-defence' justify the killing of a human being who seeks solely to live, not to threaten its mother's life? That Hays does not, and given his approach perhaps cannot, ask these questions indicates serious deficiencies in his approach. Not only does the commandment 'You shall not kill' merit more attention (one notes that this commandment informs other areas of Hays's ethical reflection), but also one finds that this commandment both requires and offers warrants for metaphysical reflection and correspondingly for natural law doctrine. In short, the 'metaphorical paradigms' offered by biblical stories read within the Christian community are insufficient outside this metaphysical questioning that arises from serious attention to the Old Testament theologies of law.

Allen Verhey

Verhey agrees with the early Fathers of the Church who 'celebrated moral truth and goodness wherever they found it' and who regarded this moral truth 'as the work of the *logos* in creation and history, the very *logos* revealed finally and decisively in the Christ whose story is told in Scripture'.[49] Thus Verhey would not seem necessarily opposed to natural law discourse in the Church, so long as that discourse remains theocentric. Verhey describes New Testament

J. Kallenberg, and Mark Thiessen Nation (1997; Notre Dame, IN: University of Notre Dame Press, 2003), 221–38.

    [49] Verhey, *Remembering Jesus*, 462.

ethics, and his own, as fundamentally 'theocratic', by which he means affirming first and foremost God's lordship in everything. For him, Christians, in communities of faith, 'remember Jesus and say among the nations, "The Lord reigns—and will reign." '[50] This affirmation of God's kingship, with the political consequences that the affirmation bears, requires Christians to be 'theocratic', although different political systems can express the 'theocratic' vision of reality.[51] While Christians cannot accomplish God's eschatological reign, they can attempt to live by the standards (charity) of God's reign and to seek— at times by prophetic rejection and at times by engagement—a politics that as much as possible manifests such charity, in the Church and in the world.[52]

Such Christian theocracy, for Verhey, is by no means an ecclesial world-domination, nor does it mean 'the political rule of a priestly or clerical hierarchy' or 'the legislation and enforcement of the positive law found in Scripture' or any earthly 'political accomplishment'.[53] Rather it expresses the radical Christian commitment to God's kingship, a kingship manifested in Christ as self-giving love and to be fully accomplished by God eschatologically. Theocratic politics means to live in the recognition that God, not human beings, is at the centre. Following the early Fathers, he suggests that 'theocratic' practices include the works of mercy, chaste and faithful 'sexual lives', and in general 'a politics of mutual instruction and discernment, of reconciliation and forgiveness, and of peaceable difference' in which persuasion, not force, serves as the legitimate instrument.[54] In seeking a politics of self-giving love, some policies can be excluded, and others promoted, by means of a process of discernment that draws upon all intellectual resources available to the (pluralist) community and measures them by Christ's story.[55] For the early Fathers living in the Roman empire, and for Verhey, 'whatever goodness and truth and justice existed was the work of Christ. The wisdom of other peoples could and did enter the deliberations—and the political deliberations—of Christians. The final test, however, for reasons given and heard in the church remained the story of Jesus.'[56] Post-Constantinian Christians were not wrong to engage pagan moral

---

[50] Ibid., 455.   [51] Ibid.   [52] Ibid., 471.   [53] Ibid., 469–70.
[54] Ibid., 457.   [55] Cf. ibid., 470–1.   [56] Ibid., 459.

truth, given the work of the *logos* in creation. Nor were they wrong 'to participate in managing a society or to consider the effects of actions and policies'.[57]

What then might be the place of natural law? Verhey's openness to 'the wisdom of other peoples' as manifestations of the work of the *logos* in creation may give space to theocentric natural law doctrine within Christian ethics. Yet, like Hays, Verhey does not discuss natural law in his book. In setting forth his biblical and theological ethics, however, he does explore what Paul might mean by 'natural' in Romans 1:26–7. Verhey seems to turn away from the idea of natural inclination, at least in its weakened and distorted form of 'orientation': 'When Paul describes homosexual acts as "against nature" (*para physin*; Rom. 1:26), he cannot mean that such acts violate a heterosexual orientation which is "natural" to and normative for human beings, or that such acts violate a heterosexual orientation which is "given" by nature to human beings (rather than chosen by them).'[58] Verhey seems doubtful there is a 'natural' and 'given' procreative inclination that belongs to human nature. He is concerned about the Humean distinction between 'is' and 'ought': the word 'natural', he states, 'always risks collapsing the distinction between the way things are and the way they ought to be'.[59]

The context of his comments about a 'natural', 'given', and 'normative' heterosexual 'orientation', however, is Victor Paul Furnish's thesis that Paul means only to rule out persons with heterosexual orientation turning, out of insatiable lust, also to homosexual acts. In this context, Verhey's comments clearly seek primarily to rule out Furnish's notion of 'orientation' as the key to Paul's meaning.[60] For Verhey, 'natural' refers back to the creation, to 'what is appropriate to the sort of embodied creatures we were created as'.[61] Jesus teaches the Pharisees regarding divorce that 'from the beginning of creation, "God made them male and female". For this reason a man shall leave his father and mother and be joined to his wife, and the

---

[57] Ibid., 463.   [58] Ibid., 236.

[59] Ibid. For critiques of the fact–value disjunction, see Lloyd L. Weinreb, *Natural Law and Justice* (Cambridge, MA: Harvard University Press, 1987); Hilary Putnam, *The Collapse of the Fact/Value Dichotomy and Other Essays* (Cambridge, MA: Harvard University Press, 2002).

[60] Verhey, *Remembering Jesus*, 236.   [61] Ibid., 237.

two shall become one' (Mark 10:6–8).[62] Verhey holds that in light of the biblical story of the creation of male and female, rather than an extrinsic law or statute, Paul, following Jesus, can understand the ' "good sex" given with the creation'.[63] The biblical story tells us what human sexuality is meant to be: 'As the knowledge and praise of God are "natural" in the creation, so are sexual relations of a man and a woman.'[64]

In Verhey's view, then, Paul's lack of a concept of 'orientation' both attunes Paul to the main lines of the biblical story of sexuality as grounded in Genesis 1–2, and blinds Paul to the complexity of homosexuality. Verhey states that 'Paul, like other writers of his day, simply assumed that people could control not only their sexual appetites but also the "orientation" of their appetites, ordering those appetites into conformity with the dictates of reason or the laws of nature or the story of creation'—the last being Paul's framework, whereas 'the dictates of reason' and 'the laws of nature' are the frameworks of other 'writers of his day', the pagan moralists. This assumption that people can order their appetites somewhat undercuts Paul's position, Verhey thinks.[65] What if persons who experience homosexual appetites do not freely choose them, but instead experience them as already given?

Verhey still wants to affirm the basic story: 'Remember the story of good sex that Jesus told, the story of "one flesh." The story of our creation as male and female still suggests, I think, that the Christian vision of good sex is the "one flesh" union of a man and a woman that gestures and nurtures the covenant made in vows, carried out in fidelity, and hospitable to children.'[66] Verhey emphasizes that Paul reaches this conclusion on the basis of fidelity to the story, not to a particular law or statute. Nonetheless, Verhey also thinks that the new understanding of 'homosexual persons'[67] (that is to say, homosexual appetites not as chosen, but as, according to Verhey, integral to one's very personhood) calls for more nuance than Paul gives. Homosexual acts may not fully fit the story, but they do not cause 'homosexual persons' to stand entirely outside the story, either. While acknowledging a 'moral preference' for heterosexual marital acts and denying

---

[62] Ibid., 213. [63] Ibid., 237. [64] Ibid.
[65] Ibid. [66] Ibid., 238. [67] Ibid.

that homosexual acts are 'a good', therefore, Verhey compares the recognition of 'homosexual persons', and thus also of 'homosexual unions', to the Protestant and Eastern Orthodox churches' permission of divorce: 'If we allow divorce in a world like this one for the sake of protecting marriage and marriage partners, and if we allow remarriage after divorce, then we must also consider allowing homosexual relationships for the sake of protecting fidelity and mutuality and the homosexual partners.'[68]

Verhey's emphasis on story, then, both privileges heterosexual marital unions among Christians, and allows for Christian homosexual unions. Since he explores the 'natural' only as presented by the biblical *story* of creation (male and female, one flesh), he does not have resources for exploring further why homosexual actions, and homosexual unions, might not belong to human fulfilment. In other words, if the story forms a template, alternative stories may logically, even if not fully fitting the story, participate in the story. Human male–male and female–female monogamous sexual relations seem to participate in the creation-story, on this view, at least as regards the presence of monogamy. Thus they may be judged, Verhey thinks, acceptable even if not ideal embodiments of Christian sexual relationships. Participation in the story is possible through monogamy, now separated from the bodiliness characteristic of the story; and Verhey affirms homosexual unions as manifesting and encouraging monogamy.

Leaving aside for the moment this troubling separation of human monogamy from human bodiliness, one might question Verhey's emphasis on story from within the biblical story itself. For instance, he gives no significant place in *Remembering Jesus* to the Torah. When he speaks of law, instead, he assumes that it is a reality merely extrinsic to the acting person. He thus assumes a typically modern rather than a fully biblical account of law. Certain biblical narratives—such as Psalm 119 and Romans 2—recognize the interior dimension of the Torah. In contrast, Verhey writes, 'The Christian theocrat also knows that morality outreaches the grasp of legal sanctions. Morality is

[68] Ibid., 239. Compare David Novak's Jewish account of Barth on Romans 1:21–7, where Novak makes clear that Barth is much closer to Paul, and thus also to the rabbinic tradition, than are many New Testament scholars: Novak, 'Before Revelation: The Rabbis, Paul, and Karl Barth', in idem, *Talking with Christians*, 108–26.

concerned with dispositions and character as well as with external actions. Law and its sanctions focus on external actions.'[69] He goes on to compare Old Testament story and Old Testament law; in his view, the latter is a pale reflection of the former.[70] For Verhey, law has to do with 'minimal standards', and thus functions pedagogically to move the people gradually closer and closer to the demands of the story.

Thus in depicting Jesus' interpretation of the Mosaic Law, Verhey affirms, 'The imminent sovereignty of God demanded something more than an external and conventional righteousness based on observance of statutes. Jesus shifted the emphasis from *halakah* to *haggadah*, from rules for conduct to the formation of character.'[71] This shift involves moving 'from statute to narrative'.[72] Narrative includes the Torah but eventually exceeds it to the point of displacing it. As Verhey states, Jesus 'set the Law in the context of a story that began with creation, continued in covenant, and was about to climax in God's unchallenged reign. The welcome due the kingdom outreaches the grasp of legal sanctions and *halakah*.'[73]

Is not, however, this shift 'from statute to narrative, from rules for external conduct to the formation of character by the story'[74] too simplistic? When Jesus deepens the commandment against adultery to include a warning against interior lust (Matt. 5:27–8), he is not displacing the commandment. When Jesus challenges the dietary laws by warning against 'evil thoughts, murder, adultery, fornication, theft, false witness, slander' (Matt. 15:19), he points to the Decalogue as the permanent and interior heart of the Law. When a young man asks Jesus what the man must do to have eternal life, Jesus places the ten commandments at the heart of following Jesus—adding a deeper story-context to the Decalogue, but by no means displacing or downgrading the Decalogue (Matt. 19:16–22).

---

[69] Verhey, *Remembering Jesus*, 475.
[70] One notes similarities with how Schleiermacher conceives of dogma as pale second-order reflection upon the experience of Jesus' absolute God-consciousness.
[71] Verhey, *Remembering Jesus*, 407.   [72] Ibid.
[73] Ibid. Verhey is good at exposing the problems with the Torah, but he does not equally bring out its permanent aspects.
[74] Ibid., 408.

Verhey is certainly right that 'the coming kingdom required something more radical than the labored application of legal precepts to external behavior, something more penetrating than certain legal limits on the expression of human anger, lust, deceitfulness, vengefulness, avarice, and enmity'.[75] But he goes too far in reducing the Mosaic Law, with the Decalogue at its heart, to the external. In answering a Pharisee's query regarding the greatest commandment of the Law, Jesus teaches a deeper understanding of the Law: 'You shall love the Lord your God with all your heart, and with all your soul, and with all your mind. This is the great and first commandment. And a second is like it, You shall love your neighbour as yourself. On these two commandments depend all the law and the prophets' (Matt. 22:37–40, following Deut. 6:5 and Lev. 19:18). In the biblical story, the Law is never *merely* external statutes. Rather, the Decalogue, and its motive precepts (love of God and love of neighbour), possesses an interior dimension that exhibits God's wise ordering in the human creature. The Decalogue's prohibition against murder does not resound solely on the level of an external statute made intelligible and interior only within the framing biblical stories; rather, it resonates with human beings' apprehension of the eternal law for human flourishing and fulfilment, no matter how clouded this apprehension is by sin or how easily casuistry appears to overcome the prohibition. The creation of human beings includes this body–soul participation in God's wisdom.

In response to Verhey, then, I would propose that to be understood, the biblical stories require metaphysical reflection upon the created order as a teleological order known by God: that is to say, natural law doctrine. Such reflection, it seems to me, would challenge both the separation of 'monogamy' and bodiliness, and the notion that human 'personhood' can be divided in terms of 'homosexual' and 'heterosexual'. Verhey is concerned that persons engaged in monogamous homosexual relationships not be written out entirely from the Christian story, and I can agree with this goal: God alone judges human souls, and human personhood is not defined by sexuality. Christians do not give up on themselves or on others even when serious sin has become habitual. The point however is that when separated from the

<hr>

[75] Ibid., 412.

bodiliness of human sexuality, simple 'monogamy' is not a sufficient participation in what Christians mean by 'marriage'.

John Barton

Whereas Hays's and Verhey's efforts to attain a biblically grounded Christian ethics leave out natural law considerations, with consequences for their understanding of the abortion of unborn infants (Hays) and of same-sex sexual relationships (Verhey), John Barton's *Ethics and the Old Testament* argues that natural law *is* biblical.[76] As with Hays, Barton's perspective on law is framed in part by Karl Barth's theology. As he observes, 'In the twentieth century Karl Barth was particularly active in insisting that God rules the world (and the church, and the individual) by positive law, of which the Ten Commandments are the most obvious example. The good for humanity is what God decrees it to be, not what human beings can deduce.'[77] Barth's position gains its force, in Barton's view, because it preserves a theocentric account of ethics, as opposed to the effort to construct an autonomous or semi-autonomous ethics out of strictly human resources. Barton notes that '[p]eople who think the Bible to be central and indeed primary within the life of the church, which until the Second Vatican Council meant in effect Protestants',[78] fear that

---

[76] As we will see, Barton distinguishes sharply between divinely commanded law and 'natural law'. This way of framing the issue spills into other Old Testament scholars' discussions of Old Testament law. See e.g. Christopher R. Seitz, 'The Ten Commandments: Positive and Natural Law and the Covenants Old and New—Christian Use of the Decalogue and Moral Law', in Braaten and Seitz, *I Am the Lord Your God*, 18–38. After noting that Calvin and Scotus thought of the first table as 'natural law', Seitz goes on to explain his concern: 'A category like "natural law" cannot easily move the epistemological boundary established by election and the covenantal relationship itself: rather, it sees law and nature from an angle of vision granted from outside the covenant relationship of God and Israel. What would it mean to take the boundary seriously—to honor positive law as given to Israel alone—and yet to see how and why that law spills out into creation more broadly?' (25). For Seitz, the key point is that Israel's divine positive law—her knowledge of the true Creator as expressed in the Decalogue—enables Israel to understand how her divine positive law applies, in certain instances, to all creation.

[77] Barton, *Ethics and the Old Testament*, 59.

[78] Ibid. This leaves out, of course, the richly biblical Catholic tradition of theological reflection.

'natural law' is simply another way of human beings defining good and evil for themselves, rather than obeying God's law and allowing God to be the ultimate lawgiver (cf. Gen. 3:4–5). In contrast, Barton suggests, Catholic ethicists tend to think that the Protestant rejection of 'natural law' gives inadequate room for the doctrine of creation and for the capacities of human reason, as created, even after sin. Such Catholic ethicists suppose that whatever positive law might be found in Scripture will, in so far as it is true and has to do with our created nature rather than our supernatural elevation, be found first or primarily in and through our created nature. In this view, the primary source for law pertaining to our created nature should be the capacities of created nature itself, even if the insights provided by these capacities need to be confirmed, after sin, by divine positive law.

What if, however, 'natural law' is itself biblical? What if 'natural law occurs within the Bible as well as outside it'?[79] This is Barton's thesis, and he suggests that it challenges both the Barthian rejection of natural law and Catholic attempts to present the 'natural law' as a strictly philosophical project reinforced by biblical 'positive law'.[80] As examples of natural law in the Bible, he gives Amos 1–2, in which the prophet denounces atrocities (and warns of a coming divine punishment) committed by the surrounding nations but not prohibited directly by the laws of the Torah;[81] various passages in Isaiah in which the prophet condemns instances of pride, again beyond what is explicitly condemned by the Torah; and especially the injunctions of the wisdom literature. Barton remarks, 'The wisdom literature used to be regarded as marginal in biblical study, and if Barth was able to treat positive divine law as the only model within the Old Testament, that is because when he was writing biblical scholars themselves took little interest in the wisdom tradition, which they saw

---

[79] Ibid., 61.

[80] Nigel Biggar observes, however, that 'in CD III/4 it becomes quite clear that, for Barth, God's will has a certain character that is expressed in the permanent structures with which he has created human nature, and that his commands, therefore, do have certain constant features. This has often been overlooked, partly because Barth generally preferred to avoid speaking of "orders of creation" in the *Church Dogmatics*' (Biggar, 'Barth's Trinitarian Ethic', 217).

[81] A similar point is made by M. Daniel Carroll, 'Seeking the Virtues Among the Prophets: The Book of Amos as a Test Case', *Ex Auditu* 17 (2001): 77–96, although he focuses on virtue ethics rather than natural law.

as a rather foreign body within Old Testament literature.'[82] In the wisdom literature, the doctrine of creation appears as undergirding God's work even in Israel, and thus God's commandments themselves already possess a framework in the created order. Citing the biblical scholar Hans Heinrich Schmid, Barton observes the centrality of 'the creation of the world and the moral order that derives from its created character'.[83]

For the wisdom literature, as for Isaiah in his discourses against pride and Amos in his critique of atrocities, 'morality is first and foremost a matter of human beings recognizing their finite, created status and seeking a way of life which embodies their sense of belonging in the hierarchical universe whose head and origin is God'.[84] Following the wisdom literature, Barton argues that one should read the laws of the Torah in light of Genesis 1–2. God's commandments to Israel belong within a 'natural moral order of the created world'.[85] Although Barton does not here mention it, the wisdom literature's framework of creation is also adopted by Jesus. For instance, one recalls Jesus' response to the Torah's law regarding divorce (Mark 10:5–9).[86] In perfecting the divine *intention* as regards Moses' law on divorce, Jesus points to the authority of the created order as well as to his own authority as interpreter of God's created order. At other times Jesus affirms laws of the Torah as accurate expressions of God's good wisdom for human fulfilment, notably as regards the Ten Commandments (e.g. Matt. 19:17–19).

If the wisdom literature, the prophets, and Jesus find in Genesis 1–2 (creation) the context for reading the whole Torah, including God's commandments, do *all* of God's commandments in the Torah belong to the natural law? In taking up this question, Barton selects the food laws as an example, since they clearly seem to belong to divine positive law—although their status as purity laws connects them with the first three commandments of the Decalogue. As Barton puts it,

---

[82] Barton, *Ethics and the Old Testament*, 67.   [83] Ibid.   [84] Ibid.

[85] Ibid. Cf. Iain Provan, ' "All These I Have Kept Since I Was a Boy" (Luke 18:21): Creation, Covenant, and the Commandments of God', *Ex Auditu* 17 (2001): 31–46.

[86] Regarding Jesus, the wisdom literature, and creation, see e.g. Ben Witherington III, *Jesus the Sage: The Pilgrimage of Wisdom* (Minneapolis, MN: Fortress Press, 1994); Leo G. Perdue, *Wisdom and Creation: The Theology of Wisdom Literature* (Nashville, TN: Abingdon Press, 1994).

'Why is it permissible to eat sparrows but not seagulls, sheep but not camels, cod but not prawns?'[87] Observant Jews, it seems clear, have generally obeyed these precepts not out of any claim that they reflect a 'natural law' that one might expect all who share in human nature to obey, but rather because God commanded the Jewish people to obey them. And yet, as Barton points out, the food laws are often, in the scriptural texts which command the food laws, explained on the basis not of divine command but of reasons: for instance, 'pigs are unclean because they are cloven-hoofed but not ruminant. To us the "because" here is exceedingly mysterious, but it is produced in the text of Leviticus as though it makes the matter obvious.'[88] Rabbinic commentators such as Maimonides, as well as the anthropologist Mary Douglas, have similarly advanced rational explanations for each of the food laws.[89] Barton concludes that it may well be that even the food laws reflect an account of the 'natural' similar to the account of the 'natural' given by Catholic ethicists today in condemning the abortion of infants in their mothers' wombs.

The food laws, then, seem close to 'natural law' for Barton, as do many other moral teachings found throughout the Old Testament. He does not, however, count the Ten Commandments as 'natural law'. For him, they are strictly positive law, 'which the people are to obey simply because they are given by God', although their character as positive law belongs with the covenantal framework that renders such positive law less impersonal.[90] Barton tends to look upon an extrinsic requirement of obedience as the mark of positive law, as opposed to

---

[87] Barton, *Ethics of the Old Testament*, 68.   [88] Ibid., 69.

[89] Ibid., 70. See Mary Douglas, *Purity and Danger: An Analysis of Concepts of Pollution and Taboo* (New York: Penguin, 1970), as well as her recent *Leviticus as Literature* (Oxford: Oxford University Press, 1999), where she makes the case that 'Leviticus exploits to the full an ancient tradition which makes a parallel between Mount Sinai and the tabernacle' (59). Jon Levenson argues that the key to these laws is not rational explanations, no matter how persuasive, but covenantal holiness. He observes that 'the presence of apodictic laws between man and God serves as a warning against identifying the Lord of the covenant with any rational principle. Reason is not the suzerain. This category of laws, the least palatable to people of a philosophical cast of mind, stands guard against any effort to depersonalize God. It is because the covenant relationship is founded upon personal fidelity that there can be laws whose only "explanation" is the unfathomable decree of God' (Levenson, *Sinai and Zion: An Entry into the Jewish Bible* (San Francisco: Harper & Row, 1985), 53).

[90] Barton, *Ethics of the Old Testament*, 72.

natural law which he sees as not requiring 'obedience' because it arises from within the created order.[91] Moral teachings that 'rest on natural human intuitions about ethics'[92] may count as natural law, but whatever ultimately stands upon obedience to God is positive law. Given this view of natural law as 'natural human morality' incommensurate with 'God telling us what we must do',[93] Barton's affirmation that there is natural law in the Bible, important as this affirmation is in distinguishing his position from the approaches of Hays and Verhey, loses some of its force. If 'natural law' represents a zone of human autonomous ethics, a zone in which obedience to the Creator is not owed, then one can agree with Barth that such 'natural law' would be antithetical to Christian ethics—for which our lives are not our own.

Interestingly, therefore, Barton defends 'natural law' in the Bible for the same reason that Hays and Verhey give it short shrift.[94] Namely, Barton finds in 'natural law', understood as 'natural human morality', more ability to be attentive to the particularity of human life and human stories. He observes earlier in the book, 'The Old Testament, as I have argued, usually works from particular to general, and hardly ever enunciates any principles that would strike us as universal: even such general texts as the Ten Commandments turn out to be very strongly anchored in the concerns of a particular society at a particular time.'[95] Barth's emphasis on positive law may accord with the 'finished or "canonical" form' of the Old Testament, but Barton finds 'earlier stages in which morality was conceived in a much more diverse way, with the model "obedience to God's positive laws" as only one option'.[96] Barton considers the positive-law 'obedience' model not fitted to many of the nuances of the actual stories, whose world

---

[91] For discussion of the relationship of positive law and natural law, see e.g. Russell Hittinger, *The First Grace: Rediscovering the Natural Law in a Post-Christian World* (Wilmington, DE: ISI Books, 2003), especially chapters 3–5; Daniel Westberg, 'The Relation between Positive and Natural Law in Aquinas', *Journal of Law and Religion* 11 (1994–5): 1–22; Robert P. George, 'Natural Law and Positive Law', in *The Autonomy of Law: Essays on Legal Positivism*, ed. Robert P. George (Oxford: Clarendon Press, 1996), 321–34.

[92] Barton, *Ethics of the Old Testament*, 72.   [93] Ibid., 75.

[94] Barton agrees with Verhey, however, about the prohibition of homosexual acts in the Old Testament.

[95] Ibid., 17.   [96] Ibid., 76.

'is frequently much more complicated';[97] and he finds 'natural law' to be a good way of speaking about the more complex, less divine-command ethical world in which the biblical characters operate. For Barton, then, natural law is actually more attuned to the particularity of the biblical stories than divine positive law.[98]

In addition to his concern that biblical ethics recognize the biblical authors' frequent appeal to 'a kind of shared moral sense which they thought everyone had in common'[99]—thereby (somewhat paradoxically) suggesting a universal moral world more open to particularity than the divine-command worldview—Barton also explores the motivations suggested by the Old Testament for ethical behaviour. In the course of this investigation he offers some insights which could have further deepened his account of natural law in the Bible. For instance, he emphasizes that 'the Old Testament takes it for granted that people pursue the good for the sake of an end',[100] a point that could lead to reflection upon natural inclinations as presented in the Old Testament. Similarly, he recognizes that the Old Testament authors see God's law as a blessing, and obedience as a form of gratitude.[101] This point somewhat weakens the contrast he had earlier drawn between God's positive law and natural law. The same is true of his observation that in the Old Testament view, 'Keeping the law should be a delight in itself.'[102] If even the divine 'positive law' should delight and bless those who obey it, then how far removed can it be from 'natural law' properly understood? Barton, however, does not take up this line of thought.

Instead, these insights lead him back to his critique of divine-command ethics in favour of human ethical resources: 'Although it does not think philosophically, the Old Testament does use what may be called quasi-philosophical lines of thought in trying to give its

---

[97] Ibid., 75.

[98] His insistence on particularity is even stronger than that of Hays and Verhey. For instance, he criticizes Stanley Hauerwas on these grounds (he prefers Martha Nussbaum's approach) despite Hauerwas's effort to stick with the particular (see ibid., 21).

[99] Ibid., 77. Barton observes in this regard of the biblical authors: 'What they had to tell people about morality was not that God had, inscrutably, commanded this or forbidden that, but that the basic principles of ethical obligation were accessible to all irrespective of any special divine revelation' (77).

[100] Ibid., 89.   [101] Ibid., 94.   [102] Ibid.

readers adequate reasons for acting morally: it is far from relying simply on assertion or diktat.'[103] Reasonable people will thus find much of value in the Old Testament as they construct their own moral systems, or as Barton puts it, 'as we go about trying to work out our own account of what it is to lead a moral life'.[104] But this account of reasonable people constituting their own ethics is far, I would suggest, from the Old Testament's own profoundly theocentric view of morality.

David Novak

By way of introducing the insights of the Jewish theologian David Novak, let us recall our original question. Does natural law belong to biblically grounded reflection on the moral life, or is it a Greek and Roman philosophical category that remains inadequate for describing biblical realities? Are there biblical warrants for natural law reflection in Christian ethics? The answers given by Hays and Verhey, leading scholars in the field of biblically based Protestant ethics, appear to be in the negative. Hays operates from within his contrast between Barth and Niebuhr, the latter of whom represents the danger of anthropocentric rationalizing. Much like Barth, Hays emphasizes narrative particularity and divine freedom, to which he adds 'metaphorical paradigms' that assist the Church in contemporary ethical application. A metaphysical understanding of 'law', it would seem, would threaten Christian ethics by turning the Church away from both narrative particularity (assisted for Hays by metaphorical, but not metaphysical, reasoning) and divine freedom. Verhey pays somewhat more attention to law than does Hays, but for him law appears as extrinsic, minimal standards whose greater intelligibility can be found only within the biblical stories, for example the story of Christ or the story of creation. These stories, however, do not offer a route to metaphysical reflection upon 'nature' and 'law', and thus Christian

---

[103] Ibid., 97. Barton's goal, as expressed in the penultimate sentence of his book, is to show that the Old Testament documents are no less rational than the works of the ancient Greeks.

[104] Ibid. See also Barton's 'Virtue in the Bible', *Studies in Christian Ethics* 12 (1999): 12–22.

ethics is largely limited to reflecting upon which stories have primacy and how alternative stories may participate in certain ways in the 'prime-analogate' story.

In evaluating Christian ethics as understood biblically by Hays and Verhey, I pointed out the severe drawbacks of excluding 'natural law' reflection. A different biblical perspective is offered by Barton as an Old Testament scholar. He retains Hays's and Verhey's concern for narrative particularity, but he argues that attention to this narrative particularity—in the Old Testament at least, and especially in the wisdom literature and the prophets—reveals a pattern of biblical appeals to natural law. If Barton is correct, then a Christian ethics attuned to the biblical stories might not be able to avoid 'natural law'. Yet Barton offers a highly problematic definition of what counts as 'natural law'. For him, as we have seen, natural law is 'natural human morality' as opposed to 'God telling us what to do'; what demarcates 'natural law' from positive law, on this view, is the presence or absence of the stricture of obedience to God. Thus the Decalogue is strictly positive law, not natural law. Two points result from Barton's analysis. First, Christian ethics should take account of biblical appeals to natural law, law inscribed in the created order and appealed to as normative even though not directly mandated by God in the Torah. Second, however, if Barton's understanding of 'natural law' as common sense or 'natural human morality' is correct, then Hays's and Verhey's concern, rooted in the central stories of Scripture, that Christian ethics be theocentric rather than anthropocentric should, I believe, override such biblical appeals to 'natural law'.

Is David Novak able to develop the conversation any further? Novak, like Barton, gives a number of biblical instances of natural law, which he contrasts with specifically revealed law. Among these biblical instances, in which human agents exhibit knowledge of moral norms not directly revealed, are the stories of the Fall (idolatry), Cain and Abel (murder), the Flood and its aftermath (sexual corruption), Abraham (righteousness and justice), the rape of Dinah, Joseph and Potiphar's wife (adultery), and Moses and Jethro (welcome of the stranger). He concludes that these stories show 'that in Scripture itself the covenant has a universal precondition as well as a universal consequence, that it has an ontology as well as an eschatology'.[105] These stories, in other words, indicate a human apprehension of God's moral law prior to God's revealing of certain norms at Sinai. It follows that such human apprehension of God's moral law must have a place in any ethics that flows from biblical revelation.

To this point Novak's contribution is broadly similar to Barton's. How does Novak understand 'natural law'? On the one hand, responding in particular to the Kantian approach of the Jewish thinker Hermann Cohen, he rejects the notion that natural law is anthropocentric. Appealing to the doctrine of creation, he states, 'Because the nature from which we learn natural law is rooted in irretrievable creation, it is not simply what we ourselves can simply bring to presence. . . . [C]reation and its order, that is, nature, is the necessary precondition for revelation to occur.'[106] What this means is that the interhuman moral norms that Cohen takes as indicative of properly human (as opposed to divine) lawgiving are in fact inscribed within a *divine* ordering. As Novak suggests in response to Cohen's interpretation of a rabbinic text in which Cohen finds the primacy of human lawgiving: 'it is not that the realm of the divine–human relationship is being reduced to the realm of the interhuman relationship. Instead, it is quite the reverse, that is, the interhuman realm is being included in the divine–human realm. The source of the law is God, whoever its more proximate source or more proximate end might

[105] Novak, *Natural Law in Judaism*, 61. The word 'ontology' is significant here. Elsewhere he states that 'metaphysics is not the way to constitute natural law. Metaphysics is after all one type of ontology, one approach to being. A theology of revelation is another. It seems to me that the ontological constitution of natural law is better done out of a religious tradition itself, specifically out of a theological constitution of the doctrine of creation' (26). He defines metaphysics as follows: 'By "metaphysics" I mean the type of ontology beginning with Plato, and most systematically formulated by his student Aristotle, that moves up in a rational trajectory from the study of universal nature (including human nature) to what has come to be known as "natural" (as distinct from "revealed") theology (see Aristotle, *Metaphysics*, 1074b35; *Nicomachean Ethics*, 1177a10–15)' (26; cf. 157).

[106] Ibid., 144–5. See also David Novak, *The Election of Israel: The Idea of the Chosen People* (Cambridge: Cambridge University Press, 1995), 104–5. Novak makes the same point in 'Before Revelation: The Rabbis, Paul, and Karl Barth', in idem, *Talking with Christians*, 108–26. In 'Before Revelation' Novak finds 'a strikingly similar theo-logic in Paul and then in Kierkegaard and then in Barth. All of them are asserting a pre-revelational norm—the prohibition of idolatry—and all of them are at least implicitly denying that it is in any way inferred from anything like natural theology' (114).

be.'[107] This is so because of the reality of creation, a reality known of course within the covenantal community and therefore not to be set in opposition to revelation.

Novak's account of natural law is thus more theocentric than Barton's. Yet he is concerned that natural law theories can become too expansive and claim too much. Arguing against the classical approaches to Noahide law (seen as 'natural law') of Maimonides and Saadiah, he observes that 'natural law' accounts can take two forms:

One way, which is epitomized by Saadiah and Maimonides, is to speculate teleologically, namely, to reflect on what the ends of law are and how natural law precepts are the proper means to fulfill them. The 'nature' in *natural* law in this way of thinking is an all-encompassing whole, each of whose parts is a good attracting intelligent human action. The other way...is to reflect on the inherent negative limits of the human condition and to see law as the way of practically affirming the truth of that limitation of a finite creature, a limitation apprehended by its intelligence. The 'nature' in *natural* law in this way of thinking is internal structure, that is, what limits personal and communal pretensions.[108]

The second approach is the one developed by Novak. He critiques the teleological account of natural law on three related grounds.

First, he argues that the teleological account rests upon a normative 'teleological natural science', whereas in his view modern biology has shown that ultimately there is no 'final cause' or *telos* in the structures and the development of biological organisms or in the cosmos as a whole.[109] Second, teleological natural law accounts, he thinks,

---

[107] Novak, *Natural Law in Judaism*, 90. As he remarks further on, 'Only in human community can we properly wait for God. That is why natural law is manifest to us as moral law, which orders our interhuman relationships. That is what connects it to the law of God.'

[108] Ibid., 151–2. For further discussion of Maimonides on natural law, see David Novak, 'Maimonides and Aquinas on Natural Law', in *St. Thomas Aquinas and the Natural Law Tradition*, eds. John Goyette, Mark S. Latkovic, and Richard S. Myers (Washington, DC: Catholic University of America Press, 2004), 43–65. Novak's concern is that Maimonides has been too influenced by Aristotle.

[109] Novak, *Natural Law in Judaism*, 136–7. Novak's view about teleology is increasingly contested by contemporary scholars. See, for instance, Alasdair MacIntyre, *Dependent Rational Animals: Why Human Beings Need the Virtues* (Chicago: Open Court, 1999); Jean Porter, *Nature as Reason: A Thomistic Theory of the Natural Law* (Grand Rapids, MI: Eerdmans, 2005), chapter 2, especially her citations of relevant scientific literature.

do not adequately consider historical particularity. In this regard he proposes, following the Roman model of *ius gentium*, that the goal of natural law theory should be to identify 'overlappings *between* oneself and others rather than the constitution of some universal whole, totally *containing* oneself and others'.[110] Third, he emphasizes that the existence of the covenant (of Israel with God) means that 'natural law must fit into the context of the covenant', not the other way around.[111] The problem with teleological models is that they suggest that 'the human relationship with God is not only *in* the world, a point common to any theology of creation, but it is always *through* the world as well'.[112] In other words, teleological natural law theories tend toward a rationalistic naturalism, which fails to distinguish human beings' radical uniqueness vis-à-vis the natural realm. Human ethical norms become teleologically rooted in nature, rather than rooted in the unique relationship with God (covenant), just as if human beings were mere animals rather than the *imago dei*.[113] He insists that 'our relation *to* the world ... be ontologically (even if not usually chronologically) subsequent to our direct relationship *with* God'.[114]

In this third regard, Novak grants that Maimonides' teleological account is far more nuanced than is Saadiah's. Whereas for Saadiah

[110] Novak, *Natural Law in Judaism*, 139–40. For further discussion of the Roman *ius gentium*, see David Novak, *Jewish–Christian Dialogue: A Jewish Justification* (Oxford: Oxford University Press, 1989), 116.

[111] Novak, *Natural Law in Judaism*, 131.   [112] Ibid., 130.

[113] Novak argues that conceiving of the *imago dei* as specifically the human power of reason, as many Jewish and Christian theologians have done, is a mistake. This is most evident, he thinks, in the case of those who do not possess the use of reason, for instance the unborn, the severely retarded, the comatose. Identifying the *imago dei* with reason would in his view deny the humanity or at least the personhood of such individuals. In contrast, I would argue that the distinction between powers, habits, and acts addresses such concerns; a human being can possess a soul without being able to reason.

[114] Ibid., 130. Here Novak relies upon the Kantian disjunction, rather than distinction, between 'history' and 'nature': 'As Dilthey clearly saw, the way we constitute the realm of freedom and purpose (what he called *Geisteswissenschaften*) is essentially different from the way we constitute the realm of necessity and causality (what he called *Naturwissenschaften*). The greatest modern Jewish theologian to my mind, Franz Rosenzweig, whatever his critique of other aspects of modernity might have been, built on modernity's insistence on the independence of history from nature ... History, not nature, is the integral realm of persons and their interrelationships' (131).

God appears primarily as the efficient cause of the universe, to whom human beings relate in this indirect way, for Maimonides 'the authentic relationship with God is with God as the supreme *telos*, the intelligible and intelligent apex of the entire cosmos'.[115] This relationship is attained by contemplation fuelled ultimately by inspired prophecy. As Novak makes clear, in Maimonides' teleological account the relationship to God is not mediated by non-human nature or by any other person. However, Novak finds Maimonides' account, like Saadiah's, to be unsatisfying. The main reason is that Maimonides' God, like Aristotle's, is not a true covenantal partner, but rather is solely a passive teleological end.[116] Natural structures, not the acts of persons (including God) in history, are determinative. In Novak's view all teleological accounts end up in this error, which at bottom is a rationalism that occludes or rejects the God of the Bible. Here Novak's concern, to my mind, is quite similar to the anti-rationalist concerns of Hays and Verhey, and equally differentiates Novak from Barton's understanding of biblical natural law.

Novak's own account of biblically based natural law focuses upon the sin of pride. Rather than approaching natural law teleologically (ordered by inclination to the good), Novak sets forth an approach

---

[115] Ibid., 133.

[116] Ibid., 135. It should be noted that earlier Novak also strongly praises Maimonides, whom he reads as accentuating practical reason while avoiding Kant's occlusion of God: 'Practical excellence as *imitatio Dei* introduces into the history of ideas a new form of practical freedom. It is more than simple free choice because it itself introduces its own ends; it is not simply an application of standards already in place. But it is still less than what we mean by autonomy after Kant. That is because this freedom can only function in a subordinate partnership with God's creative intelligence. The limitations of human mortal creatureliness—the essential finitude of the human condition—makes this metaphysical grounding the *conditio per quam* of true practical reason. Without it, the roles of God and man would be reversed, as indeed they are for Kant and all who follow him. But for Maimonides, that would be basing practical wisdom on what is demonstrably false since he believed that the primacy of God is rationally evident. Moreover, truth is both logically and ontologically prior to good. As such, the human person participates in divine creativity first by deriving his or her wisdom from that creativity through contemplation of its effects, and then creatively applying part of it in establishing the city of God on earth. In affirming that, Maimonides gave great philosophical expression to a uniquely Jewish idea. It shows him to be a thinker who was much more than a follower of Plato, Aristotle, or Alfarabi, however much he may have learned from all of them. Both his agenda and his insights were originally Jewish' (119–20).

that is ordered by the true, whose opposite is pride.[117] Rather than beginning as Maimonides does with the *telos* of the *imago dei*, namely contemplative knowledge of God, he proposes that the *imago dei* or *tselem elohim* be understood as a limit-doctrine by which one knows solely that no this-worldly category can fit human beings. In a sense, he here brings in again teleology, but in a form that escapes the bounds of natural teleology. The *imago dei* means that human beings have a 'special status, and that it is beyond anything one could get from the world'.[118] What this 'special status' indicates is that human beings await a fulfilment that (while teleological) goes beyond this world. Human beings cannot give this fulfilment to themselves. Marked by both radical finitude and radical desire, human beings can recognize in each other both their limitation and their 'special status'. Natural law (or Noahide law), for Novak, begins with this finitude—thereby excluding all anthropocentric pride— and at the same time is able to affirm certain truths (whose content is largely negative rather than positive prescription) about what is required, as a bare limit, for human individual and communal flourishing.

On this view, revelation has a primacy because 'only in revelation do humans learn the truth from the One who is the source of that [human] worth, which is that these humans are loved by this God'.[119] And yet, prior (ontologically if not necessarily temporally) to revelation, the *imago dei* enables human beings to recognize in each other their special status expressed by their desire for fulfilment from outside the world, their inability to conceive of their ends solely in this-worldly terms. This recognition is ultimately inconceivable without the doctrine of creation, because the human desire for fulfilment from outside this world bespeaks creatureliness, radical receptivity. Likewise, the combination of finitude and desire, as lived out in history, requires human beings to learn in community 'what makes authentic human community possible, both immanently and in its

---

[117] Ibid., 153.

[118] Ibid., 172. Novak's position is thus quite different from the even more minimalist position offered by Jeffrey Stout in 'Truth, Natural Law, and Ethical Theory', in *Natural Law Theory: Contemporary Essays*, ed. Robert P. George (Oxford: Oxford University Press, 1992), 71–102.

[119] Novak, *Natural Law in Judaism*, 172.

transcendent intention'.[120] It thus forms the basis of the natural law or Noahide law.

Against all rationalism, then, natural law encompasses, from within the recognition of human finitude and transcendent desire (thus from within human *limits* rather than identifiable *ends* or *inclinations*), the historical and communal practices required for rejecting pride and fostering true desire. Natural law is biblical not because it is trans-cultural but because it emerges from within cultures. As Novak puts it, 'Instead of an attempt to find some universal phenomenon to ground natural law, it seems more authentic and more useful to see it as the constitution of a universal horizon by a thinker *in* a particular culture *for* his or her own culture.'[121] This is what Novak finds occurring in the biblical texts.

BIBLICAL NATURAL LAW: CONCLUSIONS AND PRINCIPLES

What has the above survey accomplished regarding our question about whether natural law belongs to biblically grounded ethics? First, we have observed that leading contemporary efforts to chart a biblically grounded ethics, drawing especially on the New Testament, do not advert to natural law doctrine. The New Testament contains little teaching on natural law, and those passages that might suggest such a discussion—such as Romans 1–2—are often not seen as warranting the inclusion of natural law doctrine as a constitutive element of Christian ethics. When such efforts do include discussions of 'law', law is viewed either in light of Karl Barth's divine command theory or in opposition to 'story', which provides a non-metaphysical framework for discerning norms of Christian action. 'Story' does not carry the baggage of law's extrinsic and punitive

---

[120] Ibid., 183.
[121] Ibid., 190. Cf. Stanley Hauerwas, 'Christian Ethics in Jewish Terms: A Response to David Novak', *Modern Theology* 16 (2000): 293–9. Hauerwas is concerned about 'natural law accounts of Christian ethics that separate what is required of Christians from the salvation into which we have been incorporated through the work of Jesus Christ' (294).

associations, let alone of the contested metaphysical and epistemological sense of 'natural'. In discussing this situation, I questioned
whether 'story' or narratival reflection alone is in fact as sufficient as is
claimed.

Second, we have seen that some contemporary scholars whose
ethics flows from the Old Testament have made significant room
for 'natural law'. The Christian Old Testament scholar John Barton
engages natural law as a counterpoint to Barth's emphasis on divine
positive law. He finds in natural law a way of describing biblical passages that exhibit human beings appealing to moral norms that have
been discerned by human beings rather than directly commanded
by God. This position seeks to place the Bible's moral reflection
more squarely within the human labour of articulating the good, as
opposed to seeing ethics as primarily receiving and obeying divine
revelation. The Jewish theologian David Novak wishes to retain the
primacy of revelation, but also to insist upon a prior communal
context in which revelation is received—a context whose elements
of finitude and desire mark out a 'natural law' or, as Jewish theologians describe it, a Noahide law. At the very least, this work on
Old Testament biblical texts poses a serious challenge to Christian
ethicists and exegetes who exclude natural law from their theological
reflection.

Third, throughout the above survey, it has been clear that different
notions of 'law' and 'natural law' are at work. Hays admires the
theocentricity of Barth's account of ethics as obedience to divine
positive law, but the value of this account, in Hays's view, depends
upon its strict adherence to the particularity of the biblical stories
and commands. While defending the construction of 'metaphorical
paradigms' by which to apply biblical stories and commands
to situations today, Hays strongly opposes any Christian ethical
reflection that seeks to abstract from the stories, on the grounds
that an anthropocentric rationalism will emerge from such practices
(Niebuhr). 'Natural law', one supposes, would be an instance of such
metaphysical abstraction, although Hays might clarify this point in
future work. Law simply does not have a significant place in Hays's
framework. For Verhey, law has a place, but it represents extrinsic
ethics, critiqued eschatologically by Jesus, as opposed to the intrinsic
ethics made possible by primary attention to 'story'. For Barton, the

'natural law' present in biblical texts, especially in the prophets and the wisdom literature, is the 'natural human morality' that differs strongly from obedience to 'God telling us what to do', and whose value consists largely in this difference. 'Natural law' in Barton's view is essentially human common-sense morality. Novak finds 'natural law' in the biblical stories prior to Sinai, and he argues that the distinction between 'nature' and 'history' requires a non-teleological account of natural law.

Can a constructive account of biblical natural law flow from engagement with the positions of these four thinkers? I wish to propose four constructive principles, centred upon particular biblical texts, for understanding the relationship between Christian ethics, biblical revelation, and natural law doctrine. In the chapters that follow, I will seek to make the case more fully for these principles of 'biblical' natural law.

A Teleological Natural Law

First, Scripture presents certain goods as constitutive of true human flourishing and thus of moral order. Genesis 1–2 provides one place where such teleological ordering, rooted theocentrically in God's creative providence, can be seen. Here we find in germ the human natural inclinations.

The basic inclination toward the good belongs within the context of God's blessing of his creation. After the creation of human beings, 'God saw everything that he had made, and behold, it was very good' (Gen. 1:31; cf. 1 Tim. 4:4). This goodness constitutes the basic inclination of human flourishing: the good for human beings *draws* or *inclines* human beings. Goodness, as Aquinas observes, 'has the aspect of desirable' and 'implies the idea of a final cause'.[122] The rhythm of the phrase 'And there was evening and there was morning' (Gen. 1:5, 8, etc.) indicates the wise ordering toward the common good that God is accomplishing in his harmonious creation—an ordering whose 'end' is located in God's Sabbath rest (Gen. 2:1–4).

[122] *Summa Theologiae* I, q. 5, a. 2.

God creates human beings so that they are naturally ordered to preserve the good of their human existence. Without the inclination to preserve this good, God's warning about the tree of the knowledge of good and evil would not be intelligible: 'You may freely eat of every tree of the garden, but of the tree of the knowledge of good and evil you shall not eat, for in the day that you eat of it you shall die' (Gen. 2:17). The threat of death constitutes a warning because human beings recognize human life, in its united spiritual–bodily dimensions, as a good (cf. Gen. 3:3, 19). The condemnation 'you are dust, and to dust you shall return' resounds ever more powerfully because this 'dust' has received 'the breath of life' (Gen. 2:7) directly from God, and is 'in the image of God' (Gen. 1:27).

God also inscribes within human beings an inclination toward the good of procreation and the raising of children, toward the good of the continuance of the human race: 'And God blessed them, and God said to them, "Be fruitful and multiply…"' (Gen. 1:28). This instruction to 'be fruitful and multiply' is not merely an extrinsic command, but an internal inclination toward the good, as is manifest in Eve's rejoicing, '"I have gotten a man with the help of the Lord"' (Gen. 4:1).[123] God creates human beings with an inclination toward the good of living in society: 'male and female he created them' (Gen. 1:27) and 'It is not good that the man should be alone' (Gen. 2:18). In this regard recall, too, Adam's wonderful statement, 'This at last is bone of my bones and flesh of my flesh; she shall be called Woman, because she was taken out of Man' (Gen. 2:23). Nor is this inclination, in human beings, merely animal: marital intercourse is a 'knowing' (Gen. 4:1).

God creates human beings, lastly, with an inclination toward knowing the truth, ultimately the truth about the Creator. One can see this point in God's words, 'Let us make man in our image, after our likeness' (Gen. 1:26). Created in the image and likeness of God, human beings possess a natural inclination toward knowing truth, the fulfilment of the spiritual capacity to know. Man alone has the responsibility for naming the animals (Gen. 2:19–20). The serpent

---

[123] This is the key insight, put in a light-hearted manner, in Sondra Wheeler, 'Creation, Community, Discipleship: Remembering Why We Care about Sex', *Ex Auditu* 17 (2001): 60–72.

appeals, in a disordered fashion, to this inclination toward knowing the truth: ' "You will not die. For God knows that when you eat of it your eyes will be opened, and you will be like God, knowing good and evil" ' (Gen. 3:4–5). Indeed, as Genesis progresses, we see how the human moral disorder brought about by the Fall deforms, without destroying, all of these natural inclinations.

In short, the early chapters of Genesis, within a profoundly theocentric context, reveal human beings to be intrinsically teleological, ordered to certain goods constitutive of a flourishing proper to human beings. This aspect of Genesis 1–2 can be overlooked when one views God's commands as extrinsic rather than intrinsic to the human person. Yet in appealing, with regard to marriage, to 'the beginning' (Matt. 19:4, 8), Jesus himself emphasizes the teleological dimension of Genesis 1–2. In Genesis 1–2 God's commands and actions do not set up extrinsic norms, but rather indicate, in a theocentric fashion, the intrinsic norms that express the goods constitutive of true human flourishing.

Natural Law and Divine Commands

Second, Scripture does not countenance an absolute disjunction between divine positive law and natural law. Many theologians and biblical scholars have read the Decalogue as strictly divine positive law. Certainly there is something majestic and even terrifying about the requirements of human holiness and justice, given how human beings tend, as sinners, to fail to meet these requirements. And yet, Exodus 19–20 offers a sense of human teleological fulfilment, of a law that meets the requirements of human ordering toward true human flourishing. Admittedly, the encounter with God at Sinai is nearly too much for human endurance: immediately after the enumeration of the Decalogue, we read, 'Now when all the people perceived the thunderings and the lightnings and the sound of the trumpet and the mountain smoking, the people were afraid and trembled; and they stood afar off, and said to Moses, "You speak to us, and we will hear; but let not God speak to us, lest we die" ' (Exod. 20:18–19). But Moses reassures the people that this law is not opposed to them, but rather sets forth the interior path of justice, a path of proper fear of God.

Moses tells them, 'Do not fear; for God has come to prove you, and that the fear of him may be before your eyes, that you may not sin' (Exod. 20:20).

Given the human lack of justice, the people and priests had to 'consecrate themselves, lest the Lord break out upon them' (Exod. 19:22; cf. 19:14). Sinai indeed is a meeting-point of the human and the divine: 'Then Moses brought the people out of the camp to meet God: and they took their stand at the foot of the mountain. And Mount Sinai was wrapped in smoke, because the Lord descended upon it in fire.... And as the sound of the trumpet grew louder and louder, Moses spoke, and God answered him in thunder' (Exod. 19:17–19). As a meeting-point, however, it is not *alien* to the human. The Decalogue is positive law in the sense that God commands these laws and requires the people's obedience. But on the other hand, the imagery of Sinai goes far beyond the extrinsicism of 'divine command', and reveals that God seeks to *create his people anew* in holiness. What is 'natural' is not, in the disordered condition of human sinfulness, what comes naturally or mere common sense; on the contrary, disordered human beings turn away from the very laws that order them interiorly to their flourishing.

God in giving the Decalogue connects obedience to the Decalogue with a glorious new creation in justice—a renewed creation that reverses the Fall. What might at first seem to be merely extrinsic positive law is revealed as interior to the created order and its true flourishing. As Moses tells the people during their preparation for entering the promised land, 'See, I have set before you this day life and good, death and evil. If you obey the commandments of the Lord your God which I command you this day, by loving the Lord your God, by walking in his ways, and by keeping his commandments and ordinances, then you shall live and multiply, and the Lord your God will bless you in the land' (Deut. 30:15–16). The law sets forth the path of 'life and good'; to break it is 'death and evil', not extrinsically, but intrinsically.[124] Moses therefore says that 'this commandment

[124] On the grounds that in Genesis 22 God commands the slaying of Isaac, Duns Scotus argued that only the 'first table', the commandments regarding God, have intrinsic weight; all commandments regarding the neighbour can be changed by God. Aquinas takes a very different position. The divergence between Aquinas and Scotus on this point provides impetus for the rise of anthropocentric natural law: see my 'God and Natural Law: Reflections on Genesis 22', forthcoming in *Modern Theology*.

which I command you this day is not too hard for you, neither is it far off....But the word is very near you; it is in your mouth and in your heart, so that you can do it' (Deut. 30:11, 14). The divine commandments reveal what is in the people's 'mouth' and 'heart'. As the psalmist hymns, 'Thy testimonies are wonderful; therefore my soul keeps them. The unfolding of thy words gives light; it imparts understanding to the simple. With open mouth I pant, because I long for thy commandments' (Ps. 119:129–31).

Christ Jesus takes up the Decalogue in his teaching. When a man asks him, 'Good Teacher, what must I do to inherit eternal life?' Jesus responds first by warning against idolatry, the very root of human disorder: 'No one is good but God alone' (Mark 10:18). Secondly, he recalls the Decalogue, precisely as the interior path toward full human flourishing (the inheritance of 'eternal life'), not as alien divine commands. Jesus says, 'You know the commandments: "Do not kill, Do not commit adultery, Do not steal, Do not bear false witness, Do not defraud, Honour your father and mother"' (Mark 10:19). The man is pleased to say that he has obeyed these commandments.

The path of justice befitting the capacities of human nature, however, is not sufficient for the end, the full flourishing, that Jesus has come to reveal. To attain the eternal life of intimate union with the divine Trinity, faith in and configuration to Jesus' radically self-giving love—beyond the powers of our created nature, and thus a gift of grace—is necessary. The man, trusting too much in the things of this world, is in for a surprise: 'Jesus looking upon him loved him, and said to him, "You lack one thing; go, sell what you have, and give to the poor, and you will have treasure in heaven; and come, follow me"' (Mark 10:21). Yet, while obedience to the natural law does not suffice, neither is the natural law (as set forth in the Decalogue's precepts for human flourishing) rejected or changed by Jesus. Instead, Jesus retains the Decalogue in the form given to Israel. Without obedience to these commandments, the man cannot attain his end, 'eternal life'. These commandments remain the same, even as taken up into the radical *ecstasis* or self-giving enacted by Jesus. In addition to confirming the importance of law for New Testament ethics, once again we find that no disjunction here exists between divine positive law and natural law.

A Theocentric Natural Law

Third, the Bible's understanding of law is theocentric. Law does not first pertain to 'nature' or to human 'reason'. Indeed, law's theo-centricity overcomes this apparent opposition between 'nature' and 'reason' at its root, since law flows from the divine wisdom, Creator of nature and human reason. Wisdom of Solomon calls 'sophia' or personified wisdom 'the fashioner of all things' (Wisd. 7:22). In a paean to personified wisdom, Wisdom of Solomon teaches that wis-dom possesses:

a spirit that is intelligent, holy, unique, manifold, subtle, mobile, clear, unpol-luted, distinct, invulnerable, loving the good, keen, irresistible, beneficent, humane, steadfast, sure, free from anxiety, all-powerful, overseeing all, and penetrating through all spirits that are intelligent and pure and most subtle. For wisdom is more mobile than any motion; because of her pureness she pervades and penetrates all things. For she is a breath of the power of God, and a pure emanation of the glory of the Almighty; therefore nothing defiled gains entrance into her. For she is a reflection of eternal light, a spotless mirror of the working of God, and an image of his goodness. Though she is but one, she can do all things, and while remaining in herself, she renews all things; in every generation she passes into holy souls and makes them friends of God, and prophets; for God loves nothing so much as the man who lives with wisdom. For she is more beautiful than the sun, and excels every constellation of the stars. Compared with the light she is found to be superior, for it is succeeded by the night, but against wisdom evil does not prevail. She reaches mightily from one end of the earth to the other, and she orders all things well. (Wisd. 7:22–8:1)

Personified wisdom thus fashions all things and 'can do all things' because she is 'a reflection of eternal light, a spotless mirror of the working of God, and an image of his goodness'. Thanks to her, the created world that she 'orders ... well' possesses an intelligible order toward its proper flourishing. Certainly subhuman 'nature' possesses this teleological ordering, although in subhuman 'nature' (lacking the power of reason) it is not a 'law'. As Wisdom of Solomon states, God and God's personified wisdom make rationally accessible to human beings 'the structure of the world and the activity of the elements; the beginning and end and middle of times, the alternations of the solstices and the changes of the seasons, the cycles of the year and the constellations of the stars, the natures of animals and the tempers of wild beasts' (Wisd. 7:17–20). Human beings thus discern an intelligible ordering of each thing toward its proper flourishing.

Yet human beings, as rational creatures, participate freely in their teleological ordering by knowing God's law for true human flourishing. So as to participate well, Wisdom of Solomon suggests, one must imitate Solomon in beseeching that God grant one the possession of wisdom. Solomon asks God to place God's wisdom upon him: 'With thee [God] is wisdom, who knows thy works and was present when thou didst make the world, and who understands what is pleasing in thy sight and what is right according to thy commandments. Send her forth from the holy heavens, and from the throne of thy glory send her, that she may be with me and toil, and that I may learn what is pleasing to thee' (Wisd. 9:9–10). By participating in God's wisdom, human beings are able to understand and do what is right. One cannot take this sharing in wisdom for granted; rather, given human tendency toward sin and idolatry, one must strive to share in God's wisdom, at whose heart is self-dispossession or *ecstasis*. Idolatry is the perversion of the share in wisdom that human beings are given in creation. Wisdom of Solomon bemoans idolatry in a manner taken up by St Paul in Romans 1:19–20. As Wisdom of Solomon puts it, 'For all men who were ignorant of God were foolish by nature; and they were unable from the good things that are seen to know him who exists, nor did they recognize the craftsman while paying heed to his works' (Wisd. 13:1). The first mark of sharing in God's wisdom is 'ecstatically' going out of oneself so as to know God as the provident Creator of the universe's beauty and power. Those who foolishly, through self-cleaving idolatry, fall away from this sharing in God's wisdom (law), fall into more and more sin. Wisdom of Solomon observes that the killing of infants, sexual immorality, murder, deceit, and a general 'confusion over what is good' (Wisd. 14:26) follow upon self-cleaving idolatry, and that those in this condition 'call such great evils peace' (Wisd. 14:22).

Comparing human life to a sea voyage, Wisdom of Solomon holds that God has given us the path of flourishing and that God's providence will sustain and reward those who participate through wisdom in God's providential ordering for human fulfilment (Wisd. 14:1–7). Sirach puts it this way: 'The Lord himself created wisdom; he saw her and apportioned her, he poured her out upon all his works. She dwells with all flesh according to his gift, and he supplied her to those who love him' (Sir. 1:9–10).[125] Law has its ground in God, not in human beings. Our participated wisdom cannot be understood without adverting to its divine source. We do not constitute wisdom, but rather we receive it by seeking to discern and participate in it. This attitude of receptivity Sirach sums up as 'the fear of the Lord', which Sirach calls 'the crown of wisdom, making peace and perfect health to flourish' (Sir. 1:18). God pours forth his wisdom upon us, and we must cling to this wisdom (cf. Sir. 1:19). Similarly Proverbs describes wisdom, created by God 'at the beginning of his work' (Prov. 8:22), as the source of the paths of peace and 'a tree of life to those who lay hold of her; those who hold her fast are called happy' (Prov. 3:18). Far from human beings constituting their own wisdom, Proverbs states that the Lord 'by wisdom founded the earth' (Prov. 3:19) and warns us to 'trust in the Lord with all your heart and do not rely on your own insight' (Prov. 3:5). This theocentric account of wisdom as regards human flourishing finds confirmation throughout the New Testament, but perhaps most importantly in John 1, where Jesus is presented as the incarnate Word. The Word gives 'life' and 'light', and those who receive him are created anew as 'children of God' in holiness, sharing by self-giving love in his superabundant fulfilment of the Torah of Moses.

Natural Law and the Grace of the Holy Spirit

Fourth, the grace of the Holy Spirit does not negate, but rather fulfils, the law's precepts. This is true even with regard to the New Covenant's relationship to the ceremonial and judicial laws of Israel (cf. Exod. 21–3), which as I have argued elsewhere is one of fulfilment rather than negation.[126] But it holds even more clearly for the New Covenant's relationship to the Decalogue. There is no opposition

---

[125] Markus Bockmuehl suggests that Sirach is rooted in the Torah, whereas Wisdom of Solomon is closer to natural theology (*Jewish Law in Gentile Churches*, 98–9). I would argue that Wisdom of Solomon and Sirach are even closer than Bockmuehl allows: the key for both is the doctrine of creation, which illumines, rather than displaces, the wisdom of the Torah.

[126] See my *Christ's Fulfillment of Torah and Temple: Salvation according to Thomas Aquinas* (Notre Dame, IN: University of Notre Dame Press, 2002). See also the discussion of Pamela M. Hall, 'The Old Law and the New Law (Ia IIae, qq. 98–108)', in

between this law and the life of grace; on the contrary, the grace of the Holy Spirit enables us to live according to this law. As prophesied in Jeremiah 31 and elsewhere, grace is the new creation that enables Israel, and those engrafted into her in Jesus Christ (who embodies and fulfils Israel), to observe God's commandments and thereby to be holy. As we read in Jeremiah, 'I [God] will put my law within them, and I will write it upon their hearts; and I will be their God, and they shall be my people' (Jer. 31:33). The life of grace takes up into itself the law's wisdom for human flourishing. Indeed, Christ teaches, 'Think not that I have come to abolish the law and the prophets; I have come not to abolish them but to fulfil them' (Matt. 5:17).

The grace of the Holy Spirit, furthermore, is not limited to the time after Christ. St Paul remarks, 'For it is not the hearers of the law who are righteous before God, but the doers of the law who will be justified. When Gentiles who have not the law do by nature what the law requires, they are a law to themselves, even though they do not have the law. They show that what the law requires is written on their hearts, while their conscience also bears witness' (Rom. 2:13–15).[127] The Decalogue contains moral laws that the Gentiles can know 'by nature'. This natural law for human flourishing, 'written' on our hearts by creation, can be fulfilled by those whom the grace of the Holy Spirit has turned away from sin. Thus the biblical particularity of salvation, in which Christ Jesus takes up and superabundantly fulfils Sinai, requires that the Creator be the Redeemer. The particularity of the Cross is joined to the universality of the creation of human beings in the *imago dei*.

CONCLUSION

This chapter enquired whether natural law belongs properly to biblically grounded reflection on the moral life. Taking as examples two

---

The Ethics of Aquinas, ed. Stephen J. Pope (Washington, DC: Georgetown University Press, 2002), 194–206.

[127] For discussion of Aquinas's exegesis of this passage in his *Commentary on the Epistle to the Romans*, in comparison with Luke Timothy Johnson's exegesis of the passage, see my, 'Knowing What Is "Natural": Reflections on Romans 1–2' forthcoming in *Logos*.

studies in New Testament ethics and two studies in Old Testament ethics, I sought both to expose what is gained by attending to 'law' in Christian ethics and to argue that the Bible warrants natural law discourse. Evaluating the four approaches, I suggested that they provide, both deliberately and despite themselves, sufficient evidence of the biblical warrants and the interpretive value of natural law reflection. If so, the question cannot be whether Christian ethics must *import* an extrinsic system of natural law. Rather, Christian moral theology requires a philosophically sophisticated natural law doctrine in order to do justice to the teachings of divine revelation. Hays and Verhey thus need to reconsider, in my view, the place of law within their ethics. In contrast, Barton and Novak show that Scripture has a place for natural law, but they differ significantly on what 'natural law' is. It seems to me that Barton and Novak would largely, though by no means entirely, agree on which biblical narratives contain, broadly speaking, 'natural law' reflection. Where they appear to have more serious disagreement is on second-level questions about what it means philosophically to speak of 'natural law', including whether natural law is anthropocentric or theocentric, the role of natural inclinations, and so forth. I agree with Novak's theocentric emphasis, and with Barton's teleological emphasis.

I then selected certain biblical passages for reflection on the content of 'natural law'. It seems to me that interpretation of these biblical passages—to which many more could be added—requires at least four claims about 'natural law'. Without suggesting that study of the Bible should displace philosophical study of the created order, one can suppose that some philosophical approaches will be more adequate than others to illumining what God teaches about natural law through Scripture. This supposition underlies the four points that I have proposed:

(1) the Bible's understanding of human nature presumes the existence of created human natural inclinations toward the goods of human flourishing;

(2) the disjunction that some scholars make between divine commands and natural law misunderstands the character of the Decalogue;

(3) the Bible's account of natural law is radically theocentric, rooted in God's ordering wisdom, rather than anthropocentric; and

(4) affirming the natural law does not set up a competitor or parallel track to the life of grace or adduce universal norms that make the biblical narrative unnecessary.

Whether this 'biblical' natural law works philosophically and theologically will be the central question in the remaining chapters.

2

Anthropocentric Natural Law

Understanding the modern meaning of 'natural law' requires examination of the intellectual history of the shift from a theocentric worldview to an anthropocentric one. Chapter 1, which exposed how natural law doctrine has been and can be nourished and enriched by reflection upon biblical texts and problems, proposed that a theocentric and teleological understanding of the natural law best does justice to the realities taught in Scripture. I now hope to bring to the fore a philosophical and theological case for the theocentric and teleological natural law whose lineaments, in the context of biblical exegesis, Chapter 1 sketched.

The central task in this regard is to account for the development of natural-law discourse within the mainstream philosophies of the past few centuries. Beginning with Descartes and ending with Nietzsche, I will suggest that these philosophies begin by rejecting basic aspects of natural law as biblically understood (the Creator and teleological providential ordering) and end by turning 'natural law' into the very opposite of the biblical pattern of *ecstasis*. The late medieval roots of these philosophies' anthropocentric turn have been described by Louis Dupré:

Only when the early humanist notion of human creativity came to form a combustive mixture with the negative conclusions of nominalist theology did it cause the cultural explosion that we refer to as modernity. Its impact shattered the organic unity of the Western view of the real. The earliest Ionian concept of *physis* had combined a physical (in the modern sense!) with an anthropic and a divine component. The classical Greek notion of *kosmos* (used by Plato and Aristotle), as well as the Roman *natura*, had preserved the idea of the real as an harmonious, all-inclusive whole. Its organic unity had been threatened by the Hebrew–Christian conception of a Creator who remained outside the cosmos. Yet, through his wisdom, support, and grace, he continued to be present in this world. At the end of the Middle Ages, however, nominalist theology effectively removed God from creation. Ineffable in being and inscrutable in his designs, God withdrew from the original synthesis altogether. The divine became relegated to a supernatural sphere separate from nature, with which it retained no more than causal, external link. This removal of transcendence fundamentally affected the conveyance of meaning. Whereas previously meaning had been established in the very act of creation by a wise God, it now fell upon the human mind to interpret a cosmos, the structure of which had ceased to be given as intelligible. Instead of being an integral part of the cosmos, the person became its source of meaning. Mental life separated from cosmic being: as meaning-giving 'subject,' the mind became the spiritual substratum of all reality. Only what it objectively constituted would count as real. Thus reality split into two separate spheres: that of mind, which contained all intellectual determinations, and that of all other being, which received them.[1]

This chapter's survey of the trajectory of thought from Descartes to Nietzsche has positive purposes as well: Nietzsche's passionate rejection of what has preceded him, combined with his turning biblical *ecstasis* on its head (now supposing that self-aggrandizing rather than self-giving could be the true path of *ecstasis*), points to the possibility of a recovery of key aspects of theocentric and teleological natural law. Having confronted biblical natural law with its distorted mirror image in Nietzsche, I take up in the book's final two chapters the philosophical and theological resources that seem most helpful in moving toward a contemporary expression of natural law doctrine illumined once again by biblical revelation. Before depicting the path taken by modern philosophy with respect to natural law, however, I will begin by outlining the seminal

---

[1] Louis Dupré, *Passage to Modernity: An Essay in the Hermeneutics of Nature and Culture* (New Haven: Yale University Press, 1993), 3. For Plato on 'natural right, i.e., something which is by nature just', see Leo Strauss, 'On Natural Law', in Strauss, *Studies in Platonic Political Philosophy* (Chicago: University of Chicago Press, 1983), 137–46, at 138. For Aristotle, see Fred D. Miller Jr., 'Aristotle on Natural Law and Justice', in *A Companion to Aristotle's Politics*, ed. David Keyt and Fred D. Miller Jr. (Oxford: Blackwell, 1991), 279–306. Dupré is at pains to emphasize that '[t]he fact that I attribute modern problems to modern principles does not imply that I expect their solution from a return to premodern principles' (6).

contributions of Cicero and Augustine at the origins of natural law doctrine.[2]

NATURAL LAW BEFORE THE SHIFT: CICERO AND AUGUSTINE

Cicero: The Ends and Inclinations of Human Nature

Cicero's *De officiis* discussion of the law of nature takes place within his search for the source of every 'officium' or 'duty'.[3] Here he poses many of the difficult questions of moral enquiry, such as whether the duty is absolute or less so, how the duty relates to happiness (and what happiness is), how to account for occasions when what is useful conflicts with what is right ('honestum'), and how to decide what to do when given the choice between two right actions, or between two useful actions.

In order to answer these questions, he explores the ends and powers of the human being. These ends and powers come from personified nature, regarding which Cicero sets forth a detailed theology.[4]

---

[2] I have chosen Cicero and Augustine because their approaches resonate throughout the history of natural law doctrine. Given the goals of this chapter, it is not possible to review all the ancient and patristic contributions to the doctrine of natural law. On the contributions of the Presocratics, Plato, and Aristotle—in particular Plato's integration of nature and law, *physis* and *nomos*—see Dupré's superb treatment in *Passage to Modernity*, 15–29. See also Hadley Arkes, 'That "Nature Herself Has Placed in Our Ears a Power of Judging": Some Reflections on the "Naturalism" of Cicero', in *Natural Law Theory: Contemporary Essays*, ed. Robert P. George (Oxford: Oxford University Press, 1992), 245–77; Kevin L. Flannery, SJ, 'Five Republics', in *Human Nature in Its Wholeness: A Roman Catholic Perspective* (Washington, DC: Catholic University of America Press, 2006), 34–56, at 46–7.

[3] For the Stoic and Platonic background to Cicero's account, and in particular the influence of Antiochus of Ascalon (early first century BC), see Richard A. Horsley, 'The Law of Nature in Philo and Cicero', *Harvard Theological Review* 71 (1978): 35–59.

[4] See his dialogue *The Nature of the Gods*, trans. Horace C. P. McGregor (New York: Penguin, 1972), Book II, in which the speaker Balbus (whose views are approved by Cicero at the end of Book III) outlines a Platonized Stoic view. Cicero has Balbus argue: ' "That which we call Nature is therefore the power which permeates and preserves the whole universe, and this power is not devoid of sense and reason. Every being which is not homogeneous and simple but complex and composite must have in it some organizing principle. In man this organizing principle is reason and in

The first end, with its corresponding powers, is self-preservation. The second end is the procreation and raising of offspring, with the corresponding appetite for sexual intercourse. All animals possess these ends and powers, though in different ways. The human rational animal, Cicero points out, possesses these ends and powers as 'endowed with reason, by which he comprehends the chain of consequences, perceives the causes of things, understands the relation of cause to effect and of effect to cause, draws analogies, and connects and associates the present and the future—easily surveys the course of his whole life and makes the necessary preparations for its conduct'.[5]

A third end identified by Cicero is to live in society, both as regards the family and as regards public associations; this end involves powers to 'provide a store of things that minister to his comforts and wants' and to defend courageously the family and society.[6] A fourth end, which Cicero highlights as the most important and most proper to human beings, is to know truth. In specifying this end, Cicero makes clear that it requires 'leisure from the demands of business cares' but also that not merely philosophers, but indeed everyone desires to know what is not known. Cicero connects this end with a related desire to be free from subjection 'to anybody save one who gives rules of conduct or is a teacher of truth or who, for the general good, rules according to justice'. In short, the mind enables human beings to seek ends that establish 'greatness of soul', transcending the day-to-day.[7]

animals it is a power akin to reason, and from this arises all purpose and desire. Such a power is also present in the roots of trees and of every plant that springs up from the earth. This is the power which the Greeks call the 'guiding force', and it is and must be dominant in every complex being. It follows that the being in which is found the organizing principle for the whole of nature must be the supreme being, worthy of power and dominion over all. So we see that the parts of the world (for there is nothing in the world which is not a part of the universe as a whole) have sense and reason. So these must be present to a higher and greater degree in that part which provides the organizing principle of the whole world. So the universe must be a rational being and the Nature which permeates and embraces all things must be endowed with reason in its highest form. And so God and the world of Nature must be one, and all the life of the world must be contained within the being of God" ' (134–6). See also Cicero, *De legibus*, Book I.

[5] Cicero, *On Duties*, trans. Walter Miller, Loeb Classical Library (Cambridge, MA: Harvard University Press, 1913), 1.4.11, p. 13.

[6] Ibid., 1.4.12, p. 15.   [7] Ibid., 1.4.13, p. 15.

These four ends display the particular 'power of nature and reason' ('vis naturae rationisque') that enables human beings to have appreciation 'for order, for propriety, for moderation in word and deed'.[8] While the human animal shares inclinations with other animals, the human animal pursues the lower inclinations in accord with the highest inclination, the love of truth and transcendence. Cicero connects this distinctively human union of the higher and the lower, accomplished by 'nature and reason', with the human sense for 'beauty, loveliness, harmony', a sense that takes its starting points in the visible world and rises to the invisible world of the soul.[9] The beauty, loveliness, and harmony of the soul comprise the human being's 'goodness' ('honestum'). This 'honestum' is to be found in a rightly ordered pursuit of the four ends of the human being. He concludes therefore that the 'honestum' possesses four aspects corresponding to the four ends of truth, society, procreation, and self-preservation: to know the true, to live in society justly, to live an ordered and moderated life, and to be courageous. These four aspects of the 'honestum' or human 'goodness' are the four cardinal virtues—prudence, justice, temperance, and courage.

Of these the principal one is prudence, which in seeking to know the true has to do with the 'matter' or 'subject' of virtue, namely truth. Cicero emphasizes that 'of the four divisions which we have made of the essential idea of moral goodness' ('honesti naturam'), prudence 'touches human nature most closely. For we are all attracted and drawn to a zeal for learning and knowing; and we think it glorious to excel therein, while we count it base and immoral to fall into error, to

---

[8] Ibid., 1.4.14.

[9] The standard criticism of Ciceronian natural law doctrine is that it is static and lacks awareness of the transcendent capacity of the human person, who is seen simply as a part of 'nature'. Comparing the Stoics to Aristotle, Dupré observes, 'The assumption of a cosmic harmony and of a natural teleology also dominates Stoic thinking. But while Aristotle's normative concept of nature combines the essence of the natural thing with its potential for growth (the *energeia*) and with the goal or perfection at which its development aims, Stoic thought stresses nature's normative quality without allowing much to its development' (Dupré, *Passage to Modernity*, 28). The Stoics taught that '[a] divine Logos at the core of the *kosmos* sanctified nature's norm into divine law' (ibid.), and so for the Stoics nature's norm (a law rather than mere nature) has to be rationally, not merely instinctively, followed by human beings. To this Stoic framework, Roman thinkers such as Cicero added concern for the political common good.

wander from the truth, to be ignorant, to be led astray'.[10] For Cicero, the active life is superior to the contemplative, and so the intelligence should be primarily devoted to studying things that pertain to action, both as regards 'the bonds of union between gods and men and the relations of man to man'.[11]

The virtue of justice requires from Cicero a much more extensive discussion. He has to balance two fundamental principles, 'first, that no harm be done to anyone; second, that the common interests be conserved'.[12] These principles run up against hard cases, for instance when keeping a promise would harm the one to whom the promise was given, or defensive wars, or slavery, or exceptions to the principle of private property. Cicero devotes significant work to explaining the just conduct of war, both on the part of nations and on the part of soldiers. Far from glorifying war, he comments that 'there are two ways of settling a dispute: first, by discussion; second, by physical force; and since the former is characteristic of man, the latter of the brute, we must resort to force only in case we may not avail ourselves of discussion. The only excuse, therefore, for going to war is that we may live in peace unharmed.'[13] To justice Cicero adds beneficence, which he treats in detail. He also argues that the roots of justice, as found in the 'end' of living in society, manifest 'the connection subsisting between all members of the human race', a connection based both upon the power of rational communication and upon the 'end' of procreation and the raising of offspring, which grounds familial and social life.[14] Non-rational animals cannot be said to have 'justice' because they do not have the power of rational communication, even though they do seek to procreate and raise offspring. Under justice Cicero also discusses friendship and what is owed to friends, above all to one's country as comprising the good of oneself and one's friends.

Just as Cicero connects prudence with justice, for discerning the just action requires prudence, so also he connects courage with justice, because nothing courageous can be done from unjust motives. Courage involves a particular kind of self-preservation, because it requires a willingness to perform deeds that are 'extremely arduous

---

[10] Cicero, *On Duties*, 1.6.18, p. 19.   [11] Ibid., 1.43.153, p. 157.
[12] Ibid., 1.10.31, p. 33.   [13] Ibid., 1.11.34–5, p. 37.
[14] Ibid., 1.16.50, p. 53; and 1.17.54, p. 57.

and laborious and fraught with danger both to life and to many things that make life worth living'.[15] In order to possess such a willingness one must not fear to lose one's life. Yet this lack of fear flows not from a lack of desire for self-preservation, but a desire to attain a higher form of self-preservation for oneself, one's family, and one's community. Cicero observes that 'the career of those who apply themselves to statecraft and to conducting great enterprises is more profitable to mankind and contributes more to their own greatness and renown'.[16] Here he points out, by comparing Solon and Themistocles, that the statesman's accomplishments in peacetime are not less, and indeed are often more, than the soldier's in time of war. Lastly, treating temperance under the rubric of 'decorum', Cicero commends 'the order, consistency, and self-control it imposes upon every word and deed'.[17]

Taking all the virtues together, he finds both that all flow from our natural ends, and that temperance in particular manifests this connection of reason and nature:

If we follow nature as our guide, we shall never go astray, but we shall be pursuing that which is in its nature clear-sighted and penetrating (Wisdom), that which is adapted to promote and strengthen society (Justice), and that which is strong and courageous (Fortitude). But the very essence of propriety ['decorum'] is found in the division of virtue which is now under discussion (Temperance). For it is only when they agree with nature's laws ['ad naturam accommodati sunt'] that we should give our approval to the movements not only of the body, but still more of the spirit.[18]

The bodily appetites must obey reason, and to obey reason is to be 'accommodated to nature', since nature subjects the appetites to 'the law of nature'.[19] By 'nature' Cicero personifies the power behind the teleological plan for our existence. As he says, 'For nature has not

[15] Ibid., 1.20.60, p. 69. [16] Ibid., 1.21.70, p. 73.
[17] Ibid., 1.28.98, p. 101. [18] Ibid., 1.28.100, p. 103.
[19] Ibid., 1.29.102, p. 105. See also Cicero, *De re publica*, Book III. Ernest Fortin states that 'except for a single unconfirmed report by Cicero (*De natura deorum* I.36), there is no evidence that the Old Stoics [prior to Cicero] ever used the expression "natural law." Stoicism nevertheless furnished one of the key premises of that theory, namely, the notion of a providential God who guarantees the moral consistency of the universe' (Fortin, 'Natural Law', in Fortin, *Human Rights, Virtue, and the Common Good: Untimely Meditations on Religion and Politics*, ed. J. Brian Benestad (Lanham, MD: Rowman and Littlefield, 1996), 159–64, at 160).

bought us into the world to act as if we were created for play or jest, but rather for earnestness and for some more serious and important pursuits'.[20] He emphasizes in this regard the great superiority of human nature, which is rational and thereby is not limited by the sensual and instinctive, over that of mere animals.

For Cicero, temperance follows from recognizing the dignity, as rational nature, of human nature: 'if we will only bear in mind the superiority and dignity of our nature, we shall realize how wrong it is to abandon ourselves to excess and to live in luxury and voluptuousness'.[21] This superiority of human nature pertains to all human beings, even though human beings differ widely in abilities and temperaments and in this sense should direct their labours to work that fits their natural gifts. All alike possess rationality, from which the 'honestum' or moral goodness flows.[22] Furthermore, while primarily rooted in rationality, the superiority of human nature is evident even as regards the bodily form of human beings. Cicero notes the connection between the form of human bodies and the dignity of human rationality: 'Nature seems to have had a wonderful plan in the construction of our bodies. Our face and our figure generally, in so far as it has a comely appearance, she has placed in sight; but the parts of the body that are given us only to serve the needs of nature and that would present an unsightly and unpleasant appearance she has covered up and concealed from view.'[23] He has no hesitation in this regard of speaking of nature as 'our teacher and guide'.[24]

Beginning with an account of the ends of human nature—ends fully and properly achieved through the virtues—Cicero thus exhibits the 'law of nature' as the teleological dynamisms of the human being toward the achievement of the 'honestum', human goodness and beauty. In this teleological order reason possesses the dignity of guiding the whole, but to do so reason infuses and works through the dynamisms that human animals, as bodily creatures, share with other animals, such as self-preservation, procreation and the raising of offspring, and to live in society (to the degree that this is shared with other animals). Reason never stands above these dynamisms as if they

---

[20] Cicero, *On Duties*, 1.29.103, p. 105.   [21] Ibid., 1.30.106, p. 109.
[22] Ibid., 1.30.107, p. 109.   [23] Ibid., 1.35.126–7, p. 129.
[24] Ibid., 1.35.129, p. 131.

had to be humanized; rather, it is in these dynamisms that reason, even as it exercises its task of governing the whole, finds what it means to be human. Reason's quest for truth requires the proper fulfilment of the teleologies inscribed in human nature by the ends given by, as Cicero understands it, the wise, living, and all-encompassing being that is 'nature'.[25]

Augustine: Eternal Law

Cicero wrote his treatise in order to instruct his son, and posterity in general, on how to attain the happiest possible life. Augustine most fully addresses the law of nature, in contrast, in the context of a treatise that begins with the following question: 'Please tell me: isn't God the cause of evil?'[26] Cicero's reflections arise from concerns about how to live, whereas Augustine's reflections arise from concerns regarding divine providence, free will, and sin. Thus Augustine's dilemma in his treatise *On Free Choice of the Will* regarding the moral life is as follows: 'We believe that everything that exists comes from the one God, and yet we believe that God is not the cause of sins. What is troubling is that if you admit that sins come from the souls that God created, and those souls come from God, pretty soon you'll be tracing those sins back to God.'[27] In the course of investigating this

---

[25] Cicero's understanding of 'nature' as a deity undergirds his depiction of the beneficent law of nature. In this context one might ask again whether there can be a consistent, persuasive philosophical account of natural law 'without reference to the existence of God,' as John Rist puts it (Rist, *Real Ethics: Rethinking the Foundations of Morality* (Cambridge: Cambridge University Press, 2002), 152). Rist answers 'no'.

[26] Augustine, *On Free Choice of the Will*, trans. Thomas Williams (Indianapolis, IN: Hackett, 1993), 1.1, p. 1. See also Augustine's discussion in *Of True Religion*, trans. J. H. S. Burleigh (Chicago: Henry Regnery, 1959), 31.57–8, pp. 53–6. For natural law doctrine among the Fathers before Augustine, see Friedo Ricken, 'Naturrecht I: Altkirchliche, mittelalterliche und römisch-katholische Interpretationen', in *Theologische Realenzyklopädie* (Berlin: de Gruyter, 1977), vol. 24, pp. 132–53; Brian Dunkle, SJ, 'A Development in Origen's View of the Natural Law', *Pro Ecclesia* 13 (2004): 337–51. Philo of Alexandria played a key role in the mediation of Stoic thought to second-and third-century Fathers: on Philo, who like Cicero drew upon a Platonized Stoicism, see Markus Bockmuehl, *Jewish Law in Gentile Churches* (Edinburgh: T. & T. Clark, 2000), 107–11; John W. Martens, *One God, One Law: Philo of Alexandria on the Mosaic and Greco-Roman Law* (Leiden: Brill, 2003); Richard A. Horsley, 'The Law of Nature in Philo and Cicero'.

[27] Augustine, *On Free Choice of the Will*, 1.2, p. 3.

dilemma, Augustine and his interlocutor Evodius—*On Free Choice of the Will* is written as a dialogue—come upon laws that mandate opposite things, yet are both just when applied in their appropriate circumstances. Augustine calls such laws 'temporal', signalling that they hold justly in some situations but not in others. In contrast, Augustine points out that no just society could ever mandate that the wicked flourish and the good be miserable. A law condemning the good could never be just. Augustine shows that there is, then, an 'eternal and unchangeable' law, and he connects this eternal law with God's wise and good providence.

As Augustine makes clear, God, as creator, governs the 'society' of the human race. If God is a just governor, 'then he rewards the good and punishes the wicked'.[28] God's eternal law can be perceived both when we recognize laws that hold justly under all circumstances and when we trace just temporal laws back to their source. For instance, the temporal law that mandates in justice that a 'well-ordered and serious-minded people' should be able to choose its own rulers, is reversed when the condition of the people changes significantly for the worse, so that their choice of rulers could not accomplish the aim of the common good. Augustine's point is that well-ordered people justly deserve, because of their prudence, to bear the responsibility of choosing their own rulers for the common good, whereas licentious people do not justly merit such responsibility. The temporal law can justly change as regards who bears the responsibility for choosing rulers. But the eternal law—that a well-ordered people always deserves in justice to choose its own rulers—cannot change. One can never rightly say that a well-ordered people does not merit to choose its rulers, because it pertains to well-ordered people to order themselves toward the common good. One cannot, without injustice, call good a law that would deprive a well-ordered people of the exercise of its virtue. Thus the temporal law, which can change, takes its bearings from an eternal law that does not change. As Augustine puts it, 'nothing is just and legitimate in the temporal law except that which human beings have derived from the eternal law'.[29]

---

[28] Ibid., 1.1, p. 1.   [29] Ibid., 1.6, p. 11.

What is this eternal law? So far Augustine has defined it in terms of laws whose justice can never be altered by any circumstances. Such laws provide the measure by which the justice of other laws can be gauged. These laws, as God's eternal law, are 'the law according to which it is just that all things be perfectly ordered'.[30] Since God is good, his governance of his creatures cannot be unjust. Augustine puts it in concrete terms: when we know a law that binds eternally, we know a law that corresponds to the reality that justice requires 'everything to be perfectly ordered'. Since it is just, God will establish it; God will ultimately establish the justice of perfect ordering. Otherwise God would be less than well-ordered human rulers who care for the common good. The eternal law is God's perfect ordering of all things, which he will duly bring about in justice. How do we come to know laws that belong to the eternal law, God's perfect ordering? Augustine states that the 'eternal law' is 'stamped upon our minds'.[31]

At this point Augustine turns to a discussion of what 'mind' is and how it differentiates human beings from other animals. He shows that mind or reason, as the highest power in human beings, should govern the lower powers: 'For we should not call it right order, or even order at all, when better things are subjected to worse.'[32] This brings him to a discussion of the root of sin, which he finds to consist in an interior disorder plaguing the human being due to original sin and its transmission to the whole human race. Sin flows

---

[30] Ibid.

[31] Ibid. Ernest Fortin comments that for Augustine the natural law 'is the law requiring that "all things be properly ordered in the highest degree", or that at all times the lower be subordinated to the higher both within the individual and in society at large. Human beings are properly ordered when what is most noble in them, reason, controls the spirited part of the soul, when both reason and spiritedness combine to rule the desiring part, and when reason itself is ruled by God. Thus understood, the natural law is nothing other than the "divine reason or will prescribing the conservation of the natural order and prohibiting any breach of it." It extends to all of one's activities and is coextensive with the whole of virtue. As such, it is inseparable from wisdom or properly cultivated reason. What it imposes on everyone as a moral duty is nothing short of the perfection of human nature' (Fortin, 'Augustine and the Problem of Human Goodness', in Fortin, *The Birth of Philosophic Christianity: Studies in Early Christian and Medieval Thought*, ed. J. Brian Benestad (Lanham, MD: Rowman & Littlefield, 1996), 33–4). Fortin is quoting from Augustine's *On Free Choice of the Will* (1.6.15), *Against Faustus the Manichean* (22.27), and *Letter* 91.4.

[32] Augustine, *On Free Choice of the Will*, 1.8, p. 14.

from the dominance in the human being of disordered bodily desires (cupidity) over rational knowledge and will; this disorder, of course, is primarily a disorder of the mind or soul, which has given up its authority to govern and has thereby become foolish and clouded. Indeed, the culprit is the human will, which no longer governs. A good will enables one to possess the virtues of prudence, justice, fortitude, and temperance—because a good will loves itself as good and wills what pertains to goodness—while a bad will wills those things that oppose the possession of these virtues. Thus by means of a good will, one possesses a goodness that cannot be taken away, and therefore one enjoys happiness, which consists 'in the enjoyment of true and unshakable goods'.[33]

Yet who wills to be unhappy? Augustine answers that no one does, but that to be happy one must 'will it in the right way'. One must will 'to live rightly', to be and do good.[34] This point goes back to Augustine's understanding of God's eternal law, stamped on our minds: we must be rightly ordered, or else in justice we will undergo punishment. As Augustine states, 'the eternal law . . . has established with unshakable firmness that the will is rewarded with happiness or punished with unhappiness depending on its merit'.[35] To be rightly ordered, we must conform our actions to those laws for human action which we know to be eternally just. Above all we must love the perfect Good, God himself, above any created thing. Nothing could be more just and rightly ordered than to love the infinite Good above finite goods, not only because of the ever-greater character of the infinite Good, but also because of the gratitude we owe to our Creator. Augustine thus argues that 'the eternal law demands that we purify our love by turning it away from temporal things and toward what is eternal'.[36]

Among temporal things, he numbers the body, freedom to be our own masters, family, city, and property. Each of these temporal realities is subject to temporal laws. If we use the temporal things badly, temporal laws impose temporal punishments 'by taking away

[33] Ibid., 1.13, p. 23.   [34] Ibid., 1.14, p. 23.   [35] Ibid.

[36] Ibid., 1.15, p. 25. To understand Augustine properly, one needs to read this in the context of his affirmations throughout his corpus that all created things participate in, and are fulfilled by, God's eternal presence. Louis Dupré reads Augustine, mistakenly I think, as proposing a fundamentally 'extrinsic' rather than participatory relationship of creatures to God, with a resulting overly negative view of 'nature.' See Dupré, *Passage to Modernity*, 32–3.

one or another of these goods from the one being punished'.[37] But a deeper, spiritual punishment is imposed by the eternal law: namely the punishment intrinsic to cleaving to temporal realities that are passing away, as if they were eternal realities. Such disorder results in a loss of the true spiritual good, or happiness, of the human being. Whereas the eternal law mandates that the just human being, in submitting to eternal realities, should rule over temporal realities, disordered human beings allow themselves to be ruled over by temporal realities, which disordered human beings treasure more than eternal realities.

Evaluation

For Augustine, then, what is of central interest in this discussion is the eternal law. As we have seen, he pays attention to temporal laws and to our participation in the eternal law stamped on our minds. But whereas Cicero begins with ends inscribed by personified 'nature' in human nature, and traces out the virtues required to live in accord with the natural law identified through the ends, Augustine begins by showing the existence of an eternal law of right human action that exposes the context of divine providence in which human freedom operates. Thus Augustine can be said to focus more on God's 'law', and Cicero more on human nature. Yet it would be a serious mistake to imagine that this difference overcomes their more fundamental similarities. These similarities are twofold, despite the different problems that occasion their writing.

First, they both envision a *received* ordering of ends as constituting human nature. Their accounts are, in this sense, not anthropocentric. Cicero attributes the ordering of ends to personified nature, Augustine to God. While for Augustine human beings need to be healed from sin—and Cicero is aware as well of the difficulties that plague human beings in living according to what is highest in them—both are able to argue that human perfection consists primarily in receiving, not constituting, an ordering that is present in human nature as such. This argument regarding receptivity would not be possible had they started solely from human beings as they are.

---

[37] Augustine, *On Free Choice of the Will*, 1.15, p. 26.

For Cicero, the highest good (to know the truth) does not negate the lower ones, but rather enables—as the virtues show—the human being to bring the lower ones to perfection. The lower goods require the knowledge of truth for their fulfilment, and yet the lower goods are fully appropriate to human beings rather than mere animal drives that are then humanized. For Augustine, even fallen human beings can recognize (even if not will) God as the highest Good, and other goods of human nature find their proper significance only when willed in relation to this highest Good. Augustine does not suppose that conformity to the eternal law means humanizing the animal in us, but rather that conformity to the eternal law alone enables the fulfilment of all our body–soul ends—otherwise we tend toward physical death and spiritual destruction. In this regard, Cicero and Augustine take a position that divides them from leading modern proponents of natural law.

Second, Cicero and Augustine both recognize a fundamental connection between goodness (the 'honestum') and happiness. Cicero addresses the worry that the happy life is thwarted by the very personified 'nature' that inscribes the ends, since the ends are difficult of achievement. In this regard Cicero seeks to show in detail how the virtues enable the accomplishment of the ends of human nature. Augustine treats the similar fear that God's Providence itself bears responsibility for human failure to attain the happy life. If God creates and governs the soul, is not God ultimately responsible for the soul's misery, assuming that the soul does not attain happiness? Augustine exposes how our human laws reflect unchanging eternal laws by which the pattern of true human happiness can be known to us. Just as 'nature' does not constrict us for Cicero, so also God's eternal law is not the problem. The human 'honestum' or moral goodness is a happiness that is structured upon, rather than alien to or in tension with, our desires for self-preservation, for procreation and offspring, for life in society, and for truth. Similarly God's eternal law is not an esoteric knowledge, but manifests to us that God's just ordering will be accomplished in human beings.[38]

[38] See for further discussion Anton-Hermann Chroust, 'The Philosophy of Law from St. Augustine to St. Thomas Aquinas', *New Scholasticism* 20 (1946): 26–71. Chroust observes, 'Perhaps the most fundamental and far reaching contribution of St. Augustine to legal philosophy and its further development is to be seen in his basic

THE ANTHROPOCENTRIC SHIFT: NATURAL LAW
IN MODERNITY

When did this understanding of natural law as a received imprinting whose starting points are outside the self lose its force? Brian Tierney holds that the anthropocentric shift had beginnings in the canon law of the high Middle Ages.[39] As Louis Dupré observes, however, 'Aquinas has little to say about natural rights as such, because right originates through law, and natural right through natural law. . . . Even Suarez and Grotius, who began to distinguish *ius* more clearly from law and often described it as individual right, nevertheless continued to define that right by means of law.'[40] Dupré gives the key role to the Reformers' response to the theology of Scotus and Ockham.[41]

reformulation of the impersonal supreme cosmic reason proposed by the Stoics; in his successful undertaking to ground this universal order or régime exclusively in the *personal* will and intellect of God' (26). Chroust traces the reception of Augustine (and to a lesser degree Cicero) in Isidore, Alcuin, Anselm, Abelard, John of Salisbury, Gratian, Rufinus, Peter Lombard, William of Auxerre, Roland of Cremona, Alexander of Hales, Bonaventure, Matthew of Aquasparta, Albert the Great, and others.

[39] Brian Tierney, *The Idea of Natural Rights: Studies on Natural Rights, Natural Law, and Church Law 1150–1625* (1997; Grand Rapids, MI: Eerdmans, 2001), 23. Tierney is largely responding to the extensive work of Michel Villey, with whom he disagrees: see Tierney, 'Villey, Ockham and the Origin of Individual Rights', in *The Weightier Matters of the Law: Essays on Law and Religion*, eds. John Witte Jr. and Frank S. Alexander (Atlanta, GA: Scholars Press, 1988), 1–31. Tierney interprets Ockham's late-medieval political theory in light of the work of the high-medieval canonists: for Tierney on Ockham, see idem, *The Idea of Natural Rights*, 56–7, and the extensive discussion in Part II: 'Ockham and the Franciscans', 93–203. See Michel Villey, *La formation de la pensée juridique moderne*, 4th edn. (Paris: Montchrestien, 1975); idem, *Le droit et les droits de l'homme* (Paris: Presses Universitaires de France, 1983).

[40] Dupré, *Passage to Modernity*, 141–2; cf. on the general interchangeability of 'ius' and 'lex' in Aquinas, except when Aquinas wishes to speak of the 'ius gentium' or the 'lex aeterna' (or 'lex peccati seu fomitis'), Oscar J. Brown, '*Ius* and *Lex* in Aquinas', Appendix 1 in Brown, *Natural Rectitude and Divine Law in Aquinas* (Toronto: Pontifical Institute of Mediaeval Studies, 1981), 165–74, which is largely a response to Vernon J. Bourke, 'Is Thomas Aquinas a Natural Law Ethicist?' *The Monist* 58 (1974): 52–66.

[41] Dupré, *Passage to Modernity*, 215. On the Reformers' account of natural law, as well as late-medieval developments and later Protestant approaches, see Stephen J. Grabill, *Rediscovering the Natural Law in Reformed Theological Ethics* (Grand Rapids, MI: Eerdmans, 2006). Grabill finds late medieval and Scotist elements in Calvin's voluntarist account of natural law (72). See also Susan E. Schreiner, 'Calvin's Use of Natural Law', in *A Preserving Grace: Protestants, Catholics, and Natural Law*, ed.

It seems clear that a crucial step occurred in the early fourteenth century, when John Duns Scotus separated the second table of the Decalogue from 'natural law' proper, the latter now having to do solely with human beings' relationship to God, and the former comprising a realm of 'nature' lacking an intrinsic teleological unity with the movement of the will.[42] Scotus thereby establishes separations between nature and freedom, and nature and law, that were not present in Cicero, Augustine, or the earlier medievals—or in the biblical understanding of natural law which is grounded in the theology of creation, the divine wisdom that is inscribed in the created order.

Scotus's influence appears in the seventeenth-century Dutch thinker Hugo Grotius. Grotius, Richard Tuck explains, takes as his 'basic premiss' that ' "what God has shown to be his will, that is law" '.[43] But even in his earliest work Grotius 'explained what God wants in terms of man's innate sociability, to which all further natural laws were to be related'.[44] According to Tuck, 'in that explanation we can see the first indications of what was to be his eventual untheistic theory, with man's sociability becoming the sole premiss'.[45] This 'untheistic theory' holds that natural law is true 'even if we say there is no God'.[46]

Michael Cromartie (Grand Rapids, MI: Eerdmans, 1997), 51–76, especially her point about natural law for Calvin as 'a providential bridle' (68)—whose link to Calvin's doctrine of election is brought out by Timothy George in his 'Response' in the same volume (82).

[42] For further discussion, see my 'God and Natural Law: Reflections on Genesis 22', forthcoming in *Modern Theology*.

[43] Richard Tuck, *Natural Rights Theories: Their Origin and Development* (Cambridge: Cambridge University Press, 1979), 59, quoting from Grotius's *De Jure Praedae Commentarius*, ed. H. G. Hanaker (The Hague, 1868), 7. Tuck devotes chapter 3 of his book to Grotius. Anton-Hermann Chroust proposes, mistakenly I think, that Grotius simply continues the high-scholastic tradition of natural-law doctrine: 'Hugo Grotius and the Scholastic Natural Law Tradition', *New Scholasticism* 17 (1943): 101–33.

[44] Tuck, *Natural Rights Theories*, 59–60; for the influence of Scotus see 21, 176.

[45] Ibid.

[46] Hugo Grotius, *De iure belli ac pacis*, 1.10 (English edition *On the Law of War and Peace*, trans. Francis W. Kelsey (Oxford: Oxford University Press, 1925)). The force of this claim is contested by some scholars, including Chroust and Daniel Westberg. See Westberg, 'The Reformed Tradition and Natural Law', in *A Preserving Grace: Protestants, Catholics, and Natural Law*, ed. Michael Cromartie (Grand Rapids, MI: Eerdmans, 1997), 103–17, at 112.

For the natural law historian Heinrich Rommen, Grotius is 'the turning point': 'He may be said to have marked the transition from the metaphysical to the rationalist natural law.'[47] Rommen identifies the roots of Grotius's thought in the voluntarism of Scotus and Ockham, which, Rommen argues, 'split the scholastic doctrine of natural law to its very core'.[48] Others argue that the full-blown shift occurs before Grotius: Leo Strauss points to the work of Machiavelli and Thomas Hobbes,[49] while 'new natural law' theorists such as John Finnis blame the early seventeenth-century Thomistic commentator Francisco Suárez, who influenced Grotius.[50]

[47] Heinrich A. Rommen, *The Natural Law: A Study in Legal and Social History and Philosophy*, trans. Thomas R. Hanley, OSB (German 1936, 1947; Indianapolis, IN: Liberty Fund, 1998), 62. Jerome B. Schneewind agrees: see his *The Invention of Autonomy: A History of Modern Moral Philosophy* (Cambridge: Cambridge University Press, 1998), chapters 2–4.

[48] Rommen, *The Natural Law*, 53. See also Thomas M. Osborne Jr., 'Ockham as a Divine-Command Theorist', *Religious Studies* 41 (2005): 1–22, which argues convincingly against Marilyn McCord Adams, 'Ockham on Will, Nature, and Morality', in *The Cambridge Companion to Ockham*, ed. Paul Vincent Spade (Cambridge: Cambridge University Press, 1999), 245–72; and Peter King, 'Ockham's Ethical Theory' in the same volume, 227–44.

[49] See Leo Strauss, *Natural Right and History* (Chicago: University of Chicago Press, 1953), 166, 177–202. While devoting most of his attention to Hobbes, he observes that '[i]t was Machiavelli, that greater Columbus, who had discovered the continent on which Hobbes could erect his structure' (177). See also Leo Strauss, 'The Three Waves of Modernity', in idem, *An Introduction to Political Philosophy: Ten Essays by Leo Strauss*, ed. Hilail Gildin (Detroit: Wayne State University Press, 1989), 81–98. Strauss prefers the ancients' understanding of 'natural right' or 'natural law' to Aquinas's, on the grounds that Aquinas absolutizes 'universally valid rules of action' (*Natural Right and History*, 162), whereas the ancients recognize solely a 'universally valid hierarchy of ends' (ibid.).

[50] See John Finnis, *Natural Law and Natural Rights* (Oxford: Clarendon Press, 1980), 43–7, as well as the work of Robert P. George, Joseph Boyle Jr., and others who take up the thesis proposed by Germain Grisez, 'The First Principle of Practical Reason: A Commentary on the Summa Theologiae, 1–2, Question 94, Article 2', *Natural Law Forum* 10 (1965): 168–201. Followers of this approach also include, from somewhat different angles, Martin Rhonheimer, whose approach I will discuss in more detail in the next chapter, and Anthony J. Lisska, *Aquinas's Theory of Natural Law: An Analytic Reconstruction* (Oxford: Clarendon Press, 1996). See also Finnis, *Aquinas: Moral, Political, and Legal Theory* (Oxford: Oxford University Press, 1998), and the responses of Steven Long, 'St. Thomas Aquinas through the Analytic Looking-Glass', *The Thomist* 65 (2001): 259–300; and Jean Porter, 'Reason, Nature, and the End of Human Life: A Consideration of John Finnis's *Aquinas*', *Journal of Religion* 80 (2000): 476–84. Both responses point out that Finnis overlooks Aquinas's commitments to natural teleology in moral evaluation and to the hierarchical ordering of human goods.

The figures I have chosen for particular discussion inherit and develop this late-medieval/early-modern shift: René Descartes, Thomas Hobbes, John Locke, David Hume, Jean-Jacques Rousseau, Immanuel Kant, Georg W. F. Hegel, and Friedrich Nietzsche. By the end of this chapter, the anti-'ecstatic' consequences of their widely divergent approaches to natural law should be apparent. Their approaches reduce the earlier conception of natural law—natural law as a teleological participation in the divine *ecstasis* by which human beings freely and intelligently incline to *ecstasis*—to a much more narrow and constricted vision of, in various ways, self-construction and self-assertion. Dupré describes this tragic constriction well:

Once the human self becomes detached from its cosmic and transcendent moorings, the good can hardly be more than what Hobbes calls it: 'the object of any man's appetite or desire'.... What previously had given meaning to human life precisely because it surpassed individual aspirations, now came to be conceived in terms of personal need or fulfillment. Isolated from the totality from which it drew its very content, the self had nowhere to turn but to itself.[51]

René Descartes: The 'I' and Its Machine

In his Sixth Meditation, Descartes, having demonstrated the existence of God and concluded that 'God is not a deceiver',[52] takes up the relationship of the body and soul. He argues that since God is the orderer of 'nature', nature too does not deceive. His bodily feelings therefore merit trust as being no mere illusion. First and foremost, his

---

[51] Dupré, *Passage to Modernity*, 143.

[52] René Descartes, *Discourse on Method* and the *Meditations*, trans. F. E. Sutcliffe (New York: Penguin, 1968), 158. For background to Descartes and his period, see e.g. the essays in *Descartes and His Contemporaries: Meditations, Objections, and Replies*, ed. Roger Ariew and Marjorie Green (Chicago: University of Chicago Press, 1995), especially Jean-Luc Marion, 'The Place of the *Objections* in the Development of Cartesian Metaphysics', 7–20; Richard Popkin, *The History of Scepticism: From Savonarola to Bayle*, rev. edn. (Oxford: Oxford University Press, 2003), which contains two chapters on Descartes and provides the sixteenth- and seventeenth-century background to Descartes's search for certitude (namely a 'Pyrrhonism' arising out of the Reformation and the humanist recovery of ancient Greek scepticism); Jorge Secada, *Cartesian Metaphysics: The Late Scholastic Origins of Modern Philosophy* (Cambridge: Cambridge University Press, 2000); Schneewind, *The Invention of Autonomy*, 184–93.

bodily feelings teach him that 'I am not only lodged in my body, like a pilot in his ship, but, besides, that I am joined to it very closely and indeed so compounded and intermingled with my body, that I form, as it were, a single whole with it.'[53] If it were otherwise, he points out, he would not need bodily feelings to know when he was hungry or injured. As it stands, these bodily feelings—belonging to the 'nature' given him by God—instruct him to shun pain and to seek pleasure. Beyond this, however, the senses cannot make judgements about the truth of what is perceived. The senses are too prone to error, and so the mind must evaluate the data obtained by the senses.

This proneness to error troubles Descartes. If his bodily nature inclines toward certain things which are bad for it, then how can his bodily nature have been created by the good, non-deceiving God? In response to the answer that his bodily nature is fallen and corrupt, and therefore can no longer perceive what is truly good for it, he observes that 'a sick man is no less truly the creature of God than a man in full health; and therefore it is as contradictory to the goodness of God that the one should have a deceitful and faulty nature as that the other should have'.[54] Even a badly made clock still functions in accord with the nature given it; the same should hold for bodily nature. Descartes considers 'man's body as being a machine, so built and composed of bones, nerves, muscles, veins, blood and skin', that even without mind should still function in a way that attains its own good.[55] But the machine-body appears not to function in this way: a person suffering from dropsy becomes thirsty and desires water, despite the bad effect.

Seeking to understand why this is so, Descartes compares the mind, which is indivisible, with the body as composed of parts. The various parts of the body mean that it is more easily led astray than the mind, since all the parts need to be working in harmony. The nervous system, ending in the brain, is the instrument through which bodily

---

[53] Descartes, *Meditations*, 159.   [54] Ibid., 160.

[55] Ibid., 163. Yves Simon comments, 'It goes without saying that there cannot be such a thing as natural law in a thoroughly mechanistic universe. When mechanism is associated with idealism, as it is in Descartes and in most modern philosophers— again, whether outspokenly or not—we have *values* instead of natural laws' (Simon, *The Tradition of Natural Law*, ed. Vikan Kuic (1965; New York: Fordham University Press, 1992), 50).

perception occurs. Defects in the functioning of the nervous system therefore cause defects in bodily perception. But as Descartes points out, despite the possibility of defect, without the nervous system we would have much more difficulty preserving our health. He observes that 'when we need to drink, there is generated from this need a certain dryness of the throat that moves the nerves, and by means of them, the inner part of the brain, and this movement makes the mind experience the feeling of thirst, because on that occasion there is nothing more useful to us than to know that we need to drink for the preservation of our health'.[56] Even though the bodily senses sometimes mislead us, therefore, Descartes approves them as functioning in a machine-like manner proper to their nature.

The image of the machine fascinates Descartes.[57] In the Fifth Discourse of his *Discourse on Method*, he reflects upon the complexity of human bodily nature. Such wondrous complexity, he observes, 'will not appear in any way strange to those who, knowing how many different automata or moving machines the industry of man can devise, using only a very few pieces, by comparison with the great multitude of bones, muscles, nerves, arteries, veins and all the other parts which are in the body of every animal, will consider this body as a machine'[58]—and not just any machine, but a machine constructed by God. The human body is a machine built by God for use by the human mind. Given this analogy of the machine, the question arises as to whether human beings could make human beings. Descartes denies it, on the grounds that the machine would always function as a machine, in contrast to the human mind which is not constrained by the complex pathways of bodily mechanisms. The human mind, despite its mingling with the body, is free in a way that bodies are not free: 'whereas reason is a universal instrument which can serve on any kind of occasion, these organs need a particular disposition for each particular action'.[59] No machine could be complex enough to have inbuilt responsive pathways, leading to intelligible deeds and words, to fit every situation.

In what way do the ends of this machine relate to the human person? In his Second Meditation, Descartes begins with universal

---

[56] Descartes, *Meditations*, 167.   [57] See Dupré, *Passage to Modernity*, 75.
[58] Descartes, *Discourse on Method*, 73.   [59] Ibid., 74.

doubt and then quickly proves that '*I am, I exist*, is necessarily true, every time I express it or conceive of it in my mind.'[60] Who is this 'I'? Can the 'I' be described in any significant way by the bodily and/or spiritual ends? Rather than seeking to define the 'I' in terms of the nature of 'rational animal,' which he deems too contested to be fruitful, Descartes simply describes the body as that which takes up space and is perceptible. He sees no reason, however, to suppose that the 'I' depends, in its definition, upon such qualities, which in any case he has temporarily placed under universal doubt. Rather, he proposes that the 'I' is 'precisely speaking, only a thing which thinks, that is to say, a mind, understanding, or reason'.[61] This 'I' stands above the 'assemblage of limbs called the human body':[62] it is not necessary to the 'I' that it have bodiliness, since even were bodiliness proven to be an illusion, the 'I' would be real. Pushing further, Descartes reasons that the 'I', as a 'thing which thinks', possesses certain characteristics: it 'doubts, perceives, affirms, denies, wills, does not will', as well as imagines and feels.[63] These actions have as their reference things that, while outside the mind, are known solely by the mind: 'the perception of it [the thing outside the mind], or the action by which one perceives it, is not an act of sight, or touch, or of imagination, and has never been, although it seemed so hitherto, but only an intuition of the mind'.[64] In perceiving and judging things outside the mind, therefore, the mind gains evidence primarily, not of the existence of other things, but that the mind itself exists.

And yet, by beginning with his ideas, Descartes arrives, or claims to arrive, at realities that are not himself. He argues that if he has an idea whose 'objective reality' is not in him, then he has not caused the idea, and so there must be something else in existence besides him.[65] All ideas of other human beings, angels, animals, and corporeal things all could, for various reasons, have an 'objective reality' produced by him. The only exception is the idea of God. Since the infinite is not in any way 'in' Descartes, the idea of the infinite must come from outside Descartes.[66] Having moved outside himself, Descartes also observes that his 'I' does not grant and guarantee itself existence, and from thence he proceeds to a proof of God

[60] Ibid., 103.   [61] Ibid., 105.   [62] Ibid.   [63] Ibid., 107.
[64] Ibid., 110.   [65] Ibid., 121.   [66] Ibid., 124.

as the non-contingent and infinite cause of finite existence and its conservation.[67]

Neither the 'I' nor the machine-body are identified by teleological ends.[68] Rather, they are identified by certain functions: thinking, willing, thirst, feeling pain. Since thinking is radically different from, for example, thirst and feeling pain, Descartes affirms only a 'mingling', not a profound unity, of body and soul. For Descartes, earlier philosophers and theologians had failed to produce much of use. As he states of the ancient philosophers, 'I compared the moral writings of the ancient pagans to the most proud and magnificent palaces built on nothing but sand and mud. They exalt the virtues and make them appear more estimable than anything in the world, but they do not sufficiently teach one to know them, and often what they give so fine a name to is only insensibility, or pride, or despair, or parricide.'[69] Theology is (if anything) worse, because it simply affirms that salvation is open to all who seek it and that the mysteries of faith are beyond human reason. Given this situation, in which neither philosophy nor theology teach anything practicable,

[67] For an intriguing comparison of Descartes (educated by the Jesuits) to Ignatius of Loyola—the latter as a biblical path rooted in God the providential Creator that modernity could have taken—see Dupré, *Passage to Modernity*, 224–6. Dupré shows that 'Ignatius's spiritual vision, although articulated in the anthropocentric language of modern culture, subverts, in fact, the anthropocentric attitude. The *Exercises* presents God as the foundation of human nature and the goal of its accomplishments: "Man is created to praise, reverence, and serve God our Lord...." Starting from a theocentric *Fundamentum*, they conclude with a contemplation of God's active presence in all things and an invitation to view "all blessings and gifts as descending from above" (*Omnia bona descendunt desursum*) (no. 237). The metaphor of descent and return dominates the two cardinal visions that shaped Ignatius's spirituality. In Manresa he saw the entire creation proceeding from God the Father and, via the Son, returning to its divine origin. The world became transparent of God in the light flooding from above. Fifteen years later another vision near Rome transformed that contemplative vision into one of action. Or, more correctly, it converted the apostolic action upon which Ignatius was ready to engage into contemplation. He perceived that action itself as participating in the "outgoing" movement of God's trinitarian life. Humans are called not to rest in divine quiet but to descend with the Son into the created world for the purpose of sanctifying it' (225–6).

[68] Charles Taylor writes, 'Descartes utterly rejected this teleological mode of thinking and abandoned any theory of ontic logos' (Taylor, 'Descartes's Disengaged Reason', in idem, *Sources of the Self: The Making of Modern Identity* (Cambridge, MA: Harvard University Press, 1989), 144).

[69] Descartes, *Discourse on Method*, 32–3.

Descartes seeks a new beginning in the powers of the thinking and choosing 'I' and the machine-body. Louis Dupré summarizes the results:

The difficulties Descartes experienced in establishing rules for a moral system are symptomatic of his predicament in attempting to submit it to any determination but the very act of choosing. That he never succeeded in surpassing the practical guidelines of the *morale provisoire* sketched in his early *Discourse of Method* (III) should cause no surprise in view of the total open-endedness of a will considered independent of the intellect. Another difficulty arose when he distinguished the *res cogitans* from the *res extensa* as an independent substance. The traditional rule of ethics—to live in conformity with the whole of nature—becomes hard to follow when the body is assumed to be an independent substance subject to the unchangeable laws of a mechanical universe. At that point the mind has nowhere to turn but to that internal realm where it can score none but 'ideal victories.'[70]

Given Descartes's starting points, the possibility of grounding the doctrine of 'natural law' in a unified teleology inscribed in human nature by God or by personified 'nature' no longer obtains. The 'I' and its machine are now at the centre.

Thomas Hobbes: The Power of the Commonwealth[71]

Although Hobbes agrees that all law flows in some sense from the individual 'I', he discards Descartes's appeal to the soul as rising above the bodily machine. Given the aims that Hobbes sought to attain in his political philosophy, he devotes much of his most important work, *Leviathan*, to biblical interpretation. In this context he states of the soul, 'That the soul of man is in its own nature eternal, and a living creature independent of the body, or that any mere

---

[70] Dupré, *Passage to Modernity*, 131.

[71] For the political and intellectual context of Hobbes's work, as well as his central interlocutors, see John Bowles, *Leviathan: Hobbes and His Critics* (London: Jonathan Cape, 1951); and Samuel I. Mintz, *The Hunting of Leviathan* (Cambridge: Cambridge University Press, 1962), although Mintz considers Hobbes to have been a theist. See also the excellent survey of Hobbes in Schneewind, *The Invention of Autonomy*, chapter 5: 'Grotianism at the limit: Hobbes', 82–100. On Hobbes's development as a moralist, Leo Strauss, *The Political Philosophy of Thomas Hobbes: Its Basis and Genesis*, 2nd edn. (Chicago: University of Chicago Press, 1952).

man is immortal otherwise than by the resurrection in the last day
(except Enoch [Heb. 11:5] and Elijah [2 Kings 2:11]) is a doctrine
not apparent in Scripture.'[72] In Scripture, he states, the 'soul' means
only the 'life' or the 'body alive'.[73] Philosophically, he mounts a similarly full-scale critique of the notion of a spiritual soul. Regarding
ancient philosophy, he observes, 'The natural philosophy of those
schools was rather a dream than science, and set forth in senseless
and insignificant language, which cannot be avoided by those that
will teach philosophy without having first attained great knowledge
in geometry. For nature worketh by motion, the ways and degrees
whereof cannot be known without the knowledge of the proportions and properties of lines and figures.'[74] If 'nature' is then simply
mechanism, then it comes as no surprise that moral philosophy,
including natural law, that fails to understand nature in mechanistic
terms cannot attain real insight. As Hobbes describes ancient moral
philosophy, 'Their moral philosophy is but a description of their own
passions.'[75]

Given the mechanistic character of nature, including human
nature, Hobbes rejects the notion of 'essences separated from bodies',
and concludes that 'every part of the universe is body, and that which
is not body is no part of the universe. And because the universe is all,
that which is no part of it is nothing (and consequently, nowhere).
Nor does it follow from hence that spirits are nothing. For they have
dimensions, and are, therefore, really bodies.'[76] In so far as 'spirit'
is real, it must be bodily. To call it anything else would be solely a
metaphor intending to express its honour and dignity.[77] The fact that
spirit (in so far as it exists) is bodily becomes clear, Hobbes thinks,
in the apparent contradictions into which one falls in attempting to
construe spirit as 'incorporeal', a mistake that Hobbes attributes to
Aristotelian philosophy and its descendants. Hobbes points out that
'of the essence of a man, which (they say) is his soul, they affirm it,
to be all of it in his little finger, and all of it in every other part (how
small soever) of his body; and yet no more soul in the whole body

---

[72] Thomas Hobbes, *Leviathan*, ed. Edwin Curley (Indianapolis, IN: Hackett, 1994),
ch. 38.4, p. 304.

[73] Ibid., ch. 44.14, p. 419.   [74] Ibid., ch. 46.11, p. 456.   [75] Ibid.

[76] Ibid., ch. 46.15, pp. 458 and 459.   [77] Ibid., 459.

than in any one of those parts. Can any man think that God is served with such absurdities?'[78]

Nor does Hobbes manifest any more sympathy with attempts to root law in God. Of Catholic moral and political philosophy, he remarks that such efforts to defend God's providence run aground upon the problem of evil: 'If a man do an action of injustice (that is to say, an action contrary to the law), God, they say, is the prime cause of the law, and also the prime cause of that and all other actions, but no cause at all of the injustice (which is the inconformity of the action to the law). This is vain philosophy.'[79] Additionally, given Hobbes's denial of separated spiritual substances, the notion of 'God' itself is at best problematic. In speaking of God, Hobbes does not deny his existence, but instead consistently adverts to extreme apophaticism and to a genealogy of religion. For Hobbes, the notion of deity arises in polytheism out of human fear of death and calamity, a fear which develops into a desire to 'know the causes of natural bodies, and their several virtues and operations' and thereby produces the monotheistic notion of deity.[80] Lacking an understanding of mechanistic causation, human beings blindly imagine invisible causes that they call '*spirit* and *incorporeal*' without recognizing the incoherence of these words.[81]

In contrast to these views, Hobbes proposes to build an understanding of law based upon recognizing the world as a machine-body, a 'Leviathan'. Introducing this metaphor as the structuring principle of his political philosophy, Hobbes states,

For seeing life is but a motion of limbs, the beginning whereof is in some principal part within, why may we not say that all *automata* (engines that move themselves by springs and wheels as doth a watch) have an artificial life? For what is the *heart*, but a *spring*; and the nerves, but so many *strings*; and the *joints*, but so many *wheels*, giving motion to the whole body, such as

---

[78] Ibid., ch. 46.19, p. 461.   [79] Ibid., ch. 46.31, pp. 463–4.
[80] Ibid., ch. 12.6, p. 64.
[81] Ibid., ch. 12.7, p. 65. John M. Rist rightly remarks, 'The more fundamental question broached by Grotius and set squarely on the table by Hobbes was: what if there is no voluntarist God, no metaphysical deity of a Platonist sort, no attainment of *morality* through reason?' (Rist, *Real Ethics* (Cambridge: Cambridge University Press, 2002), 158). See also Pierre Manent, *The City of Man*, trans. Marc A. LePain (Princeton: Princeton University Press, 1998), especially chapter 5, 'The Triumph of the Will'.

was intended by the artificer? Art goes yet further, imitating that rational and most excellent work of nature, *man*. For by art is created that great LEVIATHAN called a COMMONWEALTH, or STATE (in Latin CIVITAS), which is but an artificial man, though of greater stature and strength than the natural, for whose protection and defence it was intended; and in which the *sovereignty* is an artificial soul, as giving life and motion to the whole body; the *magistrates* and other *officers* of judicature and execution, artificial *joints*; *reward* and *punishment* (by which fastened to the seat of the sovereignty every joint and member is moved to perform his duty) are the nerves, that do the same in the body natural; the *wealth* and *riches* of all the particular members are the *strength*; *salus populi* (the people's safety) its *business*; *counsellors*, by whom all things needful for it to know are suggested unto it, are the *memory*; *equity* and *laws*, an artificial *reason* and *will*; *concord*, *health*; *sedition*, *sickness*; and *civil war*, *death*. Lastly, the *pacts* and *covenants* by which the parts of this body politic were at first made, set together, and united, resemble that *fiat*, or the *let us make man*, pronounced by God in the creation.[82]

Hobbes holds that there is no law outside this 'Leviathan' or earthly commonwealth, unless one wishes to call individual human appetite 'law'. Properly understood, law 'is the will and appetite of the state'.[83] This is apparent, he suggests, even in the Bible. He reads the Torah as principally a political document: 'The laws of God, therefore, are none but the laws of nature, whereof the principal is that we should not violate our faith, that is, a commandment to obey our civil sovereigns, which we constituted over us by mutual pact one with another.'[84]

Law comes about when human beings make this 'mutual pact'. For Hobbes, it is only this 'mutual pact' that constitutes a machine-body adequate for the grounding of law. Individual human machine-bodies—and here his position is close to that of Descartes—do not incline toward ends sufficient to ground law. Rather, the ends toward which machine-bodies incline are radically individualistic and

---

[82] Hobbes, *Leviathan*, Introduction. 1, pp. 3–4.

[83] Ibid., ch. 46.32, p. 464. On the power of the legislator as that which makes a dictate of reason to be a 'law' for Hobbes, see Knud Haakonssen, *Natural Law and Moral Philosophy: From Grotius to the Scottish Enlightenment* (Cambridge: Cambridge University Press, 1996), 33–4. Haakonssen offers a helpful comparison of Hobbes to Grotius, and of both to Samuel Pufendorf, the seventeenth-century German political theorist.

[84] Hobbes, *Leviathan*, ch. 43.5, p. 399.

brutish. If, as in Cicero, human beings incline to live in society, for Hobbes that may be so but only with the proviso that human beings in society will do anything to rise to the top of the social heap and dominate their compatriots. This proviso means simply that any natural inclination toward life in society results in human beings violently rending apart any and all social bonds unless compelled by force not to do so. In such a context the inclination toward self-preservation, granted by Hobbes, therefore means that each human being necessarily seeks to dominate violently over every other human being. Similarly any inclination toward procreation and the raising of children, if present, reduces to violent efforts to master 'other men's persons, wives, children, and cattle'.[85] The inclination toward truth merely gratifies and stimulates ridiculous individual pride. Each human being, says Hobbes, possesses 'a vain conceit of one's own wisdom, which almost all men think they have in a greater degree than the vulgar, that is, than all men but themselves and a few others whom, by fame or for concurring with themselves, they approve.'[86]

The problem, Hobbes argues, stems from the fact that human machine-bodies are (broadly speaking) naturally on a level with each other. He states, 'Nature hath made men so equal in the faculties of body and mind as that, though there be found one man sometimes manifestly stronger in body or of quicker mind than another, yet when all is reckoned together the difference between man and man is not so considerable that one man can thereupon claim to himself any benefit to which another may not pretend as well as he.'[87] When added to the fact that for Hobbes human ends reduce ultimately to self-preservation and pleasure, in accord with mechanistic human nature, the result of this equality can only be explosive, what he famously calls 'a war....of every man against every man'.[88] The natural condition of human body-machines is therefore one of intellectual and material desolation: 'no arts, no letters,

---

[85] Ibid., ch. 13.7, p. 76.   [86] Ibid., ch. 13.2, p. 75.
[87] Ibid., ch. 13.1, p. 74.
[88] Ibid., ch. 13.8, p. 76. As Schneewind observes with respect to Hobbes's rejection of teleology: 'Desire and aversion are thus tied directly to the motion that constitutes life. Consequently Hobbes does not think of moral philosophy in terms of the search for the human highest good or final end. Going beyond Grotius, who simply sets the issue aside, Hobbes flatly asserts that "there is no such *Finis ultimis* (utmost ayme,) nor *Summum bonum,* (greatest Good,) as is spoken of in the Books of the old Moral Philosophers" (*Leviathan* XI.1)...Hobbesian desires prevent us not only

no society, and which is worst of all, continual fear and danger of violent death, and the life of man, solitary, poor, nasty, brutish, and short'.[89]

Thus, far from flowing from natural ends, let alone from God, law is absent among human beings as naturally constituted. As Hobbes states, 'To this war of every man against every man, this also is consequent: that nothing can be unjust. The notions of right and wrong, justice and injustice, have there no place. Where there is no common power, there is no law; where no law, no injustice.'[90] However, human beings have the ability to make law and justice. In this regard, Hobbes's position again veers toward Descartes's, although Hobbes's account of rationality is materialistic. That is to say, for Hobbes as for Descartes, human reason can build something solid that goes beyond the limited resources of human nature per se. The human body-machine wants to live and enjoy pleasures free of impediments, a condition which is Hobbes's notion of 'liberty'.[91] To attain this goal, 'reason suggesteth convenient articles of peace, upon which men may be drawn to agreement. These articles are they which otherwise are called the Laws of Nature.'[92] The 'laws of nature' are not inscribed in nature by personified 'nature' or by nature's God. Rather they are constituted by reason, but only by appeal to self-interest and power. They may be called 'laws of nature' because by them human beings can sustain life and pleasures, whereas without them human beings cannot sustain life and pleasures. The 'laws' or 'articles of peace' respond to the human right to self-preservation—what Hobbes calls the 'right of nature' or 'ius naturale'—in the accomplishment of which each human being is free to do 'anything which, in his

---

from having a final end but also from having naturally common or harmonious ends' (Schneewind, *The Invention of Autonomy*, 84–5).

[89] Hobbes, *Leviathan*, ch. 13.9, p. 76.   [90] Ibid., ch. 13.13, p. 78.

[91] Ibid., ch. 14.2, p. 79.

[92] Ibid., ch. 13.14, p. 78. Dupré indicates the problems that Hobbes faces here: 'Notwithstanding his efforts to submit all of nature to uniform forces, Hobbes experienced major difficulty in trying to maintain his laws of nature within a mechanistic frame. This becomes evident in his second law of nature: "That a man be willing, when others are too—to lay down this right to all things; and be contented with so much liberty against other men, as he would allow other men against himself" (*Leviathan* I, 14, p. 190) ... In *De cive*, Hobbes more consistently acknowledged no natural law but only positive divine and human laws' (*Passage to Modernity*, 140–1).

own judgment and reason, he shall conceive to be the aptest means thereunto.'[93]

Hobbes defines these 'articles of peace' as follows: 'A Law of Nature (*lex naturalis*) is a precept or general rule, found out by reason, by which a man is forbidden to do that which is destructive of his life or taketh away the means of preserving the same, and to omit that by which he thinketh it may be best preserved.'[94] This definition orients natural law entirely around self-preservation. From this understanding of the law of nature, certain more specific precepts follow. Among them Hobbes names the duty to seek peace, the willingness to allow some limits upon one's own liberty or rights in order to secure the peace, the duty to keep one's contracts in which one has given up certain aspects of one's liberty, the duty to behave well to benefactors, the duty of attempting to get along with one's fellows, the duty to forgive offences so long as the offender has repented, the duty to inflict punishment only for correction of the offender and as a warning to others, the duty to avoid strife, the duty to acknowledge each other as 'equal by nature',[95] the duty not to claim more liberty than one allows others in the compact, the duty to deal equal judgement to human beings, the duty to distribute and enjoy goods equably, the duty to grant safe conduct to enemy negotiators who seek peace, to be willing to submit one's claims to an arbitrator, to renounce the right to arbitrate one's own or one's friends' cause, and to credit witnesses in arriving at judgements.

For Hobbes, these 'articles of peace' or 'laws of nature' ultimately reduce to a negative version of the Golden Rule, 'Do not that to another, which thou wouldst not have done to thyself.'[96] The laws of nature are binding upon all people but not in all circumstances. They only bind when a commonwealth has been securely established. Without the commonwealth, the laws of 'nature' have no grounding: 'For he that should be modest and tractable, and perform all he promises, in such time and place where no man else should do so, should but make himself a prey to others, and procure his own certain ruin, contrary to the ground of all laws of nature, which

---

[93] Hobbes, *Leviathan*, ch. 14.1, p. 79.   [94] Ibid., ch. 14.3, p. 79.
[95] Ibid., ch. 15.21, p. 97.   [96] Ibid., ch. 15.35, p. 99.

tend to nature's preservation.'[97] Such preservation is only possible in a commonwealth. And yet, given the context of a commonwealth, it can be said that these 'laws of nature are immutable and eternal'.[98] Reason can discern that without these laws, no peace, and therefore no self-preservation or pleasure, is possible. Thus these laws suffice, in Hobbes's view, for moral philosophy, which cannot be grounded in anything deeper. As he observes, '*Good* and *evil* are names that signify our appetites and aversions, which in different tempers, customs, and doctrines of men are different.'[99] No common ground for moral philosophy can be found in the more specific human ends, which are too diverse. In the 'condition of mere nature', each human being's appetite determines his or her own good or evil.[100] But common ground can be found in the most simple human end, self-preservation: 'all men agree on this, that peace is good; and therefore also the way or means of peace . . . are good (that is to say, *moral virtues*), and their contrary vices, evil'.[101] Having outlined the 'articles of peace' conceived by reason, Hobbes affirms that these articles are 'laws of nature' because without them, there will be no peace.

Yet Hobbes admits that, properly speaking, these 'articles of peace' are not quite 'laws'. They are rational deductions about what will bring about peace given the natural situation of pride and violence, but they are not laws until they bear the authority of a lawgiver. They become laws when commanded by God (through Moses) in the biblical commonwealth or when commanded by the ruler of other commonwealths.[102] Reason alone, then, cannot ground these 'laws of nature'. They flow from the power of the ruler to establish peace. They are 'laws of nature' in the sense of correcting 'nature' by the authority of the ruler of the commonwealth. Their authority as 'laws' flows ultimately not from a teleological 'nature', or from an autonomous 'reason', let alone from divine providence, but from the actual exercise of power by a specific ruler of a specific commonwealth. Natural law has here moved clearly from the biblical self-giving *ecstasis*, rooted in the teleological dynamism toward communion inscribed by God, to self-asserting power.

---

[97] Ibid., ch. 15.36, p. 99.   [98] Ibid., ch. 15.38, p. 99.
[99] Ibid., ch. 15.40, p. 100.   [100] Ibid.   [101] Ibid.
[102] Ibid., ch. 15.41, p. 100.

John Locke: Self-Preservation and Property

In contrast to Hobbes, Locke denies that the 'law of nature' is grounded by the power of the commonwealth. He affirms a 'law of nature' or 'law of reason', accessible to all human beings whether in a 'state of nature' or a commonwealth, that 'teaches all mankind, who will but consult it, that being all equal and independent, no one ought to harm another in his life, health, liberty, or possessions'.[103] By positing a law of nature independent from the existence of a commonwealth, Locke—while agreeing with Hobbes's views regarding the reasons for the formation of a commonwealth, namely fear of losing life and property—strongly criticizes absolute, arbitrary power. For Locke the only commonwealth that is not itself a 'state of war' is a commonwealth based upon the prior consent of the governed, who agree to form themselves into a community in which their lives and property cannot be arbitrarily taken away.[104] Justice, and the differentiation between good and evil, are no mere products of the commonwealth, as Hobbes would have it. Rather, given the ends of self-preservation and the procreation and raising of children, Locke finds a strict law of nature or law of reason (also called by him 'the will of God'[105]): 'nobody can transfer to another more power than he has in himself; and nobody has an absolute arbitrary power over himself, or over any other,

---

[103] John Locke, 'Second Treatise of Government', in Locke, *Two Treatises of Government*, ed. Mark Goldie (1689; London: J. M. Dent, 1993), ch. 2.6, p. 117. For summaries of Locke on natural law, see Jerome B. Schneewind, 'Locke's Moral Philosophy', in *The Cambridge Companion to Locke*, ed. Vere Chappell (Cambridge: Cambridge University Press, 1994), 199–225. See also Knud Haakonssen's *Natural Law and Moral Philosophy*; and Stephen Buckle's *Natural Law and the Theory of Property: Grotius to Hume* (Oxford: Oxford University Press, 1991), which show in detail how Locke's ideas arise from Hugo Grotius and Samuel Pufendorf and lead, via Francis Hutcheson, to David Hume.

[104] As Dupré says in this regard: 'Later British philosophers, beginning with John Locke, attempted to restore a normative, moral meaning to the notion of natural law: the "dictates of reason" may conflict with positive laws. But the more they stressed the norms inherent in an individualist concept of nature, the more they emptied their natural law of any concrete social content. Natural law thus comes to function as a rational basis of prepolitical, individual rights' (*Passage to Modernity*, 141).

[105] Locke, 'Second Treatise of Government,' ch. 11.135, p. 184.

to destroy his own life, or take away the life and property of another'.[106]

Self-preservation thus plays the central role in Locke's account of natural law. Given the teleological end of self-preservation (including property), each human being must speak the truth and keep his or her promises. Otherwise one would violate the key principle of the natural law, by threatening the self-preservation (and property) of another. Locke therefore states that 'truth and keeping of faith belongs to men, as men, and not as members of society'.[107] The 'end' of self-preservation arises from human nature as created by God. Reason discerns this end because reason is 'the common rule and measure, God hath given to mankind'.[108] Self-preservation possesses an inviolable character because human beings belong to God as God's property. Destroying or tampering with God's property would go against reason, which discerns in every human being the divine plan. Self-preservation, with its roots in God's creative providence and power, thus leads to an awareness of the need to preserve others' lives as well. Locke states,

For men being all the workmanship of one omnipotent, and infinitely wise Maker; all the servants of one sovereign master, sent into the world by his order and about his business, they are his property, whose workmanship they are, made to last during his, not one another's pleasure.... Everyone as he is bound to preserve himself, and not to quit his station wilfully; so by the like reason when his own preservation comes not in competition, ought he, as much as he can, to preserve the rest of mankind, and may not unless it be to

[106] Ibid., p. 183. For Locke's understanding of 'property' see the discussion in Ross Harrison, *Hobbes, Locke, and Confusion's Masterpiece* (Cambridge: Cambridge University Press, 2003), chapter 8.

[107] Locke, 'Second Treatise of Government', ch. 2.14, p. 122.

[108] Ibid., ch. 2.11, p. 120. Knud Haakonssen, in light of Locke's *An Essay concerning Human Understanding*, suggests that Locke's arguments significantly weaken the role of a divine legislator, in accord with Locke's Socinian theology (Haakonssen, *Natural Law and Moral Philosophy*, 58). Schneewind argues that Locke's contemporaries realized that Locke could not give an 'explanation of how we could even say and mean, let alone prove, that God is a just ruler. He could not allow for the kind of relation between God and his creatures that many Christians—he [Locke] himself among them—believed to exist...Locke's readers could hardly avoid seeing that if, like him, they embraced naturalistic empiricism about moral concepts, then they would be forced into voluntarism—unless they left God entirely out of morality' (Schneewind, *The Invention of Autonomy*, 159).

do justice on an offender, take away, or impair the life, or what tends to the preservation of the life, the liberty, health, limb or goods of another.[109]

Property, in the broad sense inclusive of life, stands as the keystone to Locke's account of natural law.

In relation to the end of self-preservation, Locke also affirms procreation and the raising of children as belonging to the law of nature. The law of nature, he specifies, requires all parents 'to preserve, nourish, and educate the children, they had begotten, not as their own workmanship, but the workmanship of their own Maker, the Almighty'.[110] He thereby grounds the relationship between parents and children in God's providential plan for preserving the human race and, as part of preservation, fostering the generational transmission of property. He observes regarding these divinely mandated duties, 'God having made the parents instruments in his great design of continuing the race of mankind, and the occasions of life to their children, as he hath laid on them an obligation to nourish, preserve, and bring up their offspring; so he has laid on the children a perpetual obligation of honouring their parents.'[111] This duty of children greatly assists the parents in their self-preservation and in the maintaining of their property. As he notes, the duty of honouring parents 'ties up the child from anything that may ever injure or affront, disturb, or endanger the happiness or life of those, from whom he received his; and engages him in all actions of defence, relief, assistance and comfort of those, by whose means he entered into being, and has been made capable of any enjoyments of life'.[112] Parents give children life and possessions, and in return children defend and support the life and possessions of their parents.

What about the other inclinations and ends that Cicero, as we have seen, identifies as constitutive of the law of nature? The status

---

[109] Locke, 'Second Treatise of Government,' ch. 2.6, p. 117.

[110] Ibid., ch. 6.56, p. 142. For the significance of this point in Locke's debate with Robert Filmer, see Harrison, *Hobbes, Locke, and Confusion's Masterpiece*, 193. On Filmer, see also Norberto Bobbio, *Thomas Hobbes and the Natural Law Tradition*, trans. Daniela Gobetti (Chicago: University of Chicago Press, 1993), 21–2; cf. Robert Filmer, *Patriarcha and Other Writings*, ed. J. P. Sommerville (Cambridge: Cambridge University Press, 1991).

[111] Locke, 'Second Treatise of Government,' ch. 6.66, p. 147.

[112] Ibid.; cf. ibid., ch. 6.74, p. 151.

of the inclination toward life in society is, in Locke, unclear at best. On the one hand, Locke does speak of an inclination toward life in society. He states, 'God having made man such a creature, that, in his own judgment, it was not good for him to be alone, put him under strong obligations of necessity, convenience, and inclination to drive him into society, as well as fitted him with understanding and language to continue and enjoy it.'[113] Yet, on the other hand, human beings remain in Locke fundamentally independent of any social bonds. Every social bond, including marriage and the commonwealth, flows from strictly voluntary consent. Thus Locke speaks of the 'voluntary compact' that constitutes marriage,[114] and affirms that once the ends of the preservation of the human race, and the transmission of property, are assured, the voluntary compact may be dissolved just as other voluntary compacts are dissolved—'there being no necessity in the nature of the thing [marriage], nor to the ends of it, that it should always be for life'.[115] Similarly, a commonwealth only comes about by the free consent of those who enter into it. He famously observes, 'Men being...by nature, all free, equal, and independent, no one can be put out of his estate, and subjected to the political power of another, without his own consent.'[116] This consent arises from the desire to preserve one's life and property. As Locke puts it, 'The only way whereby anyone divests himself of his natural liberty, and puts on the bonds of civil society, is by agreeing with other men to join and unite into a community, for their comfortable, safe, and peaceable living one amongst another, in a secure enjoyment of their properties, and a greater security against any that are not of it.'[117] Individuals make communities, and individuals can withdraw from and dissolve these communities when the

---

[113] Ibid., ch. 7.77, p. 153.   [114] Ibid., ch. 7.78.

[115] Ibid., ch. 7.81, p. 155.

[116] Ibid., ch. 8.95, p. 163. See Harrison, *Hobbes, Locke, and Confusion's Masterpiece*, 200–5.

[117] Locke, 'Second Treatise of Government,' ch. 8.95, p. 163. See also John Courtney Murray, SJ, *We Hold These Truths: Catholic Reflections on the American Proposition* (1960; Lanham, MD: Sheed & Ward, 1988), 303–14. Murray pungently remarks, 'Locke prattles a bit about the "innocent delights" attendant on the "liberty" of the state of nature. But it is difficult to see how a state could be delightful wherein every individual is a sort of little god almighty, whose power to preserve himself is checked only at the point where another little god almighty starts preserving *himself*' (304).

communities arbitrarily threaten their life and property. There are no social bonds, in short, that are more fundamental than the individual and his or her self-preservation, in which Locke always includes property.

The inclination toward life in society thus has no real or lasting place in Locke's account of natural law, since the individual always stands fundamentally aloof from any social nexus, be it marriage or the commonwealth, that would tie him or her down. Despite Locke's repeated references to God, therefore, his account of the 'law of nature' or the 'law of reason' joins with Descartes and Hobbes in building everything from the individual human being. As we have seen, even procreation and the raising of offspring finds its fundamental justification in the assistance it gives to the preservation of the individual and his or her possessions. Whereas for Descartes the key move is the division of soul and body, so that the individual human being obtains a starting point from thinking and can move from there toward an account of the reality of God and the machine-body, for Locke the key move seems to be the affirmation of individual self-preservation inclusive of property. For both Descartes and Locke, Hobbes's insistence upon the teleological significance of the commonwealth is absent. Similarly, the teleological 'end' of truth, the fundamental aspect of natural law for Cicero and the key to Augustine's reconstitution of natural law around God's eternal law, is absent in Locke's account of natural law, as it is in Hobbes's.

In short, Locke reduces natural law to the bare bones of self-preservation, inclusive of property. He thereby turns natural law radically inward upon the individual and upon the inclination most shared by human beings with other animals. In so doing, he has turned upside-down the biblical theocentric and ecstatic account of natural law, and has likewise parted ways with Hobbes's (distorted) Augustinian insistence upon the commonwealth.

David Hume: Self-Interested Feelings

Much of what Hume has to say about natural law rests, as in Hobbes, upon a materialist account of knowing. He holds that 'our ideas are images of our impressions'.[118] When elucidated, this means more than that the sensible image is never discarded in intellectual knowing; rather, knowing is simply the reverberating of sensible images either in further images, or in emotional responses. As he argues,

> Now as 'tis impossible to form an idea of an object, that is possest of quantity and quality, and yet is possest of no precise degree of either; it follows, that there is an equal impossibility of forming an idea, that is not limited and confin'd in both these particulars. Abstract ideas are therefore in themselves particular, however they may become general in their representation. The image in the mind is only that of a particular object, tho' the application of it in our reasoning be the same, as if it were universal.[119]

Human beings may act as though we can formulate universal ideas, unlimited by materiality, but in fact such ideas exceed our capacity. We can know nothing whose definition does not include material extension. In this vein Hume asks rhetorically, 'Is the indivisible subject, or immaterial substance, if you will, on the left or on the right hand of the perception? Is it in this particular part, or in that other? Is it in every part without being extended? Or is it entire in any one part without deserting the rest? 'Tis impossible to give any answer to these questions.'[120] Descartes's all-important spiritual soul thus becomes an impossibility, at least so far as human beings can know. The very notion of a non-extended reality simply is, for Hume, metaphysically 'unintelligible', although on other grounds, perhaps, one might choose to postulate it.[121]

From this starting point, Hume rejects the idea of any teleological order. He seeks to respond to '[t]hose who affirm that virtue is nothing but a conformity to reason; that there are eternal fitnesses and unfitnesses of things, which are the same to every rational being

---

[118] David Hume, *A Treatise of Human Nature*, ed. Ernest C. Mossner (1739; New York: Penguin, 1985), 54. Schneewind offers an excellent survey of Hume's political philosophy in *The Invention of Autonomy*, chapter 17: 'Hume: Virtue Naturalized', 354–77. As Schneewind states, 'The "laws of nature" that we invent to make property possible, in Hume's system, are not a specific set of statable rules. They amount to nothing but the recognition that for society to exist property must be safe and transferable. Beyond that, all is local convention. And one convention is as good as another, if both do the job' (373).

[119] Hume, *A Treatise of Human Nature*, 67.   [120] Ibid., 288.

[121] Ibid., 298.

that considers them; that the immutable measures of right and wrong impose an obligation, not only on human creatures, but also on the Deity himself.'[122] Against the first affirmation, that virtue is conformity to reason, he insists upon his famous disjunction between fact and obligation, 'is' and 'ought'.[123] This disjunction rests upon his limitation of truth to matters of fact ('*real* existence') or relations between ideas; since actions are simple facts, actions cannot in themselves be true or false morally. The naming of actions as 'good' or 'bad' results from the feelings aroused by the actions, not from reason per se.[124] Yet, as he recognizes, this rejection of moral truth depends, at a deeper level, upon showing 'that those eternal immutable fitnesses and unfitnesses of things cannot be defended by sound philosophy'.[125] He attempts to show this by arguing that since 'fitness' indicates a relation, the moral character of the relation must be demonstrable. Granting the demonstrable existence of only four kinds of relations ('resemblance, contrariety, degrees in quality, and proportions in quantity and number'), he observes that 'all these relations belong as properly to matter, as to our actions, passions, and volitions'.[126] Thus as pertaining to all creatures, they cannot in

---

[122] Ibid., 508. Jacques Maritain sets forth this teleological view, with which he agrees, in terms of 'attunement' in *The Rights of Man and Natural Law*, trans. Doris C. Anson (New York: Gordian Press, 1971), 60–1. Maritain goes on to observe that because Christians (and some ancient philosophers) know 'that nature comes from God, and that the unwritten law comes from the eternal law which is Creative Wisdom itself', they are able to have a 'firmer and more unshakable' belief in natural law than are those who do not believe in God. Yet in Maritain's view '[b]elief in human nature and in the freedom of the human being, however, is in itself sufficient to convince us that there is an unwritten law, and to assure us that natural law is something as real in the moral realm as the laws of growth and senescence in the physical' (61–2). Perhaps it might be better to say that such knowledge *should* be sufficient, but often is not.

[123] Cf. Hume, *A Treatise of Human Nature*, 521. The acceptance of this disjunction provides the key to the efforts of Germain Grisez, John Finnis, and Robert P. George (as well as, in a slightly different way, Martin Rhonheimer) to reformulate natural law theory. Robert George succinctly describes the path: 'If Grisez and his followers are correct to hold that the most basic reasons for action are not derived from facts about human nature, how are these reasons known? They are known in non-inferential acts of understanding in which we grasp possible ends or purposes as worth while for their own sakes' (George, 'Natural Law and Human Nature', in *Natural Law Theory: Contemporary Essays*, ed. Robert P. George (Oxford: Clarendon Press, 1992), 31–41, at 34).

[124] Hume, *A Treatise of Human Nature*, 510.   [125] Ibid., 514.
[126] Ibid., 515.

human beings have a particular moral character lacking in the other creatures.

But could it be that he has left out some key relations? Were anyone to come forward with other pertinent relations, he states, he would consider them so long as they met two criteria. First, the relations must only be between interior actions and external objects. They cannot be relations between distinct interior actions, or relations between distinct external objects. In this way, he rules out any relations beyond materially demonstrable ones. Second, the relations must have a necessary connection to the divine will, so as necessarily to cause particular effects in the creature.[127] He has already ruled out any demonstration of a necessary relationship between cause and effect, and so this second criterion is, in his view, particularly decisive. As examples, he takes parricide and incest. He points out that in material things, such as a sapling killing the oak from which it came or incest among irrational animals, the relations are not morally reprehensible. If one supposes that human reason makes the relations morally reprehensible, one still fails to show how the relations in themselves are morally reprehensible. As he states, 'For before reason can perceive this turpitude, the turpitude must exist; and consequently is independent of the decisions of our reason, and is their object more properly than their effect.'[128] Morality, he concludes, does not consist in any set of relations, or in any facts. Rather, morality consists in feelings that arise in human beings, pleasure indicating goodness, and unease indicating badness.[129]

---

[127] Ibid., 517.   [128] Ibid., 519.

[129] For a critique of Hume and Kant, and their later followers, on the fact–value disjunction, see John Rist, *Real Ethics*, 158–77. By contrast, Rufus Black has argued in *Christian Moral Realism: Natural Law, Narrative, Virtue, and the Gospel* (Oxford: Oxford University Press, 2000) that, in Black's words, 'the Grisez School's work' should be recognized 'as a form of Christian moral realism that both meets O'Donovan's and Hauerwas's requirements for an ethic to be Christian and preserves the critical insights and emphases of both O'Donovan's and Grisez's ethical and theological analyses. The starting-point of such a theory is the Gospel—that is, the theological account of reality arising from reflection upon Scripture' (180). It seems to me that Black's appeal to 'the orderedness of Creation' (180) and to the 'integral connectedness between the process of practical reasoning and theoretical knowledge about reality that forms the foundation of a Christian realist ethic' (181) reclaims important elements of natural law doctrine that are missing in the approach that Black otherwise defends.

This conclusion, however, hardly means that there is no 'law of nature'. On the contrary, Hume argues that our feelings, in the construction of moral norms, are not arbitrary. Rather, our feelings are natural, and the morality constructed around our feelings deserves the title 'natural law'. As he says, 'Tho' the rules of justice be *artificial*, they are not *arbitrary*. Nor is the expression improper to call them *Laws of Nature*; if by natural we understand what is common to any species, or even if we confine it to mean what is inseparable from the species.'[130] Taking up aspects of Locke's discussion of equity and property, Hume argues that even if justice has no grounding in reason, let alone in a broader teleological order, conventional 'justice' nonetheless has sufficient ground in our feelings. In his view 'we always consider the *natural* and *usual* force of the passions, when we determine concerning vice and virtue; and if the passions depart very much from the common measures on either side, they are always disapprov'd as vicious'.[131] Hume finds the community's feelings, taken as a whole, sufficient to care for equity, property, and the like. Granting that '[p]roperty must be stable, and must be fix'd by general rules',[132] he observes that human feelings, grounded in self-interest, will find the right mean: 'After men have found by experience, that their selfishness and confin'd generosity, acting at their liberty, totally incapacitate them for society; and at the same time have observ'd, that society is necessary to the satisfaction of those very passions, they are naturally induc'd to lay themselves under the restraint of such rules, as may render commerce more safe and commodious.'[133] Thus human feelings or sentiments arrive at the goal envisioned by Locke and Hobbes, without need for Locke's appeal to reason or Hobbes's appeal to the absolute power of the commonwealth.

---

[130] Hume, *A Treatise of Human Nature*, 536.

[131] Ibid., 535. For critical discussion of Hume's position here, see Alasdair MacIntyre, *Whose Justice? Which Rationality?* (Notre Dame, IN: University of Notre Dame Press, 1988), 281–325, especially 286f., which places Hume in the context of eighteenth-century Scottish thought; Rommen, *The Natural Law*, 97–101; Jean Porter, *Nature as Reason: A Thomistic Theory of the Natural Law* (Grand Rapids, MI: Eerdmans, 2005), 239f. Eighteenth- and early nineteenth-century Scottish moral philosophy finds thorough exposition in Knud Haakonssen, *Natural Law and Moral Philosophy: From Grotius to the Scottish Enlightenment*, chapters 2–9.

[132] Hume, *A Treatise of Human Nature*, 549.   [133] Ibid., 550.

The 'law of nature', then, is not 'natural' in the deepest sense, and yet its rootedness in our self-interested desire to satisfy our passions in the best possible way gives it an adequate stability. For Hume, the 'three fundamental laws of nature' are '*that of the stability of possession, of its transference by consent*, and *of the performance of promises*'.[134] Each is a 'law of nature' both for individuals and for nations[135] because each is necessary for the satisfaction of human feelings (or passions, desires, sentiments). These feelings are nature's lawgivers: 'Nothing is more vigilant and inventive than our passions.'[136] Reason does not guide the feelings by means of abstract moral principles; rather the feelings, rooted in self-interest, attune reason to the conventions necessary for the satisfaction of our desires.

Reason thereby receives its law, rather than constituting its law. As Hume remarks, 'Nature has, therefore, trusted this affair [the construction of moral conventions] entirely to the conduct of men, and has not plac'd in the mind any peculiar original principles, to determine us to a set of actions, into which the other principles of our frame and constitution were sufficient to lead us.'[137] To imagine a set of abstract principles in human reason—prior to, and ruling over, our feelings of pleasure or displeasure—would be to impose extrinsically an unnaturally rigid system upon the natural instruction that our feelings intrinsically give us as regards their satisfaction.[138] Put simply, the key is to allow self-interested feelings to work themselves out. Hume has complete trust that they will secure an ordered and happy society. From 'the necessary course of the passions and sentiments' will arise 'the moral obligation of duty' which encompasses the 'laws of justice', grounded upon the principle of self-interest in that 'we approve of such actions as tend to the peace of society, and disapprove of such as tend to its disturbance'.[139] A peaceable society thus emerges, *pace* Hobbes, precisely in following our self-interested passions. The 'natural law' arises from these feelings, freeing us from the need to ground the law of nature, as in Descartes and Locke, in any account of rationality or a 'law of reason'. Once again we are far from

---

[134] Ibid., 578.   [135] Cf. ibid., 618 on the laws of nations.
[136] Ibid., 578.   [137] Ibid.   [138] Cf. 568f., on promises.
[139] Ibid., 619.

the biblical portrait of the richly 'ecstatic' capacities of the human person created by God for communion with God.

Jean-Jacques Rousseau: Savage Man

In his most famous political discourse, *On the Origin of Inequality* (1754), Rousseau grants the importance of self-preservation, along with a second foundational principle, compassion or pity. But the 'ends' of human nature cannot, in his view, provide a basis for understanding 'natural law'. Rather, he seeks to know human nature first as it was before the ugly course of history distorted it and thereby distorted both our concepts of 'human nature' and of 'law'. He hopes that by probing back in time to the original state of nature, famously posited by Hobbes, he will find human nature and thus natural law. With most modern thinkers, he conceives of human nature as self-contained rather than ordered beyond itself, and so his 'natural law' will pertain to the fulfilment of the individual rather than to a set of relationships in which human beings find their fulfilment as members of a society or as guided toward 'ecstatic' fulfilment by an ordering established by God.

Like Hume, Rousseau believes that natural desires, once released from the detritus built up by generations of thinkers, will suffice to establish good order. But like Hobbes, Rousseau is far more negative than Hume about the present disordered state of the human passions. Comparing human nature as presently instantiated in individual human beings to a time-worn and battered statue, he places his hope in a historical quest for the pure form of that self-contained statue. As he famously remarks,

Like the statue of Glaucus, which time, sea and storms had disfigured to such an extent that it looked less like a god than a wild beast, the human soul, altered in the midst of society by a thousand constantly recurring causes, by the acquisition of a multitude of bits of knowledge and of errors, by changes that took place in the constitution of bodies, by the constant impact of the passions, has, as it were, changed its appearance to the point of being nearly unrecognizable. And instead of a being active always by certain and invariable principles, instead of that heavenly and majestic simplicity whose mark its author had left on it, one no longer finds anything but the grotesque contrast of passion which thinks it reasons and an understanding in a state of delirium.[140]

Neither passions (Hume) nor reason (Locke) can attain the goal of arriving at the fully human. While Rousseau rules out Hobbes's recourse to the absolute power of the commonwealth, the Hobbesian account of the state of nature inspires Rousseau's effort to ground 'natural law' in a study of human historical development.[141]

Given his supposition that human nature, the fullest expression of the human, is to be found in the earliest or most primitive state of nature, Rousseau admits to some concerns even regarding his own work. As he says, 'the more we accumulate new knowledge, the more we deprive ourselves of the means of acquiring the most important knowledge of all. Thus, in a sense, it is by dint of studying man that we have rendered ourselves incapable of knowing him'.[142] He thereby proposes a plan of study in hopes of avoiding this impasse. The plan is to explore what would have held when human beings, in their original state, were equal. Other thinkers, both modern and ancient, had proposed accounts of human equality, but none had thought to ground a theory of human nature upon the study of the conditions for human equality. Just like other species, Rousseau says, all the members of the human race were originally equal until the vagaries of time took their toll: 'while some improved or declined and acquired various good or bad qualities which were not inherent in their nature, the others remained longer in their original state. And such was the first source of inequality among men, which it is easier to demonstrate thus in general than to assign with precision its true causes'.[143] In other words, Rousseau does not intend to retell the biblical narrative of the Fall; he wishes simply to propose, as the basis (which he grants is tentative) for an account of human nature,

[140] Jean-Jacques Rousseau, 'Discourse on the Origin of Inequality', preface, in idem, *The Basic Political Writings*, trans. and ed. Donald A. Cress (Indianapolis, IN: Hackett, 1987), 33. For brief critical surveys of Rousseau's philosophy, see Charles Taylor, *Sources of the Self*, 356–63; Louis Dupré, *The Enlightenment and the Intellectual Foundations of Modern Culture* (New Haven, CT: Yale University Press, 2004), 162–8.

[141] On the relationship of Rousseau's thought to Hobbes's, see Leo Strauss, *Natural Right and History* (Chicago: University of Chicago Press, 1953), 266–82. See also e.g. the essays in *Hobbes and Rousseau*, eds. Maurice Cranston and Richard Peters (Garden City, NY: Anchor Books, 1972).

[142] Rousseau, 'Discourse on the Origin of Inequality', 33.   [143] Ibid.

the radical equality of human beings at the beginning. The goal is to find the contours of 'natural man' and thereby to ground properly the 'natural rights' of individuals in human society.[144]

Having proposed this starting point, Rousseau offers a criticism of earlier accounts of natural law. He observes, 'The Roman jurists—not to mention the ancient philosophers who seem to have done their best to contradict each other on the most fundamental principles—subject man and all other animals indifferently to the same natural law, because they take this expression to refer to the law that nature imposes on itself rather than the law she prescribes.'[145] What is the difference between prescribing and imposing? Rousseau teaches that whereas the ancients held that 'nature' imposes a 'natural law' equally upon human beings and all other things, the moderns hold that rational creatures prescribe the natural law, as law, for themselves. Certainly for Rousseau the modern view is preferable, since it suits human beings as intelligent and free creatures. But the modern view too contains its own set of problems. Rousseau states, 'But with each one defining this [natural] law in his own fashion, they all establish it on such metaphysical principles that even among us there are very few people in a position to grasp these principles, far from being able to find them by themselves.'[146] The 'natural law' thus becomes the esoteric province of a few wise men, and its claims to binding 'naturally' are thereby dubious. In addition, the moderns, like the ancients, perpetually disagree with one another about what 'natural law' is.

Rousseau, in short, doubts that modern accounts of 'natural law' have gone far enough beyond ancient ones: both ancient and modern, in his view, claim too much for particular societal 'ends' (e.g. the commonwealth, property) and then build up rules arbitrarily around these ends. His solution, as we have seen, is to seek to locate 'natural man', and he does so first by observing the soul. The two fundamental principles of 'natural law' that he finds there are self-preservation and compassion for others; the second principle will predominate and guide human society unless the first principle is threatened. What he calls 'natural right' flows from these two principles. Like Hume, then, he insists that human beings need no complex philosophy upon

---

[144] Ibid., 34.   [145] Ibid.   [146] Ibid., 34–5.

which to ground law and rights, although Rousseau's two principles of natural law are not Humean constructions of the passions. For Rousseau also it is crucial to observe that natural law is the prescription of human reason, which recognizes the need not to harm others unless they are seeking to harm oneself. Animals and other creatures, lacking reason, have no 'natural law', although they do have a certain 'natural right' in that the second principle of compassion gives them a certain protection.

Thus, while beginning equal, human beings eventually became unequal both physically and in social status and wealth. They began in a state in which 'natural law' and 'natural right' prevailed; they devolved into a state in which violence and lack of compassion for others prevailed. Governments based upon such violence arose, in opposition to both natural law and natural right. Such societal distortion of nature came itself to seem natural (Hobbes), despite the biblical depiction of Adam's first condition.[147] In contrast to this understanding of the 'natural', Rousseau, drawing upon accounts of the Americas, sketches natural, primitive, or savage man, with 'a robust and nearly unalterable temperament' necessary for individual survival against wild animals.[148] Illnesses, Rousseau thinks, come about largely due to the unnatural impositions of society and the corresponding loss of the strength that should have been natural to us. The 'human machine' thus naturally is strong, and to this animal frame human beings add 'freedom'.[149] Rousseau observes, 'Nature commands every animal, and beasts obey. Man feels the same impetus, but he knows he is free to go along or to resist; and it is above all in the awareness of this freedom that the spirituality of his soul is made manifest.'[150] To the bodily machine, then, Rousseau adds a Cartesian spiritual soul whose defining aspect is the ability to rise above, in free choice, the restrictions of 'nature'.[151] Thanks to free choice, the human being, and the human species, can become better by freely

---

[147] Ibid., Part One, 38.   [148] Ibid., 40.   [149] Ibid., 44–5.

[150] Ibid., 45.

[151] For the roots of this concept of freedom in fourteenth-century nominalism, see Servais Pinckaers, OP, *The Sources of Christian Ethics*, 3rd edn., trans. Mary Thomas Noble, OP (1985; Washington, DC: Catholic University of America Press, 1995). Of course Rousseau takes it much further. See also Leo Strauss, *Natural Right and History*, 294.

acting upon desires or fears (the passions), unlike mere animals who can never be other than they are.

Given this account of the soul and the bodily machine, what happened to savage man? His desires propelled him eventually toward constructing civilized societies, particularly in the northern hemisphere, since 'in general the peoples of the north are more industrious than those of the south, because they cannot get along as well without being so, as if nature thereby wanted to equalize things by giving to their minds the fertility it refuses to their soil'.[152] But Rousseau supposes, on the basis both of his sources (e.g. the Abbé de Condillac) and his philosophical speculations, that this socializing happened only very slowly. For a long time, savage man remained savage man, without art, language, property, farming, social bonds, and the like. In Rousseau's view, 'it is impossible to imagine why, in that primitive state, one man would have a greater need for another man than a monkey or a wolf has for another of its respective species; or, assuming this need, what motive could induce the other man to satisfy it'.[153]

In explicit disagreement with Hobbes, moreover, Rousseau denies that this lack of social bonds and culture would have made for a more violent existence. On the contrary, Rousseau thinks that Hobbes has imported into his account of the 'state of nature' the violence of *society*.[154] It is society that makes human beings weak and dependent, and that thereby stimulates fear and violence. Furthermore, says Rousseau, Hobbes has recognized only self-preservation and has failed to see compassion or pity, the 'innate repugnance to seeing his fellow men suffer'.[155] While natural pity is corrupted by society and especially by the egotism fostered by reasoning, natural pity cannot be entirely effaced.[156] Savage man lived by the natural maxim, 'Do what

---

[152] Rousseau, 'Discourse on the Origin of Inequality', 46.   [153] Ibid., 51–2.
[154] Ibid., 53.   [155] Ibid.
[156] Ibid., 54. Rousseau states, 'Reason is what engenders egocentrism, and reflection strengthens it. Reason is what turns man in upon himself. Philosophy is what isolates him and what moves him to say in secret, at the sight of a suffering man, "Perish if you will; I am safe and sound." No longer can anything but danger to the entire society trouble the tranquil slumber of the philosopher and yank him from his bed. His fellow man can be killed with impunity underneath his window. He has merely to place his hands over his ears and argue with himself a little in order to prevent nature, which rebels within him, from identifying him with the man being

is good for you with as little harm as possible to others,' rather than by the speculative maxim, 'Do unto others as you would have them do to you'; and it is the savage maxim that actually stands a chance at being regularly performed by a wide number of members of the human race.[157]

In short, savage man, in the state of nature, lived by the natural law of self-preservation and compassion, and did so far less violently than civilized people do in societies. Living apart from each other, savages were not the fierce and competitive animals that civilized people have become. Rousseau notes as a possible exception the social bond necessitated by the procreative desire. Among savages, he proposes, only the physical aspect of this desire existed. In contrast, the 'moral aspect', which focuses sexual desire 'exclusively on one single object', has been invented by civilized women in order to dominate men. This pernicious moral aspect 'is an artificial sentiment born of social custom'.[158] Only in society does sexual love become exclusive and therefore violent.[159] Savage man is free of entangling social bonds, whether with neighbours, wife, or children, and therefore is free to seek peacefully his self-preservation and to exercise compassion. Lacking social bonds and possessions, savage man avoids the entanglements that produce oppressive strife. As Rousseau says of savage man, 'If someone chases me from one tree, I am free to go to another.'[160] Each human being is radically independent in the state of nature, and the violence begotten by dependence does not there exist.

The true natural law met its effective downfall, *pace* Locke (and Hume), on the day that one ill-starred savage man invented private property. Rousseau observes, 'The first person who, having enclosed a

assassinated. Savage man does not have this admirable talent, and for lack of wisdom and reason he is always seen thoughtlessly giving in to the first sentiment of humanity. When there is a riot or a street brawl, the populace gathers together; the prudent man withdraws from the scene. It is the rabble, the women of the marketplace, who separate the combatants and prevent decent people from killing one another' (54–5).

[157] Ibid., 55.   [158] Ibid., 56.

[159] Ibid. Rousseau speaks of 'countries where mores still count for something and where the jealousy of lovers and the vengeance of husbands every day gives rise to duels, murders and still worse things; where the duty of eternal fidelity serves merely to create adulterers; and where even the laws of continence and honor necessarily spread debauchery and multiply the number of abortions' (57).

[160] Ibid., 58.

plot of land, took it into his head to say *this is mine* and found people simple enough to believe him, was the true founder of civil society. What crimes, wars, murders, what miseries and horrors would the human race have been spared, had someone pulled up the stakes or filled in the ditch....'[161] He takes some comfort from the fact that given the rational soul operating in the animal machine to fulfil its desires, the development was bound to happen. The desires of human beings, as the earth became more populated and as human beings developed more skills, multiplied and became harder to fulfil. Self-interest gradually led human beings toward social bonds that became centres of self-interested competition. The building of dwelling places produced the family structure, and staying in these habitations weakened the female body, resulting in greater dependence. Soon enough communities of dwelling places took shape, as well as the arts and leisure, tool- and weapon-making, agriculture, and language. The result of ever-increasing civility was, as we have seen, proportionately ever-increasing violence. Here Rousseau turns Locke on his head: 'For according to the axiom of the wise Locke, *where there is no property, there is no injury*.'[162]

After natural law was destroyed, what replaced it? Certainly violence, but also 'law'—that is, the laws of nations, 'which gave new fetters to the weak and new forces to the rich, irretrievably destroyed natural liberty, established forever the law of property and of inequality, changed adroit usurpation into an irrevocable right, and for the profit of a few ambitious men henceforth subjected the entire human race to labor, servitude and misery'.[163] At first, however, a weakened law of nature existed between the various cities or states,

---

[161] Ibid., Part Two, 60.

[162] Ibid., 64. Rousseau is brilliant at describing this emergent violence after the state of nature: 'Thus the usurpations of the rich, the acts of brigandage by the poor, the unbridled passions of all, stifling natural pity and the still weak voice of justice, made men greedy, ambitious and wicked. There arose between the right of the strongest and the right of the first occupant a perpetual conflict that ended only in fights and murders. Emerging society gave way to the most horrible state of war; since the human race, vilified and desolated, was no longer able to retrace its steps or give up the unfortunate acquisitions it had made, and since it labored only toward its shame by abusing the faculties that honor it, it brought itself to the brink of its ruin. *Horrified by the newness of the ill, both the poor man and the rich man hope to flee from wealth, hating what they once had prayed for*' (68).

[163] Ibid., 70.

so that each might preserve itself and even have compassion for the weakness and suffering of other cities or states. This instantiation of the natural law in the relationships between societies also soon came to an end, leading to 'the national wars, battles, murders, and reprisals that make nature tremble and offend reason, and all those horrible prejudices that rank the honor of shedding human blood among the virtues.... Finally, men were seen massacring one another by the thousands without knowing why.'[164] Absent natural law (the state of nature), in sum, the most horrific inequality and brutality found legal recognition. Hobbes's view of the commonwealth is here turned on its head, as is Locke's view of private property (and of contractual government), Hume's of an existing good order founded upon the passions, and Descartes's of the good brought about by the soul's ratiocination. Rousseau arrives at a complete condemnation of human society: 'with original man gradually disappearing, society no longer offers to the eyes of the wise man anything but an assemblage of artificial men and factitious passions which are the work of all these new relations and have no true foundation in nature.'[165] A comparison with savage man reveals the civilized human being, entangled in social bonds, to be a slave and a dupe in whom only the traces of natural law, and true human nature, persist. The solution is to return to the free individual of the 'state of nature', unbound by the Creator or by any 'ecstatic' ordering other than compassionate feelings.

Immanuel Kant: Practical Reason

In his *Grounding for the Metaphysics of Morals*, Kant distinguishes between 'laws of nature and laws of freedom'.[166] The former is the

---

[164] Ibid.   [165] Ibid., 80.

[166] Immanuel Kant, *Grounding for the Metaphysics of Morals*, trans. James W. Ellington, 3rd edn. (1785; Indianapolis, IN: Hackett, 1993), Preface, 1. I have chosen to focus on Kant's *Grounding for the Metaphysics of Morals*, rather than discuss other influential works such as his *Theory of Right* and *Critique of Practical Reason*, because I think that the key aspects of his philosophy's impact upon later natural law doctrine find succinct expression in the *Grounding for the Metaphysics of Morals*. For further analysis of Kant in relation to natural law doctrine, see Rommen, *The Natural Law*, 88–93; Schneewind, *The Invention of Autonomy*, 483–530.

province of empirical science, the latter of moral science. No universal law for ethical action, Kant argues, can be derived from 'anthropology', because the empirical realm cannot ground universality. Kant therefore seeks a power of lawgiving that utterly transcends 'anthropology' and pertains to a priori rationality. For any universally binding law of moral action 'the ground of obligation here must therefore be sought not in the nature of man nor in the circumstances of the world in which man is placed, but must be sought a priori solely in the concepts of pure reason'.[167]

Whereas Hume and Hobbes give up on rationality as a source for moral norms, and Rousseau seeks to reconstruct 'savage man' for historical lessons regarding the tolerance inscribed in supreme individuality, Kant returns firmly to Descartes's project, which he advances. Investigation of the individual soul, whose freedom marks its transcendence above the anthropological body-machine, will reveal the sources of universally binding law regarding human action. He thereby manages to go far beyond the 'natural law' of rules for self-preservation and property that had been the fruit of Hobbes, Hume, Locke, and even Rousseau.

Kant describes human bodily desires and inclinations as 'nature', which he contrasts with reason and will, the locus of freedom. Suppose, he says, that 'happiness' comes from obeying 'nature'. It would then seem that freedom is oddly out of place. Given a 'happiness' resulting from conformity to 'nature' (in Kant's sense of bodily desires and inclinations), natural instinct carries the creature more efficaciously toward 'happiness' than rational freedom ever could.[168] Indeed, if conformity to 'nature' were the only end of the human

---

[167] Kant, *Grounding for the Metaphysics of Morals*, 2. John Paul II comments perceptively: 'The Königsberg philosopher rightly observed that giving priority to pleasure in the analysis of human action is dangerous and threatens the very essence of morality. In his aprioristic vision of reality, Kant places two things in question, namely pleasure and expediency. Yet he does not return to the tradition of the *bonum honestum*. Instead he bases all human morality on aprioristic forms of the practical intellect, which have imperative character ... With the ethics of the categorical imperative, Kant rightly emphasized the obligatory character of man's moral choices. At the same time, however, he distanced himself from the only truly objective criterion for those choices: he underlined the subjective obligation but overlooked what lies at the foundation of morals, that is the *bonum honestum*' (John Paul II, *Memory and Identity: Conversations at the Dawn of a Millennium* (New York: Rizzoli, 2005), 36–7).

[168] As Hume recognized.

being, then rational freedom would serve no purpose other than 'to contemplate the happy constitution of his nature, to admire that nature, to rejoice in it, and to feel grateful to the cause that bestowed it'.[169] In such a situation, were rational freedom to act in a way that transcended such 'nature', for instance by subjecting such 'nature' to its governance, rational freedom would be in opposition to the creature's happiness. As Kant says, 'In a word, nature would have taken care that reason did not strike out into a practical use nor presume, with its weak insight, to think out for itself a plan for happiness and the means for attaining it.'[170] Reason and its freedom, Kant grants, pose a threat to such happiness.

Is the 'happiness' of (bodily) 'nature' the only or even the primary end of the human being? Kant argues that just as bodily desires can be seen to have teleological ends, so also does rational freedom. For Kant, 'nature [here personified as artificer] in distributing her capacities has everywhere gone to work in a purposive manner'.[171] What then is the 'end' of reason? Kant proposes that its end is 'to produce a will which is not merely good as a means to some further end, but is good in itself'.[172] The end of the bodily inclinations, or 'nature', is 'happiness', but the end of reason is *duty*, the good will.[173] The latter end is higher; 'nature' must bow to 'reason'. Kant affirms, 'While such a will may not indeed be the sole and complete good, it must, nevertheless, be the highest good and the condition of all the rest, even of the desire for happiness.'[174] *Pace* Hume and Hobbes, human beings have a higher end than the satisfaction of the bodily desires, or 'happiness'.[175] This higher end so transcends the bodily desires that the human being has no need of 'happiness'. The properly human end is duty, the good will, which can be attained with or without 'happiness', although 'happiness' can be properly pursued as a duty. Reason and will pursue duty on a level

---

[169] Kant, *Grounding for the Metaphysics of Morals*, 8.   [170] Ibid.

[171] Ibid., 9.   [172] Ibid.

[173] On 'duty' in Kant see e.g. Dupré, *The Enlightenment and the Intellectual Foundations of Modern Culture*, 133–45; John Rist, *On Inoculating Moral Philosophy against God* (Marquette: Marquette University Press, 2000), 15–17.

[174] Kant, *Grounding for the Metaphysics of Morals*, 9.

[175] Kant defines 'happiness' as 'all inclinations combined into a sum total...the sum of satisfaction of all inclinations' (12).

that transcends that of (bodily) 'nature', with its natural desires and inclinations.[176]

Kant devotes much work to explaining further the concept of 'duty'. He first denies, as we have seen, that a will is 'good' because of its effects or its power (e.g. to modulate bodily passions).[177] One cannot measure the higher by the lower; the will's effects do not have the spiritual dignity and transcendent freedom that the will itself possesses. The will measures other things, rather than other things measuring the will. With this point in mind, Kant turns to the example of the natural inclination toward self-preservation, which he terms a 'duty'. Most people, he observes, pursue the duty of self-preservation in a way that accords with the inclination ('nature') but not with the duty. This is so because actions that arise from inclination do not attain the level of actions that arise from will. The former are done for a bodily motive. Actions that arise from reason and will, in contrast, transcend the bounds of 'nature' and are therefore truly free. Only such actions possess, in the strict sense, moral worth. In one of his examples, Kant notes that when one 'performs the action without any inclination at all, but solely from duty—then for the first time his action has genuine moral worth'.[178] This moral worth, as noted

---

[176] Kant writes that 'there is nothing inconsistent with the wisdom of nature that the cultivation of reason, which is requisite for the first and unconditioned purpose, may in many ways restrict, at least in this life, the attainment of the second purpose, viz., happiness, which is always conditioned. Indeed happiness can even be reduced to less than nothing, without nature's failing thereby in her purpose; for reason recognizes as its highest practical function the establishment of a good will, whereby in the attainment of this end reason is capable only of its own kind of satisfaction, viz., that of fulfilling a purpose which is in turn determined only by reason, even though such fulfilment were often to interfere with the purposes of inclination' (9).

[177] Ibid., 7.

[178] Ibid., 11. For keen insight into the results of this proposal (and its endpoint in Nietzsche), see Pierre Manent, *The City of Man*, trans. Marc A. LePain (Princeton: Princeton University Press, 1998), chapter 6, 'The End of Nature', especially 187–203. Manent observes, 'Neither Montesquieu nor Rousseau succeeded in answering clearly and plausibly the question of how man can find in his nature a motive for obeying a law that is hostile to his nature' (188). Kant's answer—that '[i]t is only because he can obey the Law by pure respect for the Law that man is the free cause and thus enjoys autonomy' (189)—establishes in human beings a capacity similar to 'a divine power of creation' (ibid.). For Manent, Kant's solution means that '[a]t last he [man] can think what until that time he could only will: he can now think that he is neither a creature of God nor a part of Nature, that he is in short born of himself, the child of his own liberty' (ibid.). Manent argues that a key problem here is the incapacity of Kant's

above, must be understood to reside in the will, not in its effects. The grandeur of the performance of duty is precisely the good will that enables such performance and thereby manifests human spiritual freedom.

Is this spiritual freedom antinomian, as if there were no 'natural law', as Hume (for instance) supposes? In Kant's opinion the answer is most assuredly no. He explains, 'Duty is the necessity of an action done out of respect for the law.'[179] This law is not the law of inclination or bodily desire: Kant argues that the human being 'can have no respect for inclination as such'.[180] Natural inclination is self-serving; duty is free and therefore can be self-sacrificing. The will, as transcendent, cannot be determined by natural inclination or by any object of the will.[181] But there is nonetheless a law that can

account to understand human sin, since it would make no sense for autonomous reason, commanding the law, to subject itself to the motives of nature, from which it is entirely disjoined. A second problem is that in commending his account of autonomous practical reason's lawmaking task, Kant sometimes appeals to human nature and at other times utterly rejects its claims, with apparent inconsistency. In Manent's view, Kant opens up a new stage of history: the ancients affirmed obedience to the natural; Christian thought, obedience to the supernatural; and Kant obedience to neither the natural nor the supernatural, but only self-creating man (what Manent calls 'the city of man') (201). The result is the Nietzschean 'Historical Man'. As Manent brilliantly summarizes: 'He flees the law that is given to him and seeks the law he gives himself. He flees the law given to him by nature, by God, or that he gave himself yesterday and that today weighs on him like the law of another. He seeks the law he gives himself and without which he would be but the plaything of nature, of God, or of his own past. The law he seeks ceaselessly and continuously becomes the law he flees. In flight and in pursuit, with the difference of the two laws always before him, modern man proceeds in this way to the continual creation of what he calls History. In this enterprise, the nature of man is his principal enemy' (204). Manent finds in this retreat into the mistaken pride of continual self-making 'the most bombastic illusion that has ever enslaved the thinking species' (205).

[179] Kant, *Grounding for the Metaphysics of Morals*, 13.   [180] Ibid.

[181] David B. Burrell, CSC, traces this view to metaphysical positions taken by Scotus: Scotus 'sought to enshrine human freedom in a self-moving faculty—the will—which could itself "elicit" acts. Effectively separated from "outside" influences, like discernment, human responsibility was secured by making the will a first mover. Yet its effect was also to remove freedom from its creaturely context and so set the stage for modernity and Kant's particular way of insisting that "only wills can be good." We can see how this separation occurred by contrasting Scotus' account with that of Thomas Aquinas, whom he often criticized. Where Aquinas considers *will* in the line of nature, Scotus opposes the freedom of the will to the necessity of nature; where Aquinas expounds willing by analogy with reasoning and relies on the complementarity of these parallel intellectual faculties to construct the dynamics of willing as a moved

'subjectively' determine the will. This law comes from the practical reason itself. Kant expresses it in the following manner: 'I should never act except in such a way that I can also will that my maxim should become a universal law'.[182] The source of the law is one's own practical reason, which determines whether one could universalize one's action. If one cannot affirm that one's action would be right for all other people as well, then one is acting from self-interested inclination rather than from duty. Duty, as opposed to inclination, respects the law laid down by the practical reason, a law which differentiates self-interested action from free action.[183] As Kant points out, no complicated philosophy or empirical science is needed to know this law; one's practical reason perceives what courses of action are universalizable.[184]

Is, then, a philosophical account of the law—which Kant prefers to call the moral law rather than the natural law, given his understanding of 'nature'—needed? Kant thinks so, on the grounds that '[m]an feels within himself a powerful counterweight to all the commands of duty, which are presented to him by reason as being so preeminently worthy of respect; this counterweight consists of his needs and inclinations, whose total satisfaction is summed up under the name of happiness'.[185] Practical reason, in setting forth its law, is in no way

movement, Scotus gives manifest priority to will as an unmoved (or "autonomous") mover ... [O]nce the created agent is deemed to be autonomous, precisely to guarantee its capacity of initiation, then creature and creator will also be conceived in parallel, the divine activity will be termed "concursus", and the stage is set for a zero-sum game in which one protagonist's gain is the other's loss ... Kant completed the reversal Scotus began, when he [Scotus] so opposed freedom to desire that *eros* came to be seen as inhibiting free actions rather than identified as their source. How could our actions be genuinely *free*—read "autonomous"—if they originated in a response? Would not that make them *heteronomous*? We must also realize, of course, how Kant was constrained to move within an entirely different world, since once Scotus had effectively "detach[ed] the will from the lure of the good ... Christian virtue itself was being redefined as obedience to authority, just as faith itself became defined as a set of propositions." So Kant needed to find a source of good actions more interior than responding to a divine command, especially since the divine had become another entity subsisting alongside the universe, as David Braine has noted. So the makings of the distinctively modern (or "libertarian") notion of freedom began to accumulate' (Burrell, 'Creation, Metaphysics, and Ethics', *Faith and Philosophy* 18 (2001): 204–21, at 216–17).

[182] Kant, *Grounding for the Metaphysics of Morals*, 14.   [183] Ibid., 15.
[184] Ibid., 16.   [185] Ibid.

indebted to the inclinations or bodily desires, and practical reason's law promises no 'happiness' to the inclinations or bodily desires. Not surprisingly, therefore, human beings have a difficult time obeying the laws of duty. Given this situation, philosophy—a 'metaphysics of morals'—can help.[186] It can do so firstly by demonstrating that human action need not arise from self-interest, *pace* Hobbes *et al.*[187] Kant does not claim to be able to make this demonstration by means of an empirical appeal to experience. The inner principles of an action are inaccessible to such empirical appeal, even if human experience suggested, as it does not, that most people are motivated by principles other than self-interest.[188] Kant argues instead that 'the question at issue here is not whether this or that has happened but that reason of itself and independently of all experience commands what ought to happen'.[189] Even if no one had ever committed a morally good action, nonetheless practical reason may command as universal law certain actions as duties. Such law is based in the a priori structure or ideals of practical reason itself, not in any empirical inclinations ('nature'), objects, or results. Only a metaphysical account of a priori law, separated from all other factors, assists human beings in acting according to the law of duty rather than according to self-interested inclinations.

In seeking to develop such an account, Kant focuses upon 'the universal concept of a rational being in general', not upon human reason as such.[190] He determines that 'the will is nothing but practical reason', because the will chooses that which practical reason presents it as 'objectively necessary'.[191] While the will may diverge from practical reason when other factors, such as natural inclinations, exert

---

[186] Kant defines 'metaphysics of morals' as 'pure rational knowledge separated from everything empirical' (21). He calls for 'a completely isolated metaphysics of morals, not mixed with any anthropology, theology, physics, or hyperphysics' (22).

[187] Kant observes that 'there have always been philosophers who have absolutely denied the reality of this disposition in human actions and have ascribed everything to a more or less refined self-love. Yet in so doing they have not cast doubt upon the rightness of the concept of morality. Rather, they have spoken with sincere regret as to the frailty and impurity of human nature, which they think is noble enough to take as its precept an idea so worthy of respect but yet is too weak to follow this idea: reason, which should legislate for human nature, is used only to look after the interest of inclinations, whether singly or, at best, in their greatest possible harmony with one another' (19).

[188] Ibid., 19.   [189] Ibid., 20.   [190] Ibid., 23.   [191] Ibid.

pressure upon the will, when properly functioning the will submits to the commands or imperatives of practical reason. There are two kinds of 'imperatives', hypothetical and categorical, depending upon whether the action commanded is a means to a further good, or a good in itself; the former has to do with 'happiness' and its 'empirical counsels', the latter with duty.[192] Kant states that in fact the only categorical imperative is the maxim we have already encountered, 'Act only according to that maxim whereby you can at the same time will that it should become a universal law.'[193] To this categorical imperative all other imperatives of duty can be reduced. Given this framework of self-constituted law that applies universally, Kant attempts to show why suicide, lying, sloth, and selfishness are opposed to duty and thus morally wrong.

At this point, however, Kant still wants 'to prove a priori that there actually is an imperative of this kind, that there is a practical law which of itself commands absolutely and without any incentives, and that following this law is duty'.[194] His concern is that it might seem that the categorical imperative, as he has thus far established it, might pertain solely to human beings—given their particular human pre-rational and rational 'nature'—and not to all rational beings of whatever kind. At stake is the 'a priori' character of the law of practical reason in the structure of rationality per se. Otherwise philosophy loses its proper autonomy, and no 'principles dictated by reason' have truly been found.[195] In undertaking this demonstration, Kant differentiates between 'subjective' and 'objective' ends, the former arising from incentives outside the structure of rational being. He then argues that rational being is the prime exemplar of an objective end: 'Now I say that man, and in general every rational being, exists as an end in himself and not merely as a means to be arbitrarily used by this or that will. He must in all his actions, whether directed to himself or to other rational beings, always be regarded at the same time as an end.'[196] In contrast to inclinations or desires ('nature'), which have to do with means, rational beings are *persons* because they are, qua rational and transcendent, ends in themselves.[197] This point both grounds the categorical imperative (in the structure of rational

---

[192] Ibid., 25–30.   [193] Ibid., 30.   [194] Ibid., 33.   [195] Ibid., 34.
[196] Ibid., 35.   [197] Ibid., 36.

being), and fills out somewhat more its content, which Kant now states as: 'Act in such a way that you treat humanity, whether in your own person or in the person of another, always at the same time as an end and never simply as a means.'[198]

It might seem, however, that this ground—that rational being ('person') is always an end in itself—undercuts the dignity of the human will, so that the will is now measured rather than possessing the freedom of a measure. Kant argues that this is not the case. He holds, 'The will is thus not merely subject to the law but is subject to the law in such a way that it must be regarded also as legislating for itself and only on this account as being subject to the law (of which it can regard itself as the author).'[199] Were the lawgiver extrinsic to the will, then obedience would flow from some interest or incentive outside the will. But since each will *is* the lawgiver of the universal law, the will is its own object and end; it stands supremely transcendent, even as it submits. In willing the law, it remains autonomous, and therefore motivated by no extrinsic interest.[200] Since each rational being is an end in itself, the proper relation of rational beings attained by duty is not self-interested but rather evinces 'the dignity of a rational being who obeys no law except what he at the same time enacts'.[201] Lacking autonomy, rational beings would not be supremely ends in themselves and so would lack this 'dignity'. Only as supremely ends in themselves can rational beings escape the web of 'nature' in which their actions are praiseworthy as means to their own fulfilment. Kant states, 'Thereby is he free as regards all laws of nature, and he obeys only those laws which he gives to himself. Accordingly, his maxims can belong to a universal legislation to which he at the same time subjects himself.'[202] As autonomous legislator, he can be subject to his

---

[198] Ibid.   [199] Ibid., 38.

[200] Ibid., 39. Kant notes, 'In every case where an object of the will must be laid down as the foundation for prescribing a rule to determine the will, there the rule is nothing but heteronomy' (47). As he goes on to say, then, 'An absolutely good will, whose principle must be a categorical imperative, will therefore be indeterminate as regards all objects and will contain merely the form of willing; and indeed that form is autonomy' (48).

[201] Ibid., 40.

[202] Ibid., 41. He explains a bit later, 'Thus a kingdom of ends is possible only on the analogy of a kingdom of nature; yet the former is possible only through maxims, i.e., self-imposed rules, while the latter is possible only through laws of efficient causes

own (universal) law without losing—through the interested motives that extrinsic legislation, including that derived from the concept of 'a divine and most perfect will', would impose[203]—the full dignity of free self-determination.

The remainder of Kant's *Grounding for the Metaphysics of Morals* explores in further detail the absolute character of the will's autonomous freedom. He takes up such issues as one's freedom as legislator vis-à-vis one's submission to (one's own) legislation; how to negotiate interiorly the differentiation between the 'world of sense' ('nature', heteronomy) and the 'intelligible world' ('person', freedom); whether free will can be demonstrated philosophically (it cannot); and how pure reason, with no incentive outside itself, takes its start, or in other words becomes practical (he is not sure).[204] He concludes that the laws prescribed by the categorical imperative can be understood as analogous to 'laws of nature', even though, as he understands 'nature', they are not such. He thus speaks of 'the splendid ideal of a universal kingdom of ends in themselves (rational beings), to which we can belong as members only if we carefully conduct ourselves according to maxims of freedom as if they were laws of nature'.[205]

In sum, the receptivity to the Creator's teleological ordering that the Bible sees as constitutive of 'natural law' has no place in Kant. In seeking to defend the rational freedom of the human person, reduced in various ways by Hobbes, Locke, Hume, and Rousseau, he extends in a distinctive way Descartes's split between the bodily

---

necessitated from without' (43). 'Nature' is here a set of efficient causes extrinsic to human interiority.

[203] Cf. ibid., 45, 47. Gordon E. Michalson Jr. comments with respect to the relationship of Kant's theism and Kant's ethical theory: 'To be sure, Kant's own unquestioned personal religious commitment is cobbled together with this philosophical vision, yet the points of connection are not only strained but they invariably display theism in a second-order relationship to a prior and much clearer account of reason's prerogatives. The religious side of Kant's outlook is best understood as the manifestation of a sensibility rather than as the result of philosophical argumentation; no accusation of hypocrisy is necessary to make such an observation... As we have seen, his actual philosophical claims suggest in multiple contexts a transformation of appeals to God and divine transcendence into fresh ways of acknowledging reason's freely given privileges and, indeed, its very sovereignty' (Michalson, *Kant and the Problem of God* (Oxford: Blackwell, 1999), 124).

[204] For these last two points, see Kant, *Grounding for the Metaphysics of Morals*, 60.
[205] Ibid., 61.

machine ('nature' and 'inclination' for Kant) and the mind (Kant's 'freedom'). Going further than his predecessors, but along a similar anthropocentric line, he makes law something that human persons constitute rather than receive, and he presents inclination and teleology as restrictive rather than liberative.

Georg W. F. Hegel: The Historical Unfolding of Spirit

Hegel's *Phenomenology of Spirit* plays an important role in the historicizing of 'natural law' thought. In the context of his exploration of 'Spirit', his discussion of 'law' revolves around his quest to exhibit the necessary historical overcoming of all otherness by the manifestation of Spirit. As one explores such apparent oppositions, Hegel argues, one finds through necessary steps that what appears as an 'other' (e.g. nature) is at a deeper level a dimension or moment of Spirit that when properly understood manifests the ultimate unification of Spirit toward which history ineluctably tends. Similarly, laws that first appear to be 'received' from outside ourselves are found ultimately to be laws that Spirit gives to itself and thus, as we come to consciousness of ourselves as Spirit (here overcoming the opposition between individual and community), that we give to ourselves.

Clearly Hegel's way of approaching the problem, through 'consciousness', owes its fundamental debt to Kant (and ultimately Descartes). But Hegel introduces two aspects—in addition to his broader narrative of the unfolding of world-Spirit, which reflects Hegel's confidence in his abilities to describe not merely the phenomena but the noumena—not found in Kant's approach. These two are the significance of the nation, against individualism, and the place of 'divine' law. In this way Hegel retrieves, through Kant, the political concerns present in Hobbes and Locke, as well as the effort to ground truth in the 'divine'.

Hegel argues that '[t]he simple substance of Spirit, as consciousness, is divided' because 'for ethical perception a given action is an actual situation with many ethical connections'.[206] This division has

---

[206] G. W. F. Hegel, *Phenomenology of Spirit*, trans. A. V. Miller (1807; Oxford: Oxford University Press, 1977): 267. I have chosen this work, rather than his *Philosophy of Right*, on the grounds that Hegel's understanding of historically evolving

first to do with the universal and the particular. Among Hegel's key pairings of thesis–antithesis is that of 'individuality and universality'; and this thesis–antithesis pair arises prominently in ethics, with complex implications for understanding law. Hegel states that 'still more for ethical perception, which is the purified substantial consciousness, does the plurality of ethical moments become the duality of a law of individuality and a law of universality'.[207] He shows this in regard to both human and 'divine' law.

Beginning with human law, he notes, 'In the essence we are considering here, individuality has the meaning of *self-consciousness* in general, not of a particular, contingent consciousness.'[208] It follows that the 'ethical substance' under analysis regards 'absolute Spirit realized in the plurality of existent consciousnesses; this spirit is the community.... It is Spirit which is *for itself* in that it preserves itself in its reflection in individuals; and it is *implicitly* Spirit, or substance, in that it preserves them within itself.'[209] The bottom line is that this 'ethical substance' has primarily to do with the ethical community as a whole, the commonwealth. Describing Spirit as regards this 'ethical substance', Hegel holds, 'As *actual substance*, it is a nation, as *actual consciousness*, it is the citizens of that nation.'[210] Idealist philosophy thus certainly need not foster individualism, in Hegel's view. In the ethical sphere this 'actual substance' and 'actual consciousness' can take both a universal and an individual form, and yet even the individual form has to do with the community. In the 'form of individuality', Hegel affirms, this 'Spirit' is the ethical consciousness's 'actual certainty of itself in the individual as such'.[211] Taken to its

---

'Spirit' is what most influences later historicist approaches to natural law. For a brief summary of *Phenomenology of Spirit* and its significance, see Michael Allen Gillespie, *Nihilism before Nietzsche* (Chicago: University of Chicago Press, 1995). Gillespie writes, 'This attribution of ultimate reality to a self-moving and self-developing spirit opens up history as the preeminent realm of human being' (118). He goes on to show how Hegel's viewpoint in *Philosophy of Right* flows from his *Phenomenology of Spirit*: 'The *Philosophy of Right* describes the final and insuperable form of rational ethical and political life made possible by spirit's reconciliation with itself in absolute knowledge' (119). For a summary of *Philosophy of Right*, see Kenneth Westphal, 'The Basic Context and Structure of Hegel's *Philosophy of Right*,' in *The Cambridge Companion to Hegel*, ed. Frederick C. Beiser (Cambridge: Cambridge University Press, 1993), 234–69, especially 241–3.

[207] Hegel, *Phenomenology of Spirit*, 267.   [208] Ibid.   [209] Ibid.
[210] Ibid.   [211] Ibid., 268.

fullest degree, this actual certainty in the individual 'is that Spirit as government', ethical authority that 'is openly accepted and manifest to all'.[212] In the 'form of universality', the 'actual consciousness' is 'the *known* law'.[213]

However, the human law never exists without its (apparent) antithesis, the 'divine' law. The nation and its law do not exhaust the 'ethical sphere'. The action of the lawmaking nation, the realm of 'self-conscious action', is insufficient to describe the realm of law. The divine law is 'the simple and immediate essence of the ethical sphere; as *actual* universality it is a force actively opposed to individual being-for-self; and as actuality in general it finds in that *inner* essence something other than the ethical power of the state'.[214] Yet, this apparent polarity should not be taken to mean that the 'ethical substance' exists only partially in each of the two laws, human and divine. On the contrary, says Hegel, 'each of the opposites in which the ethical substance exists contains the entire substance, and all the moments of its content. If, then, the community is that substance conscious of what it actually does, the other side has the form of immediate substance or substance that simply is.'[215] He then explains in terms of the 'Family' and nation (and in particular through an analysis of male and female) how the divine law is experienced in the form of individuality and in the form of universality. Likewise, he explores the relationship of the 'person' to the community, a relationship that results in a fruitful (apparent) alienation productive of 'culture'. The 'synthesis' that he arrives at, after a lengthy discussion that treats a wide variety of topics, approaches Kantian autonomy from another direction consistent with Hegel's focus on Spirit's emergence in the world:

Absolute freedom has thus removed the antithesis between the universal and the individual will. The self-alienated Spirit, driven to the extreme of its antithesis in which pure willing and the agent of that pure willing are still distinct, reduces the antithesis to a transparent form and therein finds itself. Just as the realm of the real world passes over into the realm of faith and insight, so does absolute freedom leave its self-destroying reality and pass over into another land of self-conscious Spirit where, in this unreal world, freedom has the value of truth. In the thought of this truth Spirit refreshes

---

[212] Ibid.   [213] Ibid., 267.   [214] Ibid., 268.   [215] Ibid.

itself, in so far as *it is* and remains *thought*, and knows this being which is enclosed within self-consciousness to be essential being in its perfection and completeness. There has arisen a new shape of Spirit, that of *moral* Spirit.[216]

Hegel thereby saves the communal and eternal aspect of Kant's autonomous self-legislating will.

At this stage Hegel proceeds to discuss 'duty', so important for Kant. He begins, 'Self-consciousness knows duty to be the absolute essence. It is bound only by duty, and this substance is its own pure consciousness, for which duty cannot receive the form of something alien. However, as thus locked up within itself, moral self-consciousness is not yet posited and considered as *consciousness*.'[217] The problem with 'duty' is that it makes moral self-consciousness individualistic or 'locked up within itself', and thereby prevents moral self-consciousness from rising to the true level of 'consciousness'. Tracing the consequences of this account of 'duty', Hegel summarizes Kant's position (without naming him):

From this determination is developed a moral view of the world which consists in the relation between the absoluteness of morality and the absoluteness of Nature. This relation is based, on the one hand, on the complete *indifference* and independence of Nature towards moral purposes and activity, and, on the other hand, on the consciousness of duty alone as the essential fact, and of Nature as completely devoid of independence and essential being.[218]

Hegel then explains, and expands upon, Kant's position on 'happiness'. 'Nature' cannot give happiness, since bodily pleasure is so contingent. Yet, 'pure duty', when fulfilled, contains an aspect of enjoyment precisely in the awareness of having fulfilled duty. This enjoyment opens up space, Hegel thinks, for postulating a harmony between 'morality and Nature'.[219] Thus Hegel seeks to overcome Kant's unbridgeable antithesis between reason and bodiliness. In so

---

[216] Ibid., 363.   [217] Ibid., 365.

[218] Ibid., 365–6. For Hegel's debt to and critique of Kant's ethics (a critique that largely occupies Part II of Hegel's *Philosophy of Right*), see e.g. Peter Singer, 'Hegel', in Roger Scruton *et al.*, *German Philosophers: Kant, Hegel, Schopenhauer, Nietzsche* (Oxford: Oxford University Press, 1997), 147–50.

[219] Hegel, *Phenomenology of Spirit*, 367.

doing, however, he takes seriously the possibility that the two might be unbridgeable: 'Since, of the two moments of the antithesis, sensuousness is sheer *otherness*, or the negative, while, on the other hand, the pure thought of duty is the essence, no element of which can be given up, it seems that the resultant unity can only be brought about by getting rid of sensuousness.'[220]

He first seeks a bridge by means of a 'postulate': 'But since sensuousness is itself a moment of the process producing the unity, viz. the moment of *actuality*, we have to be content, in the first instance, with expressing the unity by saying that sensuousness should be *in conformity with* morality. This unity is likewise a *postulated being*; it is not actually *there*; for what *is* there is consciousness, or the antithesis of sensuousness and pure consciousness.'[221] Combining this postulate with the earlier postulate regarding the harmony of 'morality and Nature', Hegel argues that the key is the 'movement of *actual* conduct itself'.[222] By exploring this movement (actual moral action), with the various contradictions it involves between subject and object,[223] he hopes to arrive at a synthesis that goes beyond Kant.

To present here all the steps of his argument, which focuses upon the action of 'conscience', would take us beyond the limited goals of our overview. The central point is the ability of 'conscience' to recognize law and duty and thereby to renounce the 'being-for-self' that locks the moral self-consciousness within itself. Hegel observes that in consciously acting on the basis of duty 'this distinction between the universal consciousness and the individual self is just what has been superseded, and the supersession of it *is* conscience'.[224] In the assurance, given by conscience, of doing one's duty, one 'acknowledges the *necessary universality of the self*'.[225] This universality provides a basis for the desired synthesis. It does so because it breaks away from the earthly level, on which the thesis–antithesis operates, to a higher plane. Hegel describes conscience as a human–divine voice and power:

Conscience, then, in the majesty of its elevation above specific law and every content of duty, puts whatever content it pleases into its knowing and willing. It is the moral genius which knows the inner voice of what

---

[220] Ibid., 368.   [221] Ibid.   [222] Ibid., 369.   [223] Cf. ibid., 374.
[224] Ibid., 396–7.   [225] Ibid., 397.

it immediately knows to be a divine voice; and since, in knowing this, it has an equally immediate knowledge of existence, it is the divine creative power which in its Notion possesses the spontaneity of life. Equally, it is in its own self divine worship, for its action is the contemplation of its own divinity.

This solitary divine worship is at the same time essentially the divine worship of a *community*, and the pure inner *knowing* and perceiving of itself advances to the moment of *consciousness*. The contemplation of itself is its *objective* existence and this objective element is the declaration of its knowing and willing as something *universal*. Through this declaration the self acquires moral validity and the act becomes an effective deed. The actuality and lasting existence of what it does is universal self-consciousness; but the declaration of conscience affirms the certainty of itself to be pure self, and thereby to be a universal self.[226]

In light of this view of 'conscience', Hegel argues that the terms in a relation (e.g. morality and Nature), while appearing to be 'outside' each other, are in fact subsumed into a higher unity in consciousness, given 'the immediacy of the presence within it [consciousness] of the absolute Being as the unity of that Being and its own self'.[227] The subject–object divide is not only bridged, but exploded. And yet, such moments of higher consciousness are admittedly fleeting. This leads Hegel into a brief discussion of evil, 'uncommunicative being-for-self'.[228] As we have seen, the opposition between self and knowledge of self ('I' and 'I') must be overcome on a higher plane. Hegel concludes his section on 'Morality', therefore, by stating, 'The reconciling *Yea*, in which the two "I"s let go their antithetical *existence*, is the *existence* of the "I" that has expanded into a duality, and therein remains identical with itself, and, in its complete externalization and opposite, possesses the certainty of itself: it is God manifested in the midst of those who know themselves in the form of pure knowledge.'[229]

He has thereby, in his own estimation, overcome the polarities that trouble Kant's position, and found a basis for moral law that rises beyond the apparent splits between subject–object, individual–communal, and human–divine. Yet, in addition to the question of the truth of his notion of unfolding 'Spirit', is this resolutely immanent 'Spirit' (the communal self) able to ground a free human *ecstasis*, and

---

[226] Ibid., 397–8.   [227] Ibid., 398.   [228] Ibid., 406.   [229] Ibid., 409.

a real *telos*, that measure up to the biblical portrait of the Creator who invites all human beings to share his life?[230] I think not.

Friedrich Nietzsche: Radical Historicism and 'Life'

Hegel's moral 'law' emerges out of the evolution of consciousness (Spirit) in history—the obverse of Rousseau's suggestion that 'natural law' has to be reclaimed from the dustbin of history through an excavation of savage man. In his *On the Advantage and Disadvantage of History for Life*, Nietzsche pushes further, even while radically altering, Hegel's historicist account of 'law'.[231] He begins with an image of a grazing herd of animals. Human beings, says Nietzsche, want to live like animals, yet do not want it as animals do. This is so because animals forget the past immediately, whereas human beings do not forget: 'Man on the other hand resists the great and ever greater weight of the past: this oppresses him and bends him sideways.'[232] The forgetfulness of animals, or of the infant child, enables them to be happy in a way that eludes thinking human beings. For Nietzsche, 'The least happiness, if only it keeps one happy without interruption, is incomparably more than the greatest happiness which comes to one as a mere episode, as a mood, a frantic incursion into a life of utter displeasure, desire and privation.'[233] The only way to achieve happiness 'without interruption', however, is to forget the past and live entirely in the present.

---

[230] See in this regard Kierkegaard's sustained polemicizing against Hegel's philosophy; see also Cyril O'Regan's *Gnostic Return in Modernity* (Albany, NY: State University of New York Press, 2001); idem, *The Heterodox Hegel* (Albany, NY: State University of New York Press, 1994).

[231] I have chosen to discuss *On the Advantage and Disadvantage of History for Life*, rather than such works as *Genealogy of Morals* or *Beyond Good and Evil*, because of its particularly clear advocacy for the obverse of self-giving *ecstasis*. See also David Bentley Hart, *The Beauty of the Infinite* (Grand Rapids, MI: Eerdmans, 2003), Part I: 'Dionysius against the Crucified,' Section III: 'The Will to Power', 93–125; Pierre Manent, *The City of Man*, chapter 6; Alasdair MacIntyre, *Three Rival Versions of Moral Enquiry: Encyclopedia, Genealogy, and Tradition* (Notre Dame, IN: University of Notre Dame Press, 1990), 34–57 and 196–215.

[232] Friedrich Nietzsche, *On the Advantage and Disadvantage of History for Life*, trans. Peter Preuss (1874; Indianapolis, IN: Hackett, 1980), 9.

[233] Ibid.

Nietzsche then ponders the varying degrees to which this seems possible for rational human beings. Some people, he observes, ruin their whole lives in brooding over one past event; other people pass through catastrophe after catastrophe (whether caused by others or by their own malice), yet seem hardly affected by these disasters. Pondering on the latter, Nietzsche suggests that they are able to 'master' past events so as to dominate the past and make it submit to the present. They are thereby able to live in a present 'horizon' that is enclosed and secure. As he states, 'What such a nature cannot master it knows how to forget; it no longer exists, the horizon is closed and whole, and nothing can serve as a reminder that beyond this horizon there remain men, passions, doctrines and purposes.'[234] Such people can be truly happy, because they are enclosed into their own present moment, into which they allow only that 'history' that they have mastered to enter. The 'most powerful and colossal nature', Nietzsche holds, would be self-enclosed in such a manner. Happiness then 'depends on one's being able to forget at the right time as well as to remember at the right time; on discerning with strong instinctual feelings when there is need to experience historically and when unhistorically'.[235] Thus the just human being, overly sensitive, lives in misery, whereas the strong and brutal human being, mastering his memories and forgetting what he wishes to forget, lives happily. The positive human task is to master history, to mold it into what one desires it to be.

There are two ways, according to Nietzsche, to master history. The first is egotistical and withers the human being: this way is a strictly 'superhistorical' standpoint in which one denies that one can place any hope in history because it is ever the same. However wise this might be, it is too dull for Nietzsche. He seeks a second way, namely 'life'. 'Life', in relation to mastering history, has three modes: action and greatness ('monumental'); gratitude and preservation ('antiquarian'); compassion and liberation ('critical'). The problem with 'life' in the modern world, however, is that 'history' has become a 'science'.[236] Instead of fostering 'life', such unmastered history produces 'walking encyclopedias', a lifeless 'inwardness'.[237] Modern people have become weak, unable to act, their freedom crushed by the ability to explain

---

[234] Ibid., 10.   [235] Ibid.   [236] Ibid., 23.   [237] Ibid., 24, 26.

everything 'objectively' through the inevitable progression of historical causes.[238] Such historical explanation leaves no room for 'life', that is, for subjectively mastering history by action. Taking religion as an example, Nietzsche argues that scientific history, by exposing the illusions of piety, dispels the 'illusion of love' or 'unconditional faith in something perfect and righteous' that is required for human beings to 'create'.[239] Christian religion's giving itself over to scientific history signals the end, in Nietzsche's view, of the Christian religion as an active reality, in so far as the Christian religion ever was such— since for Nietzsche Christian eschatology 'surely stimulates the deepest and noblest powers, but is hostile toward all new planting, bold attempting, free desiring....'[240] Historical objectivity, as 'a disguised theology'[241] ultimately rooted in the hopelessness of Christian eschatology, robs human beings of the possibility of subjective 'life', and a

[238] Ibid., 31. Nietzsche argues that 'objectivity' is a mask: see 34–7. He concludes that real 'history is written by the experienced and superior man. If you have not had some higher and greater experiences than all others you will not know how to interpret anything great and high in the past. The past always speaks as an oracle: only as master builders of the future who know the present will you understand it' (38).

[239] Ibid., 39. Nietzsche states, 'Each man who is forced no longer to love unconditionally has had the root of his strength cut off: he must wither, that is, become dishonest' (39).

[240] Ibid., 39, 44. Regarding the death of Christianity Nietzsche says, 'For a time perhaps the Hegelian philosophy, still smoking in older heads, may help to propagate that innocence, say, in that one distinguishes the "Idea of Christianity" from its many inadequate "forms of appearing" and talks oneself into thinking that it is the "love play of the Idea" to reveal itself in ever purer forms until finally it achieves the certainly purest, most transparent, hardly visible form in the brain of the contemporary *theologus liberalis vulgaris*. But if you listen to these most purified forms of Christianity talk about the earlier less purified forms then the impartial listener often gets the impression that it is not at all Christianity which is being discussed but rather— well, what are we to think of when we find Christianity characterized by "the greatest theologian of the century" as the religion which allows one "to feel oneself into all actual and a few merely possible religions", and when the "true church" is said to be the one which "becomes a fluid mass which knows no outline, in which each part is found at times here at times there and everything mingles peacefully"? Again, what are we to think of?

What one can learn from Christianity, that as a result of a historicizing treatment it has become blasé and unnatural until finally a completely historical, that is, just treatment has resolved it into pure knowledge about Christianity and so has annihilated it, all this one can study in everything that has life: that it ceases to live when it has been dissected completely and lives painfully and becomes sick once one begins to practise historical dissection on it' (39–40).

[241] Ibid., 45.

utilitarian commodification becomes the sole purpose of 'history' as a scholarly discipline.

Against this situation, Nietzsche proposes to turn historicism against itself: modern historical consciousness, once historically understood, can be dismissed. The goal for Nietzsche is to recreate 'in ourselves—also through our universal history—the spirit of Alexandrian-Roman culture so fruitfully and magnificently as now to be entitled, as the noblest reward, to set ourselves the still mightier task of striving behind and beyond this Alexandrian world and courageously to seek our standards of the great, the natural and human in the ancient Greek world'.[242] This return to the spirit of 'life', an unhistorical spirit that can therefore make and mould history, marks a rejection not only of Christianity but also and especially of 'Christianity' in its Hegelian form, in which 'God became transparent and intelligible to himself inside the Hegelian craniums and has already ascended all possible dialectical steps of his becoming up to that self-revelation: so that for Hegel the apex and terminus of world history coincided in his own Berlin existence'.[243] Nietzsche finds in the Hegelian understanding of the necessary historical unfolding of Spirit, the very worst possible confinement of human beings within the inexorable 'power of history'.[244] The alleged comprehension of everything that Hegelian historical understanding makes possible is, Nietzsche thinks, ridiculous: he imagines Europeans proclaiming idiotically that ' "we are at the goal, we are the goal, we are the completion of nature" '.[245]

Rather, true human happiness and 'life' consists in fighting '*against* history' and seeking what ought to be rather than what is.[246] Such human beings, undaunted by Hegel's (or 'Christianity''s)

[242] Ibid., 46.

[243] Ibid., 47. On Nietzsche's relationship to Hegel see e.g. Karl Löwith, *From Hegel to Nietzsche: The Revolution in Nineteenth-Century Thought*, trans. David E. Green (1964; New York: Columbia University Press, 1991), 186–8; Gillespie, *Nihilism before Nietzsche*, especially 246–7.

[244] Nietzsche, *On the Advantage and Disadvantage of History for Life*, 47.

[245] Ibid., 50. Yet Nietzsche has the same aim in mind. Gillespie shows that for Nietzsche, 'In willing the eternal recurrence, the strongest man wills the will to power as a whole, becomes the will to power as a whole, and wills through it all things. He becomes the one true being, supremely powerful, thoroughly autonomous, and self-creating' (Gillespie, *Nihilism before Nietzsche*, 222).

[246] Nietzsche, *On the Advantage and Disadvantage of History for Life*, 49.

suppositions about the 'world process',[247] overcome the weight of history and begin anew, as founders. Such founders, who have existed throughout history, 'do not, as it were, continue a process but live in a timeless simultaneity...one giant calls to the other across the bleak intervals of ages and, undisturbed by the wantonly noisy dwarfs who creep away beneath them, the lofty conversation of spirits continues'.[248] Having historicized the Hegelian historicism that makes the power of history dominant over individual freedom, Nietzsche proposes that history reveals not a 'process' but rather human beings who master and mould history. As he puts it, 'the *goal of humanity* cannot lie at the end but only *in its highest specimens*'.[249] There is no 'end'; this notion, originally Christian and then the foundation of Hegelian historicism, places human beings under the power of history, and thereby evacuates 'life', that is, true happiness. Since there is no 'end', there is no 'nature': those who become fully human are those who recognize the malleability of all things ('history') and make themselves. All others remain captive to various species of 'utilitarian vulgarity'.[250] Those capable of full humanity remain 'young' by refusing to grant anything, even history, the power to master them.

Whereas for earlier modern philosophers, as we have seen, 'nature' was the restrictive force that had to be overcome, now even 'history' has to be overcome. Human beings must radically make themselves

[247] Ibid., 50. The Hegelian notion of the world process here launches Nietzsche into a parody of a now-forgotten work by Eduard von Hartmann, *Philosophie des Unbewußten* (Berlin, 1869): 'To be sure, according to his [Hartmann's] explanation we are approaching "that ideal condition in which the human race makes its history consciously": but evidently we are still a good distance from that perhaps still more ideal condition in which mankind will read Hartmann's book consciously. Once it comes to that no man will let the words "world process" slip through his lips unless these lips are smiling' (53).

[248] Nietzsche, *On the Advantage and Disadvantage of History for Life*, 53.

[249] Ibid.

[250] Ibid., 55. As he says, 'The masses seem to me worthy of notice in only three respects: first as blurred copies of great men, produced on bad paper with worn plates, further as resistance to the great, and finally as the tools of the great; beyond that, may the devil and statistics take them! What, statistics prove that there are laws of history? Laws? Yes, it proves how mean and disgustingly uniform the masses are: is one to call laws the effect of inertia, stupidity, aping, love and hunger? Well, we will admit it, but with that the following proposition is also sure: so far as there are laws in history, laws are worth nothing and history is worth nothing' (55). He goes on to connect his 'great man' proposition with what he considers to be the best aspects of Christianity.

at every moment. Nietzsche envisions a 'realm of youth'.[251] As he says, 'First give me life and I will make you a culture from it! –so calls each individual of this first generation, and all these individuals will recognize each other by this call. Who will give them life? No god and no man: only their own *youth*: unfetter it and you will have freed life along with it'.[252] Youth signifies not chronological age, but recognition of one's mastery over history, one's ability to create oneself and one's world (even if one dies trying). To be 'young' it is necessary to possess a sense both of the 'unhistorical' and of the 'superhistorical'. The former enables one to forget one's past, the latter enables one to imagine eternal and unchanging ideals. Together, the two foster 'life', creative action that is happiness, that liberates from the dominance of 'humanoid aggregates' that is history.[253] As a model of this accomplishment Nietzsche points to ancient Greek culture: 'Thus the Greek concept of culture—in contrast to the Romance concept—will be unveiled to him, the concept of culture as a new and improved nature, without inside and outside, without dissimulation and convention, of culture as the accord of life, thought, appearing and willing.'[254] Mastering history, one creates one's 'nature' anew every moment.

CONCLUDING OBSERVATIONS

Absent the biblical Creator's teleological ordering, what then are the various options that modern natural law tries to provide? To judge by our overview of eight of the most influential modern philosophers, the answers take the following directions: to distinguish between the mind and its bodily machine, the former imposing its own laws and the latter with no telos outside itself (Descartes, Kant); to constitute a commonwealth that by sheer power instantiates laws of nature, which are expressions of the desire for self-preservation (Hobbes); to rely upon self-interested human emotions to preserve order (Hume, Hobbes); to turn the focus to individualistic preservation of one's property (Locke); to throw off the violent bonds of civilization and

---

[251] Ibid., 58.   [252] Ibid., 61.   [253] Ibid., 64.   [254] Ibid.

return to a state of nature governed by pity and minding one's own business (Rousseau); to affirm the law-constituting role of each individual's practical reason (Kant) over against the threat of sub-human 'inclination' and 'nature'; to affirm the overcoming of all divisions by means of the necessary historical evolution of Spirit (Hegel); to master even history itself and freely reconstitute one's 'nature' at every moment (Nietzsche).[255]

What are these approaches lacking (in part due to their epistemological assumptions, which both belong to and frame their rejection of a metaphysics of participation)? By locating the origin of 'law' in individual human beings, rather than within the biblical creature–Creator relationship, they lack not only the sense of fruitful receptivity that comes from envisioning human beings as created by God (Augustine) or as participating in personified nature (Cicero). They also lack the integral unity of body and soul, and thus distort 'inclinations' as sub-human. Most importantly, they lack awareness of the teleology of the body–soul person as received from the Creator and therefore as aiming at interpersonal communion, both by nature and (far more powerfully) by grace. Descartes's mind cannot give itself, let alone its body-machine, a *telos* of intimate communion with another; Hobbes's commonwealth rules out true communion; Hume and Locke focus strictly upon the goods of this world; Rousseau's effort to retrieve anti-social savage man, while at least offering an ideal, rejects real communion; Kant grounds everything upon autonomous individual reason; and Hegel and Nietzsche, in differing ways, cannot escape the grip of this-worldly history. No real *ecstasis*—giving oneself to others as a participation in the radically distinct, creative divine

---

[255] Thomas Hibbs summarizes the trajectory: 'The modern exaltation of freedom at the expense of nature and of our living relationship to a personal God begins by urging upon us the Herculean task of self-legislation but ends up reducing freedom to farce. If there is nothing either external to me or within my nature in light of which I might appraise my choices, then every choice validates (and thereby trivializes) itself' (Hibbs, *Virtue's Splendor* (New York: Fordham University Press, 2001), 62). Hibbs recognizes, as we will see in the next chapter, that those who would retrieve Aquinas's insights on human nature have to do so by recovering an adequate notion of the 'good'. Otherwise 'Aquinas's emphatic statement that the will necessarily desires happiness (*ST*, I, 82, 1) sounds constraining to modern ears' (ibid., 63). For Aquinas, as Hibbs points out, 'The more we participate in the order established for us by God, the more free we are. This freedom is more than a liberation from an external and self-alienating law; it is, rather, a discovery of who and what we are as creatures' (59).

self-giving—is possible once one begins with human beings as the source and origin of law. Natural law, understood anthropocentrically, constricts and narrows the human person.[256] This constriction of human *ecstasis* can be recognized even if one also grants that the modern thinkers we have surveyed here would view the constriction as an unavoidable fact of life, or even as a good.

By contrast, an understanding of the human being as God's creature who is 'ecstatically' ordered to the particular flourishing or perfection that is personal communion with God—an understanding informed by the biblical narrative—provides the key to renewal of a doctrine of natural law that adequately attends to the 'ecstatic' fulfilment of human personhood. A theocentric and teleological natural law doctrine offers a better understanding of natural inclinations and rational freedom than modern anthropocentric accounts offer. It can also integrate contemporary insights regarding the dignity of the human being and the significance of history for any concept of 'nature'. Drawing upon the thought of Aquinas, the two chapters that follow enter into this constructive project toward the renewal of a 'biblical' natural law doctrine.

---

[256] As Guy Mansini, OSB, remarked to me, it is telling that the positions of these modern philosophers can be discussed without ever a mention of friendship.

3

Natural Law and Natural Inclinations

What are natural inclinations, and how do they relate to natural law? The centrality of this question appears through our survey of modern philosophical approaches to the natural law. As we have seen, Descartes and Kant leave no place for natural inclinations: Descartes denies any teleology to the body-machine, while Kant supposes that natural inclination crimps human freedom and the dignity of rationality. In various ways Hobbes, Locke, and Hume all suppose that the only human natural inclinations truly at play are our self-interested desires for property and self-preservation, with a correspondingly truncated teleology. Hegel and Nietzsche historicize human 'nature', in which any inclination is subsumed into the historical world process (Hegel) or the fight to rise above history's implacable dynamisms (Nietzsche).

Thus how each modern thinker views 'inclination' to a significant degree determines his approach to natural law. Thomas Aquinas, whose understanding of natural law flows from Scripture as well as from such thinkers as Cicero and Augustine, is in this regard no different. His presentation of the content of the natural law depends largely upon his understanding of natural inclinations.[1] For Aquinas the creature is never 'neutral': powers are always inclined toward an end—ultimately the creator God—that draws and defines them.[2]

---

[1] For further discussion of this point, in critical dialogue with the 'new natural law theory' of Germain Grisez, see Douglas Flippen, 'Natural Law and Natural Inclinations', *New Scholasticism* 5 (1986): 284–316. Grisez responds to Flippen in 'Natural Law and Natural Inclinations: Some Comments and Clarifications', *New Scholasticism* 6 (1987): 307–20.

[2] See Russell Hittinger, 'Natural Law and Virtue: Theories at Cross Purposes', in *Natural Law Theory: Contemporary Essays*, ed. Robert P. George (Oxford: Oxford

Inclination belongs to our rational apprehension of being. As he states, 'Now as *being* is the first thing that falls under the apprehension simply, so *good* is the first thing that falls under the apprehension of the practical reason, which is directed to action: since every agent acts for an end under the aspect of good.'[3] Aquinas observes that this dynamism toward the good is 'the first principle in the practical reason' from which follows 'the first precept of law, that *good is to be done and pursued, and evil is to be avoided*.'[4] He unfolds this natural inclination toward the good by specifying four further natural inclinations, arranged in an ontological hierarchy, each of which expresses an aspect of the purposive natural inclination toward the human good. Natural inclination in human beings does not conflict with freedom: human nature inclines purposively to 'ends' that the person attains through the rational exercise of free will. Indeed without inclination one could not imagine how free will could be directed toward particular objects.[5]

The precepts of the natural law, that is to say what reason 'naturally apprehends as man's good',[6] are based in this created teleological structure of natural inclinations toward ends. As Aquinas puts it, 'good has the nature of an end, and evil, the nature of a contrary, hence ... all those things to which man has a natural inclination, are naturally apprehended by reason as being good, and consequently as objects of pursuit, and their contraries as evil, and objects of avoidance. Wherefore according to the order of natural inclinations, is the order of the precepts of the natural law.'[7] Natural inclinations and

---

University Press, 1992), 42–70. As Hittinger explains his central point, 'While the older teleological theories permitted natural-law analysis to play both roles—to explicate the goods embedded in human actions as well as their completions—the modern rejection of teleological thinking guarantees that a natural-law doctrine of *recta ratio* must restrict itself to discourse about natural goods or values. It will prove very difficult to include the virtues in this discourse' (43).

[3] *Summa Theologiae* I–II, q. 94, a. 2.   [4] Ibid.

[5] Cf. *Suppl.*, q. 41, a. 1 (*IV Sent.*, d. 26, q. 1, a. 1).

[6] I–II, q. 94, a. 2. Cf. Kevin Flannery, SJ's detailed argument that one of Aquinas's goals in this key article is 'to depict natural law as possessing the same general structure as an Aristotelian science' (Flannery, *Acts Amid Precepts: The Aristotelian Logical Structure of Thomas Aquinas' Moral Theory* (Washington, DC: Catholic University of America Press, 2001), 26).

[7] I–II, q. 94, a. 2. An excellent summary of Aquinas's natural law doctrine is found in Jean-Pierre Torrell, OP, *Saint Thomas Aquinas*, vol. 2: *Spiritual Master*, trans. Robert

reason's apprehension of the precepts of natural law belong to the same teleological ordering of the human being as created.

Is such a perspective, informed as it is by the Bible's understanding of reality, viable in the context of modernity? Recent Thomistic approaches to articulating a contemporary natural law doctrine have sought to engage the questions about nature, freedom, and history raised by modern philosophy. How does the natural law arise in the human person? How do freedom and the natural inclinations relate? In what way should the rational character of natural law be described? Is natural law *discerned* by human reason as a normative order inscribed in nature? Or is natural law *constituted* historically by the judgements of practical reason, which transform and elevate (humanize) inclinations found in nature by reorienting these inclinations to the personal ends known by spiritual creatures?

These questions arose as well in our reflection on Scripture. Thus in seeking to develop a contemporary account of natural law whose philosophical and theological precisions are adequate to reality as illumined by biblical revelation, we need to engage more directly these questions, which arise from modern efforts to locate natural law in natural inclinations or in the human mind. This chapter undertakes this task by means of a dialogic approach that seeks to listen to the diversity of contemporary Thomistic viewpoints. I have chosen three representative accounts, by Martin Rhonheimer, Servais Pinckaers, and Graham McAleer respectively. Rhonheimer emphasizes the independence or freedom of practical reason in constituting the natural law from the data provided by the natural inclinations.

Royal (Washington, DC: Catholic University of America Press, 2003), 282–90, which rightly places the natural law in the ('ecstatic', to use Graham McAleer's term) context of Aquinas's theology of friendship, the common good, and the communion of the Church. After presenting a lengthy excerpt from I–II, q. 94, a. 2, Torrell observes, 'Anyone who reads this with even a minimum of care will find it astonishing. While other spiritual writers speak volubly about fighting nature so that grace may triumph, Thomas says, on the contrary, that everything in line with nature is good in itself. Created by God, it is in itself oriented toward the good; it is sin that goes against nature. The same attitude was at work in Thomas's recognition of the natural character of the passions in themselves ... [W]e should also note how it is common possession of human nature that inclines men to live in society; by underscoring three times that there is a *communicatio* at the base of each *inclinatio*, Thomas finds here the *koinônia* postulated by Aristotle at the starting point of all social amity' (285–6).

He desires to affirm the fully personal and free activity of human beings in working out their own salvation through moral knowing and moral action. Pinckaers argues that a nominalist understanding of 'nature' places nature in conflict with reason and thereby undercuts the theology of the natural law. For this reason Pinckaers devotes significant effort to retrieving a positive account of the natural inclinations. Lastly, McAleer begins with the metaphysical and teleological structure of human bodiliness, so as to locate the natural law within an ecstatic (and historical) framework adequate to the human person's participation in God.

By emphasizing the constitutive role of practical reason, Rhonheimer's approach to natural law and natural inclinations possesses similarities to that of the 'new natural law theory' proposed by Germain Grisez and developed further by John Finnis, Robert George, and others.[8] Pinckaers, for his part, engages the metaphysical fabric of natural law doctrine: the hylomorphic unity of the body–soul composite; the nature of the good; and perfection, happiness, and friendship as constitutive of the doctrine of natural law and natural inclinations. McAleer's work relates closely to John Paul II's *Theology of the Body*. Among those still interested in 'natural law' doctrine, Rhonheimer's view, which accepts Hume's critique and creatively builds upon Kant's solution, represents the most common position. While I will therefore present his view in some detail, I will argue that Pinckaers and McAleer, by exhibiting a far richer account of natural inclinations, offer a better way forward. The fundamental issue might be summed up in the following manner: If natural law is primarily received from the Creator rather than primarily constituted by the moral agent, does this undercut the dignity of human freedom?

---

[8] Cf. Rhonheimer's *Natural Law and Practical Reason: A Thomist View of Moral Autonomy*, trans. Gerald Malsbary (New York: Fordham University Press, 2000), which contains a new preface and postscript that offers a brief intellectual autobiography and responds to critical reviews of the German edition, *Natur als Grundlage der Moral*, which appeared in 1987. This postscript identifies the influence of Grisez and Finnis upon Rhonheimer and illumines the broader discussion (largely among German-language scholars) that provided the context for his approach. *Natural Law and Practical Reason* critiques both what he considers to be the 'physicalist' action theory of many traditional Thomists and the revisionist theories of 'autonomous morality'. For discussion of this book, see the insightful critical review in *The Thomist* 66 (2002): 311–15 by Stephen L. Brock.

Or, put another way, how does receptivity relate to a freedom shaped, as the Bible teaches, by the vocation of *ecstasis*?

MARTIN RHONHEIMER: PRACTICAL REASON's CONSTITUTIVE ROLE AS THE *IMAGO DEI*

Martin Rhonheimer has devoted a number of books and articles to setting forth his account of natural law and natural inclinations.[9] In a recent article, he provides a helpful overview of his position. The main task of this section will be to present Rhonheimer's position as set forth in his recent overview.

He begins by describing the dilemma faced before Vatican II by Catholic ethicists who examined natural law doctrine, at that time quite influential in Catholic moral teaching particularly as regards sexual ethics. Taking Josef Fuchs as an example, he observes that Fuchs found in the Magisterium's appeals to natural law not one but two concepts of natural law. On the one hand, natural law appeared in texts of the Magisterium as an objective reality inscribed in the 'order' or 'nature' of things: the locus of natural law was in this natural order. In particular, natural law in human beings was inscribed in human body–soul nature. On the other hand, other Magisterial texts seemed to locate the natural law in human knowing. In seeking to unite these two sets of texts, Fuchs proposed that the natural law is primarily inscribed in the natural order of things and secondarily known by human reason.[10]

---

[9] See *Natural Law and Practical Reason*. See also his *Praktische Vernunft und Vernünftigkeit der Praxis: Handlungstheorie bei Thomas von Aquin in ihrer Entstehung aus dem Problemkontext der Aristotelischen Ethik* (Berlin: Akademie Verlag, 1994); idem, *La prospettiva della morale: Fondamenti dell'etica filosofica* (Rome: Armando, 1994); idem, *Die Perspektive der Moral: Philosophische Grundlagen der Tugendethik* (Berlin: Akademie Verlag, 2001); idem, 'Contraception, Sexual Behavior, and Natural Law: Philosophical Foundation of the Norm of *Humanae Vitae*', *The Linacre Quarterly* 56 (1989): 20–57.

[10] Martin Rhonheimer, 'The Cognitive Structure of the Natural Law and the Truth of Subjectivity', *The Thomist* 67 (2003): 1–44, at 1–2. See Josef Fuchs's *Natural Law: A Theological Investigation*, trans. H. Reckter and J. Dowling (New York: Sheed & Ward, 1965), written before *Humanae Vitae* and the corresponding shift in Fuchs's position. The terms of the post-Vatican II debate are perhaps best expressed by Charles E. Curran's 'Natural Law in Moral Theology' (1970), reprinted in *Readings*

Rhonheimer finds here an unfortunate dualism of 'objective' and 'subjective'. He argues that this dualism reveals the presence of fundamentally incompatible views of the natural law, one Stoic, the other Catholic. He describes the Stoic view, which he attributes most fully to Cicero, as follows:

one could make the objection that God in fact reveals himself 'in nature' and that reason is participation of the eternal law of God precisely to the extent to which it knows and makes its own an order that is inserted into nature.... This is the Stoic notion, which influenced the tradition of natural law that came down to us through Roman law. The idea, typical of Stoa, that the eternal law is to be identified with the cosmic order and that it is therefore decipherable through a knowledge of nature, of which man is a part, opens the way to a notion of law and natural right that in the Western tradition has been very important.[11]

The Stoic view contains part of the truth, Rhonheimer grants, but it is led astray by its lack of knowledge of human reason's participation in divine reason. As Rhonheimer remarks, 'For the Stoics, human *ratio* is not the participation and image of a transcendent *ratio*, but a *logos* that is inherent in nature itself. The human *ratio* thus becomes a kind of reflection of what nature already contains in terms of inclinations and ends; man, in *oikeiosis*, rationally assimilates this natural order.'[12] In other words, for the Stoics—so Rhonheimer claims—human reason does not possess a transcendent dimension; human rationality

---

in *Moral Theology*, no. 7: *Natural Law and Theology*, ed. Charles E. Curran and Richard A. McCormick, SJ (New York: Paulist Press, 1991), 247–95. Aware of Germain Grisez's effort to ground natural law on practical reason alone but unpersuaded by the ethical teachings derived by Grisez from this theory, Curran outlines the problem of 'physicalism' that he thinks infects *Humanae Vitae*: 'The Thomistic natural law concept vacillates at times between the order of nature and the order of reason. The general Thomistic thrust is towards the predominance of reason in natural law theory. However, there is in Thomas a definite tendency to identify the demands of natural law with physical and biological processes. Thomas, too, is a historical person conditioned by the circumstances and influences of his own time. These influences help explain the tendency (but not the predominant tendency) in Thomas to identify the human action with the physical and biological structure of the human act. A major influence is Ulpian, a Roman lawyer who died in 228' (254–5).

[11] Rhonheimer, 'The Cognitive Structure of the Natural Law and the Truth of Subjectivity', 16–17. For discussion, see Jean-Marie Aubert, *Le droit romain dans l'oeuvre de saint Thomas* (Paris: J. Vrin, 1955).

[12] Rhonheimer, 'The Cognitive Structure of the Natural Law and the Truth of Subjectivity', 17.

bears no mark that distinguishes it radically from the rest of the cosmic order, and thus human rationality is called to apprehend, rather than ultimately transcend, the rest of the cosmic order. Human action on the Stoic view should blend in with cosmic teleologies, should be normed by the order intrinsic to the whole cosmos, rather than standing above the cosmos and discerning human norms not in the cosmos but ultimately in itself as a participation in God's reason.[13]

Against those who emphasize the influence of Stoicism, Rhonheimer argues that the Catholic tradition begins not with the cosmos as normative but with human reason, radically distinct from the cosmos, as normative. He explains, 'For the Fathers of the Church, the *imago* of this God in the world is neither nature nor the cosmic order: the image of the Creator is present solely in the spiritual soul of man, in particular in his intellect and thus in his acts of practical reason. Practical reason does not simply reflect "nature"; rather, in being an active participation of the divine intellect, human reason in its turn illuminates nature, rendering it fully intelligible.'[14] Human rational 'nature' and non-rational 'nature' are radically distinct, because in

---

[13] See also Rhonheimer, *Natural Law and Practical Reason*, 66, for a similar discussion.

[14] Rhonheimer, 'The Cognitive Structure of Natural Law and the Truth of Subjectivity', 18. Rhonheimer comments in the introduction (1987) to *Natural Law and Practical Reason*: 'What is meant when we speak of human nature as the foundation of moral normativity? What are the methodological principles for a normative ethics that make use of natural-law arguments? The key to answering these questions, it will be maintained, can be found by attending to the personal structure of the natural law—a structure that becomes clear in Thomas only in the context of a theory of the practical reason. The natural law will be shown to be the *law of the practical reason*, and this is why a theory of the *lex naturalis* is precisely a theory of the practical reason. Furthermore, the independence of the practical reason vis-à-vis the theoretical reason must be established, and it must be shown how the practical reason can be a subject of ethics at all' (xviii). He sounds the same notes in the new preface to the English translation (2000): 'I am convinced that a discourse on natural law is a discourse on practical reason. What distinguishes a natural-law doctrine from any other kind of theory about practical reason, however, is that it contains a view of practical reason as embedded in specific natural inclinations of the human person. Nevertheless, a doctrine of natural law is not a doctrine about natural inclinations but precisely one about practical reason, which is shown to be practical in so far as it works in a context determined by natural inclinations. Being so tightly bound up with practical reason, any conception of natural law necessarily includes an understanding of moral autonomy' (viii). He goes on to say that 'the legitimate demands of moral autonomy for "self-legislation" are fully satisfied by the *participated autonomy* of moral experience and by the conception of a natural law that is constituted through the practical reason'

human nature alone one finds the *imago dei*. The *imago dei*, the intellect and its acts of knowing, does not take orders from non-rational nature; rather the *imago dei* humanizes non-rational nature (present in the human person) by ordering it, and thereby exercises its proper task as *imago dei*, reflective of God's transcendence and law-giving authority. In other words, as God is to the created universe, so is the *imago dei* to non-rational creation. Human reason, as not merely part of nature but as *imago dei*, gives the 'law' to 'nature', rather than receiving the law from nature. This is so ultimately because human reason (itself 'natural' as created) can give a natural law that, while taking up nature, transforms and elevates it in light of human reason's unique participation in God and awareness of an eternal destiny.

In explicating this point, which he takes to be the witness of the Catholic tradition and most especially of Thomas Aquinas, Rhonheimer argues that he is not denying, in a Cartesian manner, the significance of human animality. He carefully explains: 'It is certainly the case that man is a "person" thanks to his spirituality, but the "human person" is all that is formed by the spirit and body in a unity of substance. Man is not an embodied spirit since he does not belong to the order of spirits. Man belongs to the order of animals, and before anything else he is an animal.'[15] Yet animality, bodiliness, means something different for human rational animals than it does for non-rational animals. Animality or bodiliness itself is transformed by the fact that the human body is animated by a spiritual soul. This means that the human rational animal carries 'out not only spiritual acts but also all the other acts of his animal character in a way that is impregnated with the life of the spirit and thus under the guidance of reason'.[16] Just as human animality is transformed by this guidance

---

(xx). His position in these earlier writings is the same as in 'The Cognitive Structure of Natural Law and the Truth of Subjectivity.'

[15] Rhonheimer, 'The Cognitive Structure of the Natural Law and the Truth of Subjectivity', 19. Here one might wish that Rhonheimer had said 'rational animal' or 'human animal' rather than 'an animal'.

[16] Ibid. See for expositions of Thomistic hylomorphism, Thomas S. Hibbs, 'Introduction', in Thomas Aquinas, *On Human Nature*, ed. Thomas S. Hibbs (Indianapolis, IN: Hackett, 1999), vii–xxi; Jean-Pierre Torrell, OP, *Saint Thomas Aquinas*, vol. 2: *Spiritual Master*, trans. Robert Royal (Washington, DC: Catholic University of America Press, 2003), 253–9; idem, *Saint Thomas Aquinas*, vol. 1: *The Person and His Work*, trans. Robert Royal (Washington, DC: Catholic University of America Press, 1996),

of reason, so also human rational acts are corporeal acts: the spiritual acts of human beings are performed through the body, not despite the body. As Rhonheimer states, 'This applies to all the acts both of the speculative intellect, which without a body are not possible for us, and of the practical intellect, which without the natural inclinations could not be practical and move towards action.'[17] Rhonheimer's account of the human person seeks to remain attuned to the integral body–soul constitution of human nature. The human 'person' is never simply the soul and its spiritual acts, but is always body and soul in a radical 'unity of substance'.

Precisely because of this integral body–soul unity, however, the 'human good' can never be discerned simply by looking at either the body or the soul alone. Rather, the 'human good' will be grasped by properly judging the transformation of the bodily dynamisms and of the soul's dynamisms by their integral union. It cannot be denied that human beings have animal bodily dynamisms, such as the natural inclination for self-preservation or for sexual inter-course, but in human beings these dynamisms cannot be understood merely in terms of the 'naturalness' of the non-rational animal level. Rhonheimer distinguishes between this 'naturalness' and the natural inclinations understood as transformed and elevated in the human person. As he notes, 'Every natural inclination possesses *a natura* its own good and end (*bonum et finis proprium*). However, at the level of their mere naturalness, does following the tendency to conserve oneself or the sexual inclination also mean following the good and end *due* to man? How can we know what is not only *specific* to these inclinations according to their particular nature but also *due* to the person, that is to say, at the moment of following these inclinations, good for man *as man*?'[18]

187–90; Gilles Emery, OP, 'L'unité de l'homme, âme et corps, chez S. Thomas d'Aquin', *Nova et Vetera* (French) 75 (2000): 53–76.

[17] Rhonheimer, 'The Cognitive Structure of the Natural Law and the Truth of Subjectivity', 19.

[18] Ibid., 19–20. See for a similar account John Finnis, *Natural Law and Natural Rights* (Oxford: Oxford University Press, 1980). Finnis writes, 'Having thus stressed the inclinations which, prior to any rational control of ours, underlie all our effort, including our effort to make our efforts intelligent and reasonable, Aquinas turns to that aspect of our participation of God's practical reason which I mentioned earlier: our power of understanding. For, by this power, we grasp the basic forms of good (and thus the basic principles of natural law); the data for this act of understanding

The answer, Rhonheimer thinks, is the natural law. The natural law takes up the level of 'mere naturalness', the bodily aspects of the natural inclinations, and exposes the fully *human* good determined by practical reason as the *imago dei*, a participation in divine reason. Practical reason, which as noted above both is 'nature' (as created) and transcends non-rational 'nature' as the *imago dei*, can establish the natural law because practical reason, in a unique way, imitates and participates in the divine reason establishing eternal law. Rhonheimer explains:

> But how can one say that the natural law, understood as practical reason which naturally moves towards good, *constitutes* the moral order? Precisely because the *lumen rationis naturalis* so much spoken about by St. Thomas Aquinas is created *ad imaginem* by divine reason. Specifically, because the natural law is a real participation of the eternal law—and this, in the particular case of the rational creature, in an active way—the natural law can be considered properly as *constituted* by natural reason, just as the entire order of good is at its origins constituted by divine reason which is the eternal law.[19]

In other words, God establishes or constitutes the moral order for his creatures in his eternal law. Thus human beings must have, as rational creatures in the image of God, a parallel constitutive role in constituting the moral order. This parallel role involves humanizing

include the desires and inclinations which we experience, but like all understanding, this act of understanding goes beyond the data as experienced, to concepts accessible or available not to experience but only to understanding' (402).

[19] Rhonheimer, 'The Cognitive Structure of the Natural Law and the Truth of Subjectivity', 20. For a more detailed account of 'The Natural Law as Participation in the Eternal Law' in Rhonheimer's work, see e.g. *Natural Law and Practical Reason*, 64–70. Rhonheimer consistently makes clear that what differentiates his position from Kant's is that Rhonheimer holds that 'the "space" in which the human reason is efficacious as lawgiver is not to be thought of as "free space" from within which, somehow, nothing has been foreseen or ordained, so that this "space" would not itself be subject to any law' (65). In *Natural Law and Practical Reason* as in 'The Cognitive Structure of Natural Law and the Truth of Subjectivity', Rhonheimer takes the truth that law exists only in minds to mean that there is no morally normative 'natural order'. Thus in *Natural Law and Practical Reason* he writes, 'On the contrary—and this is something that must be emphasized to counter the naturalistic fallacy—this law that pertains to human behavior exists only in the mind of God, and not in created nature. This order (established through the *lex aeterna* and constituted, for the realm of human actions, through the *lex naturalis*) is not at all a "natural order", but rather an "order of reason" (*ordo rationis*) that exists from eternity in God, and which is then constituted, by the mediation of the human reason, in acts of the will and in particular actions' (66).

the level of 'mere naturalness', inscribed in the non-rational natural inclinations, by means of the transforming and elevating judgements of practical reason.

Although practical reason is also 'natural' (thus 'natural law'), it differs from and in a certain sense stands above—although significantly always working through—the animal or bodily level of 'mere naturalness'. Practical reason's role is constitutive of the natural law, but as Rhonheimer goes on to explain this constituting is (as befits the *imago*) also and indeed fundamentally a participation: 'This participation displays itself not only in subjection to the eternal law, but also by its participation in the specific ordering function of the eternal law that *constitutes* the moral order, even if human reason, as only participated and created cognitive light, does this not by creating any truth at all but by *knowing it* and thereby *finding it* in its own being, essentially constituted by the natural inclinations as well.'[20] The body–soul constitution has not been forgotten: practical reason, in constituting the natural law out of the material of the natural inclinations, 'knows' and 'finds' what is good for the kind of body–soul 'unity of substance' that is the *human* being.

Rhonheimer thus attempts to move beyond Fuchs's 'dualism' between the natural law as objectively in an 'order of nature' and the natural law as subjectively in us. For Rhonheimer, the natural law, as moral knowledge, 'is really "subjective." Its objectivity—and thus the objectivity of the moral norms based upon it—consists in the fact that in this natural knowledge of human good the *truth* of subjectivity is expressed.'[21] There is no need ultimately to contrast 'nature' and 'reason' because the two are one in natural (created) reason, although the contrast between 'mere naturalness' and nature as transformed and elevated by the engagement of human reason remains. Similarly, there is no need to be concerned about a contrast between 'subjective' and 'objective', because the practical reason's subjective knowledge,

---

[20] Rhonheimer, 'The Cognitive Structure of the Natural Law and the Truth of Subjectivity', 20–1. In this regard Eberhard Schockenhoff criticizes Rhonheimer for being still too concerned to find norms in bodily nature: see Schockenhoff, *Natural Law and Human Dignity: Universal Ethics in an Historical World*, trans. Brian McNeil (Washington, DC: Catholic University of America Press, 2003), 159–60 fn. 65.

[21] Rhonheimer, 'The Cognitive Structure of the Natural Law and the Truth of Subjectivity', 3.

when truly participating the divine reason, is precisely the 'objective' order.

Furthermore, Rhonheimer shows that appeals to human 'nature' cannot in themselves determine natural law, because in order to know what human 'nature' is, we must know the human good. In order to understand human beings, we must know what perfects their abilities and actions. We cannot know this solely by identifying human beings' characteristic ends, as we could with non-rational animals. As Rhonheimer says, 'In the case of man, who acts on the basis of freedom, that which takes place regularly and with "normality" is not a criterion by which to determine his good. Human persons act on the basis of reason and thus with freedom, since reason is "open to many things" and can have "various notions of good"—false ones as well as true.'[22] Thus ethics goes beyond the philosophy of nature; the only question is how ethics does so. Rhonheimer argues that ethics goes beyond the philosophy of nature by means of 'natural law', in which the *human* good, and thus human nature, is known. Human practical reasoning, in constituting the human good, thereby constitutes the natural law: 'the human good is not simply an object "given" to intellectual acts. The very nature of the intellect...means that what is really good for man is, in a certain sense, constituted and formulated only in the intellectual acts themselves. The human and moral good is essentially a *bonum rationis*: a good *of* reason, *for* reason, and formulated *by* reason.'[23] Human 'nature' and human 'reason' cannot be contrasted in terms of objective–subjective, because human reason is constitutive of human nature.

Rhonheimer thinks that his account of the natural law as constituted by human practical reason should be recognized as that of the Catholic tradition. To this end, he calls particularly upon Thomas Aquinas and Leo XIII, in light of John Paul II's *Veritatis Splendor*. Paragraph 44 of *Veritatis Splendor* refers to the discussion of natural law in Leo XIII's encyclical *Libertas Praestantissimum*. The paragraph of Leo's encyclical from which John Paul II quotes is as follows:

Foremost in this office comes the *natural law*, which is written and engraved in the mind of every man; and this is nothing but our reason, commanding us to do right and forbidding sin. Nevertheless all prescriptions of human

---

[22] Ibid., 5–6.   [23] Ibid., 6.

reason [*praescriptio rationis*] can have the force of law only inasmuch as they are the voice and interpreters of some higher power on which our reason and liberty necessarily depend. For, since the force of law consists in the imposing of obligations and the granting of rights, authority is the one and only foundation of all law—the power, that is, of fixing duties and defining rights, as also of assigning the necessary sanctions of reward and chastisement to each and all of its commands. But all this, clearly, cannot be found in man, if, as his own supreme legislator he is to be the rule of his own actions. It follows therefore that the law of nature is the same thing as the *eternal law*, implanted in rational creatures, and inclining them *to their right action and end*; and can be nothing else but the eternal reason of God, the Creator and Ruler of all the world.[24]

Rhonheimer argues that Leo XIII is here defining natural law as our practical reason: natural law 'is not "human nature" or "an order of nature"; nor is it a norm encountered in the nature of things. It is something "written and engraved in the heart of each and every man." It is "human reason itself" because it commands us to do good and forbids us to sin.'[25] Continuing his exegesis of the

---

[24] Leo XIII, *Libertas Praestantissimum*, in *The Great Encyclical Letters of Pope Leo XIII (1878–1903)* (Rockford, IL: Tan Books, 1995 (reprint of 1903 Benziger Brothers edition)), 140. On Leo XIII's political thought, see Russell Hittinger, 'Pope Leo XIII (1810–1903)', in *The Teachings of Modern Christianity on Law, Politics, and Human Nature*, vol. 1, ed. John Witte Jr. and Frank Alexander (New York: Columbia University Press, 2006), 39–74.

[25] Rhonheimer, 'The Cognitive Structure of the Natural Law and the Truth of Subjectivity', 8. See also Robert P. George, 'Kelsen and Aquinas on the Natural Law Doctrine', in *St. Thomas Aquinas and the Natural Law Tradition: Contemporary Perspectives*, ed. John Goyette, Mark S. Latkovic, and Richard S. Myers (Washington, DC: Catholic University of America Press, 2004), 237–59, at 244–5. George follows Germain Grisez's 'The First Principle of Practical Reason', *Natural Law Forum* 10 (1965): 168–201; and John Finnis's *Natural Law and Natural Rights*, 46–9 and elsewhere. However, George's presentation does not grasp Aquinas's account of the relationship of speculative and practical knowing, as Steven Long makes clear in his essay in the same volume, 'Natural Law or Autonomous Practical Reason: Problems for the New Natural Law Theory', 165–93. On this point, see also Ralph McInerny, 'The Primacy of Theoretical Knowledge: Some Remarks on John Finnis', in his *Aquinas on Human Action* (Washington, DC: Catholic University of America Press, 1992), 184–92; Kevin Flannery, *Acts Amid Precepts: The Aristotelian Logical Structure of Thomas Aquinas' Moral Theory* (Washington, DC: Catholic University of America Press, 2001), 199. The Humean opposition that George enforces between the 'is' and the 'ought' cannot be squared with a theology of God the providential Creator: as John Courtney Murray, SJ, puts it, 'The order of being that confronts his [man's] intelligence is an order of "oughtness" for the will; the moral order is a prolongation of the metaphysical

passage, Rhonheimer finds that natural law, 'human reason itself', is also called the 'prescriptions of human reason'. It seems clear to him that Leo XIII is referring to the 'set of determined judgments of the practical reason'.[26] Thus natural law, despite the Stoic claim that gained momentum with the rise of modern science, is not 'natural regularities, orientations, and structures, knowable to man and then applicable at a practical level'.[27] Rather, although there are indeed such natural orders in creation that manifest God's ordering wisdom, 'natural law' refers not to this natural order, known by speculative knowledge, but strictly to the judgements of practical reason about human acts.[28]

For Aquinas, Rhonheimer states, the case is the same: ' "law" is an *ordinatio rationis*, or rational prescription, that is to say an imperative act of reason that directs, in a given sphere, human acts to their end, which is always a certain good'.[29] The key here is that natural law belongs to human reason, not to an order outside human reason. As Rhonheimer points out, *Veritatis Splendor* twice quotes Aquinas's point that natural law is 'nothing other than the light of

order into the dimensions of human freedom' (Murray, *We Hold These Truths* (1960; Lanham, MD: Sheed & Ward, 1988), 328). As Romanus Cessario also observes regarding Hume's position, 'One is constrained to note that these conclusions presuppose a prior abstractive reduction of nature to a factive surd, drained of necessity, intelligibility, and teleological structure' (Cessario, *Introduction to Moral Theology*, 39 fn. 97). At issue is whether 'the good as end draws' (ibid., 45–6) in a way that orders practical reasoning.

[26] Rhonheimer, 'The Cognitive Structure of the Natural Law and the Truth of Subjectivity', 9.

[27] Ibid.

[28] *Veritatis Splendor* (1993) emphasizes Leo XIII's conclusion: 'It follows therefore that the law of nature is the same thing as the *eternal law*, implanted in rational creatures, and inclining them *to their right action and end*; and can be nothing else but the eternal reason of God, the Creator and Ruler of all the world' (see *Veritatis Splendor*, § 44). This 'implanting' and 'inclining' indicate a fundamentally receptive dynamism. Otherwise, since Leo teaches that the natural law and the eternal law are the same, the constitutive action of practical reason would not only constitute the natural law, but also the eternal law. In developing its concept of 'participated theonomy', *Veritatis Splendor* observes, 'The rightful autonomy of the practical reason means that man possesses in himself his own law, received from the Creator. Nevertheless, *the autonomy of reason cannot mean* that reason itself *creates values and moral norms*' (§ 40).

[29] Rhonheimer, 'The Cognitive Structure of the Natural Law and the Truth of Subjectivity', 10.

understanding infused in us by God, whereby we understand what must be done and what must be avoided'.[30] Quoting Aquinas's statement in *Summa Theologiae* I–II, q. 90, a. 4, ad 1—'The natural law is promulgated by the very fact that God instilled it into man's mind so as to be known by him naturally'—Rhonheimer concludes that for Aquinas the natural law is 'natural' not because of a natural ordering of things, but ' "because the reason which promulgates it is proper to human nature," in the same way that the intellect that has been given to man by the Creator is a part of human nature. It is a law that man through his intellectual acts establishes, formulates, or promulgates naturally.'[31]

The crucial aspect is that an 'order of nature' does not establish the moral pattern for human reason, but rather human reason 'establishes, formulates, or promulgates' its own moral pattern. Yet human reason is, as Leo XIII and Aquinas agree, not autonomous: rather as the *imago dei* human reason is subjected and referred to the divine reason. As Rhonheimer puts it, 'God teaches man his own true good in an imperative way, that is to say, in the form of law, through man's own cognitive acts.'[32] Since human beings' practical reason is a participation in the divine reason, its judgements manifest and establish God's eternal law in a natural manner. The natural law is human beings' participatory 'possession' of the eternal law 'in a cognitive and active way', as the judgements of practical reason.[33] It follows, as Rhonheimer says, that 'practical reason, because it is the natural law and proceeds on the basis of the natural law, is really the authoritative guide for action, imposes duties, and formulates rights'.[34] Since practical reason is a participation in God's reason (eternal law), human beings can be said to possess a 'real autonomy' in establishing and promulgating the natural law, but an autonomy that is participated—what Rhonheimer and *Veritatis Splendor* call 'participated theonomy'.[35] In this regard, Rhonheimer appeals to a set of texts from Aquinas, particularly from *Summa Theologiae* I–II,

---

[30] Ibid., citing *Summa Theologiae* I–II, q. 94, a. 2; and *Veritatis Splendor* §§ 12 and 20.

[31] Ibid., 11.   [32] Ibid., 12.   [33] Ibid.   [34] Ibid.

[35] Ibid., 13. Compare David Novak's Jewish approach to 'theonomous morality'—focusing on the commandments of the Torah—in his *Jewish–Christian Dialogue: A Jewish Justification* (Oxford: Oxford University Press, 1989), 141–56.

q. 91, a. 2, in which Aquinas holds that 'the natural law is none other than the participation of the eternal law in the rational creature' that enables human beings to participate actively in divine providence.

Thus while the natural law refers not to an 'order of nature' but to the divine reason, the natural law truly is human reason; human beings promulgate the natural law, even if this promulgation is a participation in the eternal law. This promulgation takes place in the judgements of human practical reason, which as communicating the 'known good of reason' are binding upon the knower. Indeed, such promulgation occurs whether or not the person knows that his or her judgements are participatory in the eternal law. When human beings recognize the participated character of their judgements, they discover that their experienced autonomy is in fact a participated theonomy.

Rhonheimer devotes special attention to the 'locus classicus' of *Summa Theologiae* I–II, q. 94, a. 2, whose treatment of natural inclinations we have briefly summarized above. Focusing upon this article, Rhonheimer seeks to show that Aquinas affirms three points. First, the work of practical reason in constituting the natural law does not take its starting point from speculative reason. This is important because otherwise one might say that speculative reason presents practical reason with an 'order of nature'.[36] Second, the natural law is a practical knowing that integrates the natural inclinations. The importance of this point consists in its affirmation of the body–soul constitution of the human person. Third, practical reason transforms and elevates the dynamisms of the natural inclinations: while the natural inclinations certainly constitute the human good, nonetheless this is so only as 'these inclinations with their goods and ends are regulated and ordered by reason, that is to say integrated into the whole of the corporeal–spiritual being of the human person, and thereby also transformed'.[37] Only as *transformed* do the natural inclinations constitute the natural law. This point is crucial because it upholds both the differentiation of the practical reason from the level of 'mere

---

[36] Here Rhonheimer agrees with Germain Grisez. The opposite position has been well expressed by Steven Long in his 'Natural Law or Autonomous Practical Reason: Problems for the New Natural Law Theory'.

[37] Rhonheimer, 'The Cognitive Structure of the Natural Law and the Truth of Subjectivity', 21.

naturalness', and because it upholds the priority of the practical reason as governing the natural inclinations of the human being, rather
than allowing for the latter to set the course for the former. Practical
reason retains its transcendence and its ordering ability, as befits the
imago dei.

As regards the first point, Rhonheimer focuses upon Aquinas's
claim that the precepts of the natural law are to practical reason
as first principles of demonstration (e.g. non-contradiction) are to
speculative reason. It follows, he suggests, that these principles are
first principles arising in the experience of 'good', not derived from
speculative knowledge. As Rhonheimer says, 'The practical principles, having their own point of departure, which is not derived, are
thus immediately intuited (otherwise they would not be *principles*, as
St. Thomas affirms).'[38] In this immediate intuition, not dependent
upon speculative knowledge, we grasp the first principle of practical
reason which is also the first precept of the natural law: 'good is to
be done and pursued, and evil avoided'.[39] The first principle, as a
precept, is already intrinsically immersed in moral action.

Regarding the second point, Rhonheimer sets forth his particular understanding of the relationship of practical reason and natural inclinations. Practical reason, founded upon its first principle,
understands experientially the particularly *human* ends of human
natural inclinations, and thereby constitutes the natural law. Again
Rhonheimer insists that practical reason undertakes this task alone:
'This is a genuine experience of the human subject, an experience
that is eminently and essentially *practical*, and that is not derived
from any other form of knowledge. It is the originating experience of
itself as being moving towards good in the multiplicity of the natural
inclinations specific to man, and is, therefore, of a practical and moral
character.'[40] This practical experiential knowledge, which constitutes
the natural law, is prior to any 'ethical reflection' or definition of
'human nature', which cannot be fully known outside this 'natural
law as natural knowing of good'.[41] Rhonheimer quotes Aquinas in

---

[38] Ibid., 22.   [39] Ibid., 23.   [40] Ibid., 24–5.

[41] Ibid., 25. With regard to the work of John Finnis, Ralph McInerny draws a
distinction that also applies here: 'What Finnis wants to say is that we must have first
acted, have engaged in action, before we can develop an account of action. I think he
is absolutely right about this. It is not simply that theoretical accounts depend upon

support of the view that the natural law is constituted by the practical reason's experiential engagement with the natural inclinations: 'reason naturally grasps everything towards which man has a natural inclination in considering them goods, and as a result as something to pursue with works, and their contrary as an evil to be avoided. Thus, the order of the precepts of the natural law follows the order of the natural inclinations.'[42]

The third point hinges upon Aquinas's answer to the second objection of I–II, q. 94, a. 2. The objector proposes that since 'the natural law is consequent to human nature', which is one in its whole and many in its parts, there must be only one precept of the natural law or else even concupiscible inclinations would be caught up in the natural law. Aquinas responds: 'All the inclinations of any parts whatsoever of human nature, e.g., of the concupiscible and irascible parts, in so far as they are ruled by reason, belong to the natural law, and are reduced to one first precept, as stated above: so that the precepts of the natural law are many in themselves, but are based on one common foundation.'[43] Rhonheimer cites this text and italicizes 'as they are regulated by reason' (his translation). For Rhonheimer, the meaning of the 'as they are regulated by reason' is that the constitution of the human person requires a crucial distinction between natural inclinations 'in their pure naturalness' and natural inclinations as regulated by practical reason. Natural law includes the natural inclinations only as regulated by practical reason. This regulation, as we have seen, takes the form of practical reason's identifying the truly *human* ends of the natural inclinations. And it is the natural inclinations as thus regulated in the judgements of practical reason that belong to the 'natural law', which is none other than the judgements of practical reason.

Rhonheimer is thus concerned to deny that the natural inclinations, qua natural inclinations ('in their pure naturalness'), belong

---

sensory experience. Rather, the point is that the theoretical and practical knowledge with which we begin is not had in the same mode as that formalized in theoretical and practical sciences' (McInerny, 'The Primacy of Theoretical Knowledge', in *Aquinas on Human Action*, 190). That speculative reason grounds practical reason does not mean that what we think of as 'ethical reflection' has taken place.

[42] I–II, q. 94, a. 2; cited in Rhonheimer, 'The Cognitive Structure of the Natural Law and the Truth of Subjectivity', 26.

[43] I–II, q. 94, a. 2, ad 2.

to the natural law. Rather, they belong to the natural law only in so far as practical reason takes them up into its judgements, which are the natural law. The key point remains that practical reason must establish the norm for the natural inclinations, rather than discerning in the natural inclinations an already established norm. Appealing to Aquinas's understanding of natural law as a rational participation in eternal law, Rhonheimer observes that 'in participating through the possession of the *lumen rationis naturalis* in the eternal law—the ordering reason of God—man is not simply guided by the different natural inclinations towards their own acts and ends, but possesses, at a rational level, a specific natural inclination *ad debitum actum et finem*', to the *due* act and end.

Here Rhonheimer appeals also to his understanding of Aquinas's account of the moral object as constituted by reason. Since we cannot delve fully into Rhonheimer's position on the moral object, it will suffice to observe that he emphasizes the distinction between its 'formal' and 'material' constitution.[44] The same goes for the practical reason's relationship to the natural inclinations in constituting the natural law. The practical reason provides the 'form', and the natural inclinations the 'matter'. The latter, Rhonheimer stresses, are '*natural*' and thereby (one infers) they refer to nature rather than, as do human reason and natural law, to God. It would be a case of 'physicalism' to suppose that the natural inclinations, qua natural inclinations, belong to the natural law. On the contrary, they belong to the natural law only when taken up in the judgements of practical reason. As Rhonheimer states, 'The naturalness of good, as it is formulated in the natural law, cannot, however, be reduced to the simple

---

[44] For a full exposition of his position, see especially his 'The Perspective of the Acting Person and the Nature of Practical Reason: The "Object of the Human Act" in Thomistic Anthropology of Action', *Nova et Vetera* 2 (2004): 461–516. As Rhonheimer explains his position: 'Speaking *materially*, we can say that the various elements that compose the exterior act are like a "materia circa quam", a matter around which the action develops and that specifies it as a particular *type* of action. Considered *formally*, however, that is, as the object of a human act and as an end—as the object, that is, of a voluntary act—this "materia circa quam" is the same exterior act as *bonum apprehensum et ordinatum per rationem*. Only in this way can the *material circa quam* be understood as a moral object, and only in this way, as St. Thomas explicitly states, does it specify the act *morally*. This shows that the "moral object" is not, for Thomas, properly an "object of the exterior act", but always and exclusively the object of the interior act of the will and, for this reason, a *forma a ratione concepta*' (476). The problem here lies largely in Rhonheimer's use of 'exclusively'.

naturalness of the individual natural inclinations and their good, ends, and acts. Such a reduction would be equivalent to reducing the *genus moris* of an act to its *genus naturae*, to confusing the "moral object" and the "physical object" of a human act.'[45] Practical reason's regulating and ordering of the natural inclinations to their *human* end, through rational judgements about the good, is the natural law.

Thus Rhonheimer arrives, through his analysis of I–II, q. 94, a. 2, at a set of important conclusions. Since 'law', as Aquinas says in q. 90, consists in 'universal practical judgments (propositions) of practical reason, ordered to acting', it follows that the natural law is the practical reason's judgements as regards the ends of the natural inclinations. These judgements constitute, rather than discern, the 'natural moral order'. As such, they make moral action possible. Yet they do not do so in a strictly autonomous fashion, because in fact they make manifest God's eternal law.[46] And through this experiential engagement of practical reason, speculative reason gains as objects of speculative knowledge the 'natural moral order' and 'human nature'.

Rhonheimer goes on to give some examples of how the natural law, constituted by practical reason's engagement with the natural inclinations, differs from the natural inclinations qua natural inclinations. The natural inclination to self-preservation, for example, becomes when worked upon by the practical reason 'not only the simple natural inclination in its pure naturalness'.[47] This is seen when human

[45] Rhonheimer, 'The Cognitive Structure of the Natural Law and the Truth of Subjectivity', 28.

[46] Ibid., 30–1.

[47] Ibid., 32. For a position similar to Rhonheimer's, see Oscar J. Brown, *Natural Rectitude and Divine Law in Aquinas* (Toronto: Pontifical Institute of Mediaeval Studies, 1981). Brown cites some texts from Aquinas's *Commentary on the Sentences*, as well as I–II, q. 95, a. 4, ad 1, to defend the claim that 'it must be up to reason—in the sense of practical *scientia discursiva*—to order those instinctual tendencies, to arrange those various human goods, in a definite value hierarchy. That activity of practical reasoning will doubtless constitute the properly human component in natural law or, better, practical mind will be as form to the matter of natural inclinations in a specifically human "natural law" (*recta ratio, ius gentium*)' (41). To deny the rational character of natural law (as well as the perfecting of the natural inclinations in the virtues) would be foolish, but the risk here is that form and matter will be understood as extrinsic to each other, so that the human natural inclinations are not already, in their very constitution, caught up into the *humanum*, with all that this entails for the understanding of their role in natural law.

beings sacrifice their own lives for others. Similarly, the natural inclination to procreate, when taken up by practical reason, 'is more than an inclination found in pure nature'.[48] Without the transformative work of practical reason upon the natural inclination as natural, human sexual relationships would be mere animality. Instead, Rhonheimer observes, 'This natural inclination, grasped by reason and pursued in the order of reason—at the personal level—becomes love between two people, love with the requirement of exclusiveness (uniqueness) and of indissoluble faithfulness between *persons* (i.e., it is not mere attraction between bodies!), persons who understand that they are united in the shared task of transmitting human life.'[49] Absent the work of practical reason, the natural inclination would be simply the 'mere attraction between bodies' that animals partake in; taken up by practical reason, the natural inclination is made to serve *persons*. Thus bodily aspects of sexual intercourse cannot as such, Rhonheimer argues, be morally normative (e.g., one supposes, appeals to the bodily suitability of male–female rather than male–male intercourse). Such 'relations of fittingness', which are 'natural' because they come from natural *reason*, can be normative only as taken up by 'practical reason, which alone is able to order these relations of fittingness towards the end of virtue, which is the good of the human person'.[50] As Rhonheimer concludes, therefore, 'in the case of man, what "nature has taught all animals" is not even sufficient to establish any dutifulness or normativeness'.[51] As a rational animal, the human being differs profoundly from the animals: 'If the animal does what its nature, endowed with a richness of instincts, prescribes

---

[48] Rhonheimer, 'The Cognitive Structure of the Natural Law and the Truth of Subjectivity', 33. Despite Rhonheimer's efforts (noted above) to affirm hylomorphism, what 'pure naturalness' or 'pure nature' means as regards the human hylomorphic creature remains in question. 'Pure naturalness' does not seem to be the right term, because the human natural inclinations are never in a pre-human state.

[49] Ibid. A contrast between the 'personal level' and the natural inclination's level seems implied.

[50] Ibid., 35. Here human reason and human bodily nature seem opposed, at least until reason has (extrinsically to bodily nature) accomplished its work. Leon Kass offers a quite different perspective in his *The Hungry Soul: Eating and the Perfecting of Our Nature* (Chicago: University of Chicago Press, 1999).

[51] Rhonheimer, 'The Cognitive Structure of the Natural Law and the Truth of Subjectivity', 33.

to it, it performs its function. Can the same be said of man?'[52] The answer to this rhetorical question is no.

Rhonheimer thus warns against attempts to deduce 'rights' from a natural order or from human nature, as if rights could be discerned in nature. Rather, rights derive from 'a reading of the natural structures in the light of the principles of the natural law'.[53] Moral norms come from natural law, the work of reason, not from nature per se. Once one understands this point, and seeks the natural law not in an extrinsic natural order but rather in 'the natural judgments of the natural reason of each man', then one sees also how 'natural law' upholds the dignity of each person's subjectivity, in which the (participated) autonomy of subjective rational self-possession joins with the establishment of an objective moral norm.[54] And once the profound interiority of the natural law is grasped, one can also apprehend more fully the connection between the natural law and the moral virtues. Just as the natural law belongs to the interior work of reason, so too do the moral virtues. The acquisition of the moral virtues enables the person to live by the rule of practical reason, by the natural law. Thus 'the precepts of the natural law are precisely the principles of prudence. The "truth of subjectivity," of which the natural law at the level of principles is the foundation, is ultimately guaranteed through the possession of the moral virtues.'[55] Vice, in contrast, obscures the natural law.

In brief: If I understand Rhonheimer correctly, his work seeks to provide philosophical underpinnings for how human beings, in the natural law, are able to order their natural inclinations freely to ends that befit the *imago dei*, and thus ultimately to the ends revealed biblically in Christ Jesus. Rhonheimer finds in practical reason the practical power of ordering natural inclinations to the ends that befit the human person whose destiny, while linked with nature,

[52] Ibid.   [53] Ibid., 36.   [54] Ibid., 37–8.

[55] Ibid., 38. For further discussion of prudence and natural law, see Daniel Westberg, *Right Practical Reason: Aristotle, Action, and Prudence in Aquinas* (Oxford: Clarendon Press, 1994), 239–44; Romanus Cessario, *Introduction to Moral Theology*, 93, 128–44. See also Vernon J. Bourke's distinction between *prudentia* and *scientia practica*, which he argues have been conflated by Grisez and Finnis (Bourke, 'The Background of Aquinas' Synderesis Principle', in *Graceful Reason: Essays in Ancient and Medieval Philosophy*, ed. Lloyd P. Gerson (Toronto: Pontifical Institute of Mediaeval Studies, 1983), 345–60, at 358–60).

transcends nature as communion with the Trinity. Approached this way, one might recognize in the practical reason's 'humanizing' task a philosophical grounding for the free and noble participation of the human person in the missions of the Word and the Holy Spirit, in which the natural ends are taken up, enfolded, and transformed. On this view, natural law is no mere receptivity to the created order, but rather is the human being's proper ability to give the gift of self (and ultimately to do so in the order of grace). Seen in this way, one can understand why Rhonheimer so prizes, in his understanding of natural law, the notion of the practical reason humanizing the natural inclinations. The practical reason's active, constitutive work enables the human person to transcend merely natural (intra-cosmic) ends. Put succinctly, Rhonheimer wants to find a place for the person's *constitutive self-giving*, not only in the biblical order of grace, but indeed firmly within the order of human nature, the order of natural law.

What questions might one put to Rhonheimer's position? First, does his account of the 'imago dei' as an image precisely in its *constitutive* power adequately appreciate the role of receptivity and contemplation in human rationality?[56] Related to this question, does he separate the 'practical' from the 'speculative' aspect of reason too firmly, out of concern that human reason norm non-rational nature, rather than human reason receiving a norm from non-rational nature? Second, does his view of a level of 'pure naturalness' in the human body, for example what he calls a 'mere attraction between bodies', properly understand the hylomorphic unity of the (hierarchically ordered) inclinations in the human person? Since

---

[56] For a rich discussion of the 'imago dei' and natural law, see Craig A. Boyd, 'Participation Metaphysics, the *Imago Dei*, and the Natural Law in Aquinas' Ethics', *New Blackfriars* 88 (2007): 274–87. On the *imago dei*, see Servais Pinckaers, OP's 'Ethics and the Image of God', in Pinckaers, *The Pinckaers Reader: Renewing Thomistic Moral Theology*, ed. John Berkman and Craig Steven Titus (Washington, DC: Catholic University of America Press, 2005), 130–43. Surveying the contemporary theological scene, Pinckaers writes, 'We are dealing now with a blind image that no longer seeks to know and to see the One whom it images. The theme of the image is robbed of its entire contemplative dimension, as is morality' (142–3). See also Michael Dauphinais, 'Loving the Lord Your God: The *Imago Dei* in Saint Thomas Aquinas', *The Thomist* 63 (1999): 241–67; Jean-Pierre Torrell, OP, *Saint Thomas Aquinas*, vol. 2: *Spiritual Master*, trans. Robert Royal (Washington, DC: Catholic University of America Press, 2003), 'Image and Beatitude', 80–100, as well as Torrell's abundant bibliographical references.

these bodies are *human* bodies, the bodily natural inclinations are already caught up in the form of the spiritual soul in such a way that the person, as created, manifests a unified ordering, not a disjointed encounter in which the spiritual element must humanize the animal element.[57]

Elsewhere, however, Rhonheimer has made it clear that he does not think that these questions, with their implied criticisms, evince an understanding either of his project or of other attempts, such as the influential work of Germain Grisez and John Finnis, to emphasize the role of practical reason.[58] But it should be clear that the central issues of modern natural law doctrine have here been raised: above all, the relationship of 'nature' and 'freedom', understood historically. Are there other ways to respond to the heritage of the modern thinkers, with on the one hand their reductions of human nature (Hobbes, Hume) and on the other hand their privileging of practical reason

---

[57] Aquinas states that 'we must gather from the form the reason why the matter is such as it is' (*ST* I, q. 76, a. 5). See also John Paul II, *Veritatis Splendor*, § 48 (emphasis in the original): 'one has to consider carefully the correct relationship existing between freedom and human nature, and in particular *the place of the human body in questions of natural law*. A freedom which claims to be absolute ends up treating the human body as a raw datum, devoid of any meaning and moral values until freedom has shaped it in accordance with its design.' A key question, then, is whether the human body, in its human bodily teleologies, has normative moral significance even 'prior' to the work of the practical reason. *Veritatis Splendor* continues (§ 48): 'Consequently, human nature and the body appear as *presuppositions or preambles*, materially *necessary*, for freedom to make its choice, yet extrinsic to the person, the subject and the human act. Their functions would not be able to constitute reference points for moral decisions, because the finalities of these inclinations would be merely "*physical*" goods, called by some "pre-moral."' At issue, in other words, is the status of 'the finalities of these inclinations'. As *Veritatis Splendor* goes on to observe, 'To refer to them, in order to find in them rational indications with regard to the order of morality, would be to expose oneself to the accusation of physicalism or biologism. In this way of thinking, the tension between freedom and a nature conceived of in a reductive way is resolved by a division within man himself. This moral theory does not correspond to the truth about man and his freedom. It contradicts the *Church's teachings on the unity of the human person*, whose rational soul is *per se et essentialiter* the form of his body' (§ 48). For insightful commentary, see David L. Schindler, 'The Significance of World and Culture for Moral Theology: *Veritatis Splendor* and the "Nuptial-Sacramental" Nature of the Body', *Communio* 31 (2004): 111–42.

[58] See Rhonheimer's response to Jean Porter's brief book review of his *Natural Law and Practical Reason* (the book review appeared in *Theological Studies* 62 (2001): 851–3), in 'The Moral Significance of Pre-Rational Nature in Aquinas: A Reply to Jean Porter (and Stanley Hauerwas)', *American Journal of Jurisprudence* 48 (2003): 253–80.

(Kant) as in some sense the historical manifestation of transcendent freedom (Rousseau, Hegel, Nietzsche)? In comparing Rhonheimer's position on natural law and natural inclinations to Servais Pinckaers's and Graham McAleer's, I will ask whether their approaches better achieve Rhonheimer's goal of affirming the biblical dignity of the human person as a free moral agent who acts in self-giving ('ecstatic') love as a soul–body unity.[59] Do they provide a better path for 'biblical' natural law doctrine?

SERVAIS PINCKAERS: RECLAIMING NATURAL LAW AFTER NOMINALISM

In describing what he calls the fourteenth-century 'nominalist revolution', Servais Pinckaers observes of William of Ockham: 'A significant feature of Ockham's critique of the Thomist conception of freedom was his rejection of natural inclinations outside the kernel of the free act. Notably, he rejected the inclination to happiness, which pervades the moral doctrine of the *Summa Theologiae* and, in

---

[59] Cf. *Veritatis Splendor*, § 48: '*The person, including the body, is completely entrusted to himself, and it is in the unity of body and soul that the person is the subject of his own moral acts. The person, by the light of reason and the support of virtue, discovers in the body the anticipatory signs, the expression and the promise of the gift of self*', in conformity with the wise plan of the Creator'; § 50: 'At this point the true meaning of the natural law can be understood: it refers to man's proper and primordial nature, the "nature of the human person", which is *the person himself in the unity of soul and body*, in the unity of his spiritual and biological inclinations and of all the other specific characteristics necessary for the pursuit of his end.' This unity is difficult to achieve: the natural law is neither a set of biological norms, nor a humanizing of the animal element in man. It is a rational participation in the eternal law that manifests the human body–soul teleology. Rhonheimer reads § 48 in light of § 78, which treats the moral object. For his account of the moral object see e.g. *Natural Law and Practical Reason*, 87–94, 410ff., and more recently 'The Perspective of the Acting Person and the Nature of Practical Reason: The "Object of the Human Act" in Thomistic Anthropology of Action'. As I read § 78, it seeks to ward off proportionalism and consequentialism by noting that, in describing the object of human action, one must describe a human act (thereby a unity of body and soul) rather than 'a process or an event of the merely physical order, to be assessed on the basis of its ability to bring about a given state of affairs in the outside world'. Rhonheimer takes this 'merely physical' as an approval of his understanding of human bodiliness as a purely physical realm that is then humanized.

keeping with all previous tradition, forms its initial moral question.'[60] As Pinckaers shows throughout his *The Sources of Christian Ethics*, the question of happiness forms the heart of ancient and patristic moral theory, in contrast to modern focus upon duty and obligation. Two principles of ancient moral theory stand out for Pinckaers as fundamental for patristic–medieval Christian understanding, which takes them up in light of God the Creator, the Father who creates through his Word (John 1). The first of these is '*sequi naturam*, or conformity with nature, which must positively not be understood as a biological inclination, for it chiefly concerned rational nature, which was characterized by a longing for the enjoyment of the good, of truth, and of communication with others'.[61] The second is happiness. Given the theology of creation in the Word, the Fathers understood that 'nature' is no neutral zone but rather that 'the following of nature harmonized with the scriptural following of God and Christ',[62] with the seeking of beatitude promised by Christ in the Sermon on the Mount. Pinckaers observes that 'the entire tradition of the Fathers adopted and fully maintained the two principles of *sequi naturam* and the primal longing for happiness'.[63]

In contrast, as Pinckaers summarizes in some detail, Ockham and the fourteenth-century 'nominalists' rejected nature and 'happiness' as antithetical to freedom, understood as 'the choice of contraries' ('freedom of indifference').[64] Pinckaers summarizes the tensions that emerged in moral theory, and that are easily documented in modern thinkers, as the following polarities: either freedom or law; either freedom or reason; either freedom or nature; either freedom or grace; either human freedom or God's freedom; either subject or object; either freedom or the passions; either my freedom or others' freedom; either the individual or society.[65] For our purposes, we can

---

[60] Servais Pinckaers, OP, *The Sources of Christian Ethics*, 3rd edn., trans. Mary Thomas Noble, OP (1985; Washington, DC: Catholic University of America Press, 1995), 244. For comparison of Ockham with Scotus on this point, see Thomas M. Osborne Jr., *Love of Self and Love of God in Thirteenth-Century Ethics* (Notre Dame, IN: University of Notre Dame Press, 2005).

[61] Pinckaers, *The Sources of Christian Ethics*, 334. The 'new natural law' theory developed by Germain Grisez and John Finnis strongly dissociates this principle from Aquinas's theology of natural law.

[62] Ibid.   [63] Ibid., 335.   [64] Ibid.   [65] Ibid., 351.

focus on the polarities of freedom and nature and freedom and law. Why did these polarities gain acceptance?

Regarding freedom and nature, Pinckaers notes that prior to the fourteenth century, in the patristic–medieval tradition, 'the natural inclinations to goodness, happiness, being, and truth were the very source of freedom. They formed the will and intellect, whose union produced free will.'[66] Freedom thus emerges from nature, given that our nature is spiritual nature and therefore is inclined to being, good, and truth. As I would put it, such nature is never neutral, but rather is a complex ordering toward ends. Ontologically prior to any exercise of freedom or rationality, the human being already tends or inclines toward the Good who creates. The ontological order that is human nature is teleological to its core. This complex teleological constitution is the fundamental given of human creatureliness, not constructed by human rationality or freedom. Human rationality both speculatively and practically discerns the natural, unified ordering of human nature, which is constituted by bodily and spiritual inclinations and thereby always teleologically drawn. In contrast, Ockham sees such inclinations, in so far as they are ontologically 'prior' to freedom, as constricting freedom and thereby undermining the dignity of the free rational creature.

Ockham argues, Pinckaers notes, that 'freedom dominated the natural inclinations and preceded them, because of its radical indetermination and its ability to choose contraries in their regard. From this point of view, it could be said that freedom is more apparent when it resists natural inclinations.'[67] To the tradition prior to the fourteenth century, within which Pinckaers highlights Aquinas, such an understanding of freedom as constitutive of the human would make no sense, since freedom emerges from within natural inclinations to ends. If certain objects (being, goodness, truth) did not draw the intellect and will toward their own fulfilment (happiness), there would be no rational and free action. After Ockham, however, the situation is reversed: if human beings do not themselves constitute what counts as their 'nature', building upon a natural substratum, to be sure (one that requires humanization), then their freedom is imperilled. This natural substratum becomes the place where 'natural

---

[66] Ibid., 245.   [67] Ibid.

inclinations' receive consideration in moral theory: 'natural inclinations, no longer included within the voluntary act, were something short of freedom and were relegated to a lower level in the moral world, to the order of instinct, sensibility, or to a biological ambience'.[68] Radically differing from freedom, this substratum becomes humanized only when taken up into the dynamisms of rational freedom. We can see that the hierarchical, teleological ordering of the body–soul person is, in this view, not ontologically given in the created order, but rather constituted by the acting person, even if constituted on the basis of certain created givens. A morally significant ordering is therefore opaque to reason, operating speculatively, before reason acting to attain the good humanizes and orders the various inclinations that it perceives in the experience of moral agency.

Contrasting Ockham and Aquinas, then, Pinckaers states:

The most decisive point of Ockham's critique of St. Thomas's teaching on freedom was the breach between freedom and the natural inclinations, which were rejected from the essential core of freedom. According to St. Thomas, freedom was rooted in the soul's spontaneous inclinations to the true and the good. His entire moral doctrine was based on the natural human disposition toward beatitude and the perfection of good, as to an ultimate end. A person can never renounce this natural order of things, nor be prevented from desiring it. For Ockham, the state of being ordered to happiness, however natural and general, was subject to the free and contingent choice of human freedom. This meant that I could freely choose or refuse happiness, either in particular matters presented to me or in general, in the very desire which attracted me to it, owing to the radical indifference of my freedom.[69]

Human freedom, after Ockham, thus constitutes human nature, freely choosing among, and giving order to, the natural inclinations. Human freedom governs over even the inclinations toward good and happiness, because these inclinations must not restrict human beings in responding to God's commands. As Pinckaers goes on to point out, such an understanding of 'human nature' as constituted by human freedom, rather than as the source of human freedom, radically transforms the understanding of 'human nature'. Human nature and natural inclinations come to be seen as referring primarily to

[68] Ibid.   [69] Ibid., 332–3.

bodily inclinations, 'impulses of a lower order, on the psychosomatic plane'.[70] Freedom receives the task of integrating these bodily inclinations, no longer belonging to a unified (hierarchically ordered) body–soul teleology, with the spiritual dynamisms of the free person. Pinckaers observes, 'The harmony between humanity and nature was destroyed by a freedom that claimed to be "indifferent" to nature and defined itself as "non-nature." ... These [natural] inclinations appeared as the most insidious threat to the freedom and morality of actions, because they were interior and influenced us from within.'[71] This threat to freedom is mollified only when freedom itself, prior to any metaphysically given order in which freedom emerges from within nature, gives order and intelligibility (law) to the profusion of competing natural inclinations.

If freedom and nature (natural inclinations) thus became polarized, what of freedom and law? Pinckaers remarks upon how the fourteenth century's voluntarist conception of law—law as the expression of the will, rather than as the expression of the lawgiver's wisdom together with his will—led to fear of the eternal and divine law as an imposition of divine will threatening human freedom. Similarly, the divine law itself, for fourteenth-century thinkers, must not restrict divine freedom, and therefore must be fundamentally relative and open to God's modifications. As Pinckaers notes, this conception of law as grounded radically in God's arbitrary freedom results in an 'irreducible' tension in human life, an 'untenable' situation for human beings confronted by 'divine arbitrariness'.[72] It is no surprise, then, that in later moral theories divine lawgiving is displaced by human lawgiving. Indeed, Pinckaers identifies already in the fourteenth-century theories a guiding anthropocentrism, in contrast with the theocentric worldview of the patristic–medieval thinkers. As he puts it, 'We can see in it [the nominalist shift] the direct, clearly deduced, and fully deliberate result of placing humanity

---

[70] Ibid., 333. For a response to this view, see Stephen L. Brock, 'Natural Inclination and the Intelligibility of the Good in Thomistic Natural Law', *Vera Lex* 6 (2005): 57–78.

[71] Pinckaers, *The Sources of Christian Ethics*, 333.

[72] Ibid., 344, 345. For a study of Aquinas's understanding of human moral rectitude and the 'divine law', exhibiting Aquinas's debt to Augustine, see Laurent Sentis, 'La lumière dont nous faisons usage. La règle de la raison et la loi divine selon Thomas d'Aquin', *Revue des sciences philosophiques et théologiques* 79 (1995): 49–69.

in a central position. This was the core of freedom of indifference.'[73] Beyond the metaphysical givenness of the creature now stands self-constituting freedom, even if this freedom remains in a submissive relationship to divine freedom. Pinckaers concludes, 'Beneath freedom of indifference lay hidden a primitive passion—we dare not call it natural: the human will to self-affirmation, to the assertion of a radical difference between itself and all else that existed.'[74] Human freedom as self-constituting, as establishing its own 'norm or law', radically divides not only human beings from the Creator, but also human freedom from the remainder of body–soul powers, those that do not have to do directly with the transcendent operation of free human action.[75]

Given this implicit anthropocentrism, it is no wonder that the Reformers reacted against unguarded appeals to a law of nature. In order (among other reasons) to escape this anthropocentrism, the Reformers shaped a Protestantism that, in Pinckaers's words, 'has spontaneously started with faith, Scripture, and the Word of God, and has been somewhat suspicious and critical of the human and of reason'.[76] The first task for natural law thinking is to critique this anthropocentrism, this false understanding of freedom. As Pinckaers remarks, 'Particularly in our times, ethicists are tempted to reduce Christian ethics to the rules of natural reason.'[77] A properly theocentric understanding of the natural law and natural inclinations places them within the broader context not only of eternal law, but of eternal law specified as divine law, the Decalogue and the 'law' of the grace of the Holy Spirit. This theocentric order requires beginning with the divine Creator and Redeemer, rather than with the human being, in seeking to understand the teleological constitution of the human being. For this reason, Pinckaers states, 'In the *Summa Theologiae* St. Thomas always took God, and the things of God, as his starting point, since God was the principle and source of all things in the order of being and truth. . . . His treatise on laws started with the eternal law, the highest origin of all authentic legislation.'[78] It is grace that enables human beings, tempted to place themselves first, to place God first.

---

[73] Pinckaers, *The Sources of Christian Ethics*, 338.   [74] Ibid.
[75] Ibid., 339.   [76] Ibid., 291.   [77] Ibid., 292.   [78] Ibid.

At the end of *The Sources of Christian Ethics*, Pinckaers devotes a chapter entirely to the natural inclinations. They are particularly important, he says, because '[t]hey form the basis of natural law and the source of energy that broadens and develops in the virtues.'[79] As we have seen, Pinckaers holds that our understanding of the natural inclinations has been profoundly distorted by nominalist polarities, especially the alleged opposition between freedom and nature. Reiterating his earlier comments, he states, 'If we think of freedom as something dependent only on our voluntary decision, and totally indeterminate before we take that decision, then we will be led to think of the natural as something necessarily predetermined. In this view, it is hard to see how we can reconcile the natural and the free.'[80] The 'natural' here consists in more than the bodily inclinations; even the natural inclinations of the soul come to seem restrictive, in so far as they are not ordered and constituted by the free acting person. Quoting Jacques Leclerq's mid-twentieth-century account of Thomistic ethics, in which Leclerq strives to separate metaphysics (understood as a restrictive teleology) and ethics (understood as personal freedom), Pinckaers shows how thinkers come to 'see the natural inclinations of both intellect and will as tendencies both blind and coercive.'[81]

Although above we have examined much of Pinckaers's answer to this misunderstanding, it is worth pausing more directly, with Pinckaers, upon the character of the natural inclinations. He emphasizes that they are the metaphysical source, inscribed in our very being, of human intellectual and ethical spontaneity and freedom. Describing the natural inclination to the good, which according to Aquinas is the root of all the natural inclinations, he calls it 'a primitive élan and attraction that carries us toward the good and empowers us to choose among lesser and greater goods'.[82] There is no 'nature' that is not already tending or inclining, however distantly, toward

---

[79] Ibid., 400. Cf. in this regard Romanus Cessario, OP, *Introduction to Moral Theology*, 91. See also Nicholas Ingham, OP, 'The Rectitude of Inclination', *The Thomist* 60 (1996): 417–37.

[80] Pinckaers, *The Sources of Christian Ethics*, 400–1.   [81] Ibid., 401.

[82] Ibid., 402. See also Stephen L. Brock's 'Natural Inclination and the Intelligibility of the Good in Thomistic Natural Law'. For helpful consideration of the 'good' see Jan A. Aertsen, 'Natural Law in the Light of the Doctrine of the Transcendentals', in *Lex et Libertas*, ed. Leo Elders, SVD, and K. Hedwig (Vatican City: Libreria Editrice Vaticana, 1987), 99–112.

the Good who creates and attracts every 'nature'. There is no non-teleological nature (a point that, as Alasdair MacIntyre and others have shown, natural science is increasingly recognizing).[83] Indeed, Pinckaers says of the inclination to the good that 'this inclination should be described as higher than morality and supremely free, even a sharing in the freedom, goodness, and spontaneity of God'.[84] Similarly the inclination toward truth, above all the truth about God, is—ontologically prior to all reasoning—a 'radiant splendor, a sort of alpha ray of the mind allowing us to share in the divine Light'.[85] At the metaphysical roots of our being, we find an ordering toward the good and true. This fundamental ordering is received, not constituted, by the creature, but this fact does not limit the freedom of the creature. On the contrary, the inscribed ordering toward fulfilment makes sense of freedom and structures it so as to render it not arbitrary. The inscribed ordering marks out the 'end' of freedom and exposes the God-centred character of reality.

If such natural inclinations are truly liberating, what about inclinations such as hunger, thirst, and the sexual urge? Whatever one might say about natural inclinations at the heart of human spiritual dynamisms toward the true and the good, surely natural inclinations that involve bodily urges must be seen as limiting freedom and as therefore difficult to reconcile with the picture of natural inclinations that Pinckaers offers. Yet, Pinckaers praises Cicero's depiction of the natural inclinations as providing 'the best possible introduction to the teaching of the Angelic Doctor on natural inclinations'.[86] How can this be?

Cicero's significance, Pinckaers suggests, only becomes clear once one has metaphysically understood the natural inclination toward the good, the natural inclination that lies at the root of all others. The notion of the 'good' requires reclamation: 'Under the influence of modern ethical theories, we have come to think of the good as

---

[83] See Alasdair MacIntyre, *Dependent Rational Animals: Why Human Beings Need the Virtues* (Chicago: Open Court, 1999); see also the scientific references cited by Jean Porter in chapter 2 of her *Nature as Reason: A Thomistic Theory of the Natural Law* (Grand Rapids, MI: Eerdmans, 2005).

[84] Pinckaers, *The Sources of Christian Ethics*, 402–3.   [85] Ibid., 402.

[86] Ibid., 406. Torrell cites Pinckaers approvingly in this regard: see Torrell, *Saint Thomas Aquinas*, vol. 2: *Spiritual Master*, 286.

whatever conforms to moral law and its precepts, and evil as the contrary. Moral law being viewed as a series of imperatives dictated by a will external to ourselves, the concept of good reflects the concept of moral obligation. It tends to become equally static and extrinsic.'[87] Far from extrinsic, the good in fact is at the heart of our movement and freedom. It can only be defined 'in terms of the attraction it exercises, the love and desire it arouses. The good is the lovable, the desirable.'[88] The lovable is prior to our love; every nature is teleologically ordered and attracted, precisely through being in act to the degree that it is. Insofar as any nature is in act, it is being attracted and drawn by the good. The good is metaphysically constitutive of every nature, since act, in so far as it is in act, tends toward the good. Thus there is no level of 'mere nature' that lacks an intrinsic teleological ordering. As Pinckaers observes, 'The break between metaphysics and ethics was a direct effect of nominalism. Caught up in the current of a moral system based on individual freedom, the notion of the good was henceforth confined within the limits of the dispute between freedom and law fixed by the theory of obligation.'[89]

In seeking to reunite the metaphysical ordering of the human person toward the good and the person's ethical agency, Pinckaers connects the good with the desire for perfection. As he says, 'The very notion of the good implies the idea of perfection, of an excellence that attracts; from this comes a desire for the perfection of the one so drawn. Naturally, perfection will vary as beings differ.'[90] Perfection is both the fullness of the good, and the fullness of a creature's sharing in the good. Human perfection, then, is 'happiness'. Happiness and the good are reciprocal terms: as Pinckaers says, 'the good was the cause of happiness, and happiness was the plenitude of the good. Yet

---

[87] Pinckaers, *The Sources of Christian Ethics*, 408. See Michael Waldstein's rich conception of the 'good' in his 'Dietrich von Hildebrand and St. Thomas Aquinas on Goodness and Happiness', *Nova et Vetera* 1 (2003): 403–64; cf. Christopher V. Mirus, 'Aristotle's *Agathon*', *Review of Metaphysics* 57 (2004): 515–36. See also Alasdair MacIntyre's insistence that understanding Aquinas's account of the human 'good' requires reading not merely the *Summa Theologiae*'s treatise on law, but also its treatise on happiness and indeed the entire *prima pars*: MacIntyre, *Three Rival Versions of Moral Enquiry: Encyclopedia, Genealogy, and Tradition* (Notre Dame, IN: University of Notre Dame Press, 1990), 134–5.

[88] Pinckaers, *The Sources of Christian Ethics*, 409.   [89] Ibid., 409–10.

[90] Ibid., 412.

they could be distinguished by a certain nuance: the good resided in the objective reality, while happiness subsisted in the subject who experienced the good.'[91] In addition to 'perfection' and 'happiness', Pinckaers considers the good in a third way, as an 'end'. Teleology, or 'finality', describes the pattern by which the creature is drawn 'ecstatically' to fulfilment and perfection by its proper good and happiness, which it acts to attain. At this stage Pinckaers also distinguishes between the 'love of concupiscence' and the 'love of friendship', the latter being the full portrait of the good as an 'end' since it is love of a good that is supremely 'lovable in itself and for itself'.[92] This good will be what Aquinas terms an 'honest' good, beyond the goods sought by Epicureans or utilitarians since, as the perfection of moral excellence, it 'deserves to be loved for its own sake'.[93] Lastly, Pinckaers, following Aquinas, observes that the good 'radiates' or generously bears fruit.

In light of this expansive metaphysical account of the good and creaturely sharing in it, Pinckaers turns to ethical agency.[94] He is attuned to the unity of the various goods of the person in the fulfilment or perfection of the person in happiness, the plenitude of goodness proper to the person. He also emphasizes the hylomorphic unity of the human person. The different components of human nature 'are joined together in a natural unity comparable to the unity of the members of the body, to use the classic analogy. The rational part encompasses the biological and psychical parts, giving them a new dimension and capacities. St. Thomas gives strong emphasis to this association when he discusses the substantial unity of the human composite.'[95] In the human person, there is no level of *merely* bodily

---

[91] Ibid., 413.   [92] Ibid., 415.   [93] Ibid.

[94] It is this metaphysical framework, so necessary for any understanding of created 'nature', that Susan F. Parsons calls for—but, outside of faith, calls into question—in her 'Concerning Natural Law: The Turn in American Aquinas Scholarship', in *Contemplating Aquinas: On the Varieties of Interpretation*, ed. Fergus Kerr, OP (London: SCM Press, 2003), 163–83.

[95] Pinckaers, *The Sources of Christian Ethics*, 422. G. Simon Harak, SJ, explains this point: 'We have often heard Thomas's definition of the human being as a rational animal. Thomas does not mean to say that we have a body into which a soul is inserted. We are not "fallen angels"—intellective souls placed into physical bodies. Nor are we, on the other hand, animals to which an intellect has been added. Recall what Thomas said about animal (sensate) *appetitus* in relation to natural *appetitus*. The same is true in the case of the intellective *appetitus*. As a composite of body and

inclination that then must be humanized by the rational soul, as though the soul were sitting on top of an animal. Rather, it is because the human natural inclinations are already *human* that they are fulfilled in the virtuous ordering of the person. The human natural inclinations as such express an integrated, hierarchical ordering that pertains as a whole to the fulfilment of the person's freedom and capacity for truth.

For instance, the rational natural inclination to self-preservation serves our freedom by giving us a love for being and living, a 'spontaneous, natural love of self' that makes possible the self-giving precept 'Love thy neighbor as thyself.'[96] Without the natural attunement of the person to the good of being and living, the person would have no basis for appreciating being and living as goods for others. Were self-preservation not experienced as naturally good, we would stand isolated from God's own infinite love of his divine being and life, and thus would lack 'participation in the love with which God loves himself in his own essence and in his works, causing him to will the conservation and perfection of all beings, loved by him'.[97] Thus self-preservation serves human creatures precisely in their body–soul fulfilment as called to love.

Similarly, the natural inclination to procreation and the raising of offspring belongs to human beings as rational animals. This means, once again, not that human rationality has to order and elevate an animal drive, but rather that human animality is already rational animality, human bodies, not 'mere' bodies. Pinckaers argues that 'the natural processes of sexuality . . . have a vital connection with the deep relationships between man and woman', and that 'the orientation of sexuality to fruitfulness is intimately connected with the

intellective soul, the human being is a completely different species. The intellective power of the soul suffuses or permeates—or, better, animates—the whole composite being' (Harak, *Virtuous Passions: The Formation of Christian Character* (New York: Paulist Press, 1993), 66). See also Pinckaers's 'Reappropriating Aquinas's Account of the Passions', in Pinckaers, *The Pinckaers Reader: Renewing Thomistic Moral Theology*, ed. John Berkman and Craig Steven Titus (Washington, DC: Catholic University of America Press, 2005), 273–86.

[96] Pinckaers, *The Sources of Christian Ethics*, 424.   [97] Ibid., 426.

demand for fruitfulness which precedes what we might call the law of giving, written at the heart of every love'.[98] In other words, the inclination to procreation, like that to self-preservation, grounds an 'inclination toward the other' that belongs to human fulfilment—a fulfilment that has bodily as well as spiritual dimensions. Indeed, in human beings the inclination's bodily dimension indicates its spiritual dimension; even the bodily dimension does not lack an interior ordering toward self-gift, fulfilled in the virtue of chastity. While after the Fall human sexuality, like all the natural inclinations, has to be restored and perfected by grace (in the case of sexuality through the virtue of temperance) from a distorted self-seeking tendency, sexuality does not represent an animal dimension of the person that rationality must extrinsically order and 'humanize'. On the contrary, the natural inclination to procreation, including its bodily dimension, expresses human flourishing in the 'ecstatic' gift of self. Even renunciation of marriage, which might seem to be a rejection of the bodily inclination, has as its *ratio* the begetting and nourishing of spiritual children for the kingdom of God, spiritual paternity and maternity in the bridal Church. The bodily dimension does not simply disappear as meaningless even when bodily consummation of sexuality is renounced.[99]

The natural inclinations to truth and to live in society even more clearly belong to the fulfilment in happiness of human rationality and freedom. As rational animals and political animals, human beings seek to know and enjoy the good in friendship. Pinckaers emphasizes that the natural desire to know is no mere desire for encyclopedic mastery of facts or ideas, but rather is a desire to attain to first causes

[98] Ibid., 441. In agreeing with Daniel Mark Nelson's critique of Aquinas's affirmation of the immorality of homosexual acts, Pamela Hall raises the possibility that 'the inflexible linking, or even the equation, of the goods of sexuality with procreation is an impoverished way of deliberating about this particular *inclinatio* (Hall, *Narrative and the Natural Law*, 125 fn. 41). But it would seem to me that the 'impoverishment' would actually occur only in views that *take away* the procreative aspect of human sexuality.

[99] This point is crucial for accounts of the priesthood. See e.g. Sara Butler, 'Women's Ordination and the Development of Doctrine', *The Thomist* 61 (1997): 501–24.

and thus to the creative Good.[100] The natural inclination to live in society, *pace* the post-nominalist reduction of human beings to individuals set upon maximizing their freedom in competition with each other, affirms the centrality of *friendship* for happiness.

For Pinckaers, in short, the account of the good and the natural inclinations is the fount from which descriptions of moral agency—the free person who acts on the basis of the known good (which includes speculative and practical dimensions of knowing[101])—take their direction. The teleological ordering of the human person finds its fulfilment in the supremely virtuous person, who participates fully in the goods that God has ordained for the human person. As Pinckaers puts it,

> Thanks to these inclinations, which make up our spiritual nature, we have a firm basis, anchored in freedom itself, for undertaking the construction of a moral system. We are able to show how we can welcome the Word of God and the work of grace in all openness, for they form the New Law, and it is chiefly from them that Christian ethics proceeds. Thus from this human pole, natural law, we are carried to the divine pole revealed to us in the teaching of Christ.[102]

From the inclinations to the virtues and the gifts of the Holy Spirit, moral theory revolves theocentrically around the work of God as the ground of human action and fulfilment. Ultimately the work of Christ and the Holy Spirit fulfils the natural law in us and elevates us to communion with the Trinity. Pinckaers concludes, 'This is why Christian theology must begin with faith and the Gospel, which reveal to us, beyond sin, our heart and our true nature, such as they were in the beginning and as they shall once more become through the grace of Christ.'[103] Natural law doctrine is rightly formulated in light of the absolute and ongoing primacy of God's creative work in us, a reality that, as Pinckaers says, the Gospel manifests.

---

[100] Cf. in the context of Augustinian, Neoplatonic, and Scotist positions, Jan A. Aertsen, 'Aquinas and the Human Desire for Knowledge', *American Catholic Philosophical Quarterly* 79 (2005): 411–30.

[101] Cf. Pinckaers, *The Sources of Christian Ethics*, 418–19. While properly emphasizing practical reason, Pinckaers observes, 'The known good includes, therefore, all the knowledge of goodness that we can gain through study, education, reflection, perception, and, above all, personal experience' (419).

[102] Ibid., 464.   [103] Ibid.

GRAHAM McALEER: METAPHYSICAL *ECSTASIS* AND THE NATURAL LAW

In his *Ecstatic Being and Sexual Politics*, McAleer proposes to join 'Thomas's natural law and his metaphysics of the body'.[104] What McAleer means by Aquinas's 'metaphysics of the body' is that for Aquinas the 'flesh' (our bodiliness) is naturally 'ecstatic'. It seems to me that McAleer's approach, influenced in particular by John Paul II's *Theology of the Body*, adds a valuable third angle, closely allied with that of Pinckaers, from which to explore how contemporary natural doctrine may be enriched by biblical revelation.

For McAleer, the foundations for a doctrine of natural law should be sought first in an account of human bodiliness, not first in an account of human rationality. The earlier chapters of McAleer's study outline this metaphysics of the body. Investigating the moral significance of human bodiliness, he begins at the level of form and matter. Contrasting Aquinas with Averroes and Giles of Rome, he observes, 'In his concept of the *concreatum*—and it is unusual in the period— Thomas argues that matter and form are always already internally related; in other words, that desire is always already united to its object.'[105] If form–matter composites are two distinct realities extrinsically bonded together, domination and violence would belong to the very character of nature, 'a *metaphysical* original sin'.[106] Not only is Aquinas's understanding of the form–matter composite characterized metaphysically by interior 'peace', but also *being*, as *good*, is characterized by a movement of self-diffusion. Thus at the metaphysical

---

[104] G. J. McAleer, *Ecstatic Morality and Sexual Politics: A Catholic and Antitotalitarian Theory of the Body* (New York: Fordham University Press, 2005), 62. McAleer makes reference to Alasdair MacIntyre's *Dependent Rational Animals* (Chicago: Open Court, 1999). One might see also Thomas S. Hibbs, *Virtue's Splendor*, 26–55. On John Paul II's *Theology of the Body*, see the introduction by Michael Waldstein to his new translation of *Theology of the Body* (Boston: Pauline Books and Media, 2006).

[105] McAleer, *Ecstatic Morality and Sexual Politics*, 2. Unlike Aquinas, Averroes thought of material composites as 'congregatum', in which matter exists prior to form and thus is not interiorly constituted by form (6). Giles of Rome, returning to the Averroist tradition, similarly advanced the view of material composites as 'aggregatum', in which matter again has metaphysical independence of form. In this 'Averroist-Augustinian' metaphysical tradition, the interior unity of the substance is lost, and what remains are two substances always threatening to break apart.

[106] Ibid., 7.

roots of human bodily desire, one finds an *ecstasis* that is intrinsic to human fulfilment. McAleer observes, 'Creatures are intrinsically structured to an other-directedness through which they yet attain their own proper good (ST I, q. 19, a. 2): they are thus internally ecstatic, a consequence of their being good and so interiorly propelled to communicating that good: *bonum est diffusivum sui*.'[107]

Applying this metaphysics of the body to the human natural inclinations—to know truth, to live in accord with reason, to enjoy pleasures (concupiscence as virtuously formed in temperance), and to preserve oneself (the irascible appetite as virtuously formed in courage)—McAleer argues that these are fulfilled in *ecstasis*. Summarizing this aspect of his argument, he states that 'when concupiscence imitates God more, sensuality becomes ecstatic, opening to a wider good. Through the virtuous life, and finally and definitively in beatitude, bodily desire rises to God in ever greater intelligibility, universality, and generosity.'[108] Reason when properly functioning governs 'politically' by seeking the common good of all the parts of human nature; this political governance supports the teleology present in bodiliness, by leading it into its fulfilment in self-diffusiveness.

McAleer grants that the human body, while metaphysically not a locus of combat, is also not solely metaphysically 'ecstatic' or self-diffusive. In his view, the human body possesses a 'double aspect': both a natural propensity toward domination because of bodily individuation, and a natural propensity toward *ecstasis*.[109] As the Council of Trent teaches, McAleer observes, the body's self-centred tendency is

---

[107] Ibid., 15.

[108] Ibid., 19. Cf. Hans Urs von Balthasar, 'Nine Propositions on Christian Ethics', in Heinz Schürmann, Joseph Cardinal Ratzinger, and Hans Urs von Balthasar, *Principles of Christian Morality*, trans. Graham Harrison (German 1975; San Francisco: Ignatius Press, 1986). Balthasar writes regarding Kant's categorical imperative: 'because of its formalism, it is obligated to oppose abstract "duty" against the "inclination" of the senses, whereas in reality it is a question of encouraging the person's absolute "inclination" toward absolute good to triumph over contrary particular affections. What man appropriates to himself with a view to the absolute norm (*oikeiosis*, in Stoic terms) coincides with self-expropriation in favor of the divine good and the good of one's fellow man' (100).

[109] McAleer contrasts his view with that of postmodern thinkers such as Foucault and Merleau-Ponty, and feminist thinkers such as Luce Irigaray and Donna Haraway, who celebrate the body as a place of combat and resistance. His argument draws upon Brian O'Shaughnessy and is indebted as well to the postmodern thinkers Levinas and Nancy. McAleer's arguments find corroboration and development in the essays

present even before original sin turned the body's *pronitas* into a full-fledged disordered *inclinatio*. Rightly ordered sensuality, he argues, requires 'a wounded body' or a 'liquefaction' of the body, a body that in vulnerability forgoes 'some of its integrity or particularity that had excluded the other'.[110] What he means by this becomes particularly clear in his discussion of contraceptive sexual intercourse. Given original sin and the disordered *inclinatio* toward self-centredness, he agrees with Augustine that sexual intercourse cannot be separated from the 'violence' of the *libido dominandi*. Thus acts of sexual intercourse, to be rightly ordered, must be constituted by bodily participation in the order of *ecstasis*, 'the objective law of the self-diffusion of the good'.[111] Lacking the bodily *ecstasis* that belongs to the 'formality' of procreation, contraceptive sexual intercourse promotes the violent *inclinatio* toward self-centredness. As McAleer says, '*Humanae Vitae* then would have us replace a formality (*inclinatio*) of domination by a formality of procreation and the self-diffusion of the good.'[112] Such 'bodily diffusion' in sexual intercourse cannot reject 'the formality of procreation'.[113]

Given this metaphysics of bodily *ecstasis*, taken up in the *ecstasis* of the whole person, McAleer critiques such thinkers as John Milbank and Stanley Hauerwas for their rejection of natural law in favour of revelation, as if natural law were an autonomous zone whose truth threatens the relevance of revelation. He connects their thought with Scotus's conception of natural law as divine positive law, a list of rules.

in *Women in Christ: Toward a New Feminism*, ed. Michele M. Schumacher (Grand Rapids, MI: Eerdmans, 2004).

[110] McAleer, *Ecstatic Morality and Sexual Politics*, 52.   [111] Ibid., 125.

[112] Ibid., 126.

[113] Ibid., 130. McAleer's position on contraceptive sexual intercourse contrasts with Rhonheimer's. For Rhonheimer's view, see most recently his response to Benedict Guevin, OSB, in 'On the Use of Condoms to Prevent Acquired Immune Deficiency Syndrome: Argument of Martin Rhonheimer', *National Catholic Bioethics Quarterly* 5 (2005): 40–8; cf. Rhonheimer's 'The Truth about Condoms', *The Tablet* 258.8545 (10 July 2004): 10–11; idem, 'Contraception, Sexual Behavior, and Natural Law: Philosophical Foundation of the Norm of *Humanae Vitae*', *The Linacre Quarterly* 56 (1989): 20–57; idem, *Natural Law and Practical Reason*, 109–38. Jean Porter gives a helpful summary of Rhonheimer's view, which has remained consistent throughout his career, in her *Nature as Reason*, 190. For responses to Rhonheimer, see Luke Gormally, 'Marriage and the Prophylactic Use of Condoms', *National Catholic Bioethics Quarterly* 5 (2005): 735–49; Janet E. Smith, 'The Morality of Condom Use by HIV-Infected Spouses', *The Thomist* 70 (2006): 27–69.

In contrast, he argues that in fact the natural law is our participation in the pattern of *ecstasis* that governs the universe. Natural law is not a competitor to divine law, but rather exposes created nature's sharing in the ecstatic being of its Creator. The ultimate rational order is an ecstatic communion. In this theocentric understanding of natural law, which McAleer finds in Aquinas, 'natural law is a description of ecstatic being in another register. As such, natural law is a participation in God according to Pseudo-Dionysius's dictum *bonum diffusivum sui est.*'[114] Since natural law is a participation in God, and God is self-giving goodness and wisdom, natural law partakes of this ecstatic character. All created reality, including human bodiliness, has inscribed within it this ecstatic ordering to its own fulfilment. Human reason shares receptively in God's knowing of this ecstatic ordering in creation, and this sharing, as imprinted in our minds, is natural law.

If 'natural law' in this sense is both our mind's participation in the eternal law and our discernment of a natural (ecstatic) order in creation, is this account 'physicalist'? It certainly presupposes a natural teleological order that is ethically normative. It is not 'physicalist', however, because it presupposes God's eternal law, the divine creative intellect, as the structuring principle. As McAleer puts it, 'natural law is the argument that an objective moral law *structures* nature.'[115] This objective moral law is none other than, as God's eternal law, the law of charity or ecstatic self-diffusion as the path to fulfilment of being. McAleer thus compares the natural law to Emmanuel Levinas's theory of 'rapport social'. Drawing upon Levinas's *Ethics and Infinity*, he states, 'The "deposition of sovereignty" through "being-for-the-other" (EI, 52) is the role of natural law understood by Thomas on the model of the Deposition [of Christ]. Natural law is a participation in the charity that is God and ecstatic being and by which a person cares less for his own good and rather more for the good of the other.'[116] In other words, natural law is the pattern of ecstatic being that human

---

[114] McAleer, *Ecstatic Morality and Sexual Politics*, 66.

[115] Ibid., 68. Cf. Adrian Reimers's emphasis on John Paul II's theocentric and teleological account of human nature, including human bodiliness: Reimers, 'Karol Wojtyla on the Natural Moral Order', *National Catholic Bioethics Quarterly* 4 (2004): 317–34.

[116] McAleer, *Ecstatic Morality and Sexual Politics*, 70.

beings, participating in God's eternal law, discern in ourselves as well as in all of creation. It is this ecstatic ordering, natural law teaches, that constitutes creaturely fulfilment. Our created 'ends', whether self-preservation, procreation and raising of offspring, living in society, knowing the truth about God, and so forth, are joined to our ecstatic being so that we find the fulfilment of our inclinations solely through giving ourselves into the hands of others. The precepts of the natural law require living according to this pattern of self-diffusive or ecstatic love. As McAleer says, 'The wound of love is the order of nature: hence, Thomas is fond of citing I Tim (1, 5) *finis praecepti est caritas* (Quod. V, q. 10, a. 19).'[117]

Does this account of natural law conflate the 'natural' with what is beyond the capacity of nature unaided by grace, thereby either rendering useless the adjective 'natural' or else making requisite, for the fulfilment of created human nature, the absolutely gratuitous gift of grace? McAleer at times seems to think that such a conflation is unavoidable: 'In arguing that the Cross is the eternal law ordering the natural law, I am well aware that I propose that the end of nature and the end of charity are one and the same.'[118] One might likewise ask whether McAleer's account makes of Christ's Cross not an utterly unique sacrifice, but simply the highest instance of the natural law's teaching on ecstatic being and human fulfilment. For McAleer, 'the normative structure of the human body [according to Aquinas], its appetites and those of the whole person, is Christ's wounded body on the Cross.... Thomistic natural law is Christological.'[119] Or as he states a bit later: 'In Thomas's mind, Christ's diffusion of himself on the cross is paradigmatic of the ecstatic structure of Being.... Acknowledging this demands that the Cross be raised to a metaphysical significance.'[120]

---

[117] Ibid. One might contrast this position with that of Eberhard Schockenhoff, who finds in the Ten Commandments and the Sermon on the Mount the basis for a universal philosophical ethics. In his view, the history of Europe evinces just such progress toward universalizing what began as a biblical ethics (see Schockenhoff, *Natural Law and Human Dignity*, 285–6). This effort to locate 'human rights and the idea of the natural law' in the innate dignity of each person's humanity rather than in the eternal wisdom of the provident Creator with respect to the common good reduces the scope of natural law's accounting for human ends.

[118] McAleer, *Ecstatic Morality and Sexual Politics*, 81.   [119] Ibid., 75.

[120] Ibid., 80.

As I have suggested, I agree with McAleer's profound point—often missed in studies of natural law—that 'Thomas does see nature as such as ecstatic. The human body is ecstatic in the same way as the most rudimentary existences, and as animals, though to be sure, structured by other ecstatic appetites *as well*. Nature, because being is diffusive of itself, always possesses at least a vestige of "the dimension of the infinite." '[121] In the sense that the 'precepts of the natural law make the human body ecstatic, satisfying pseudo-Dionysius's dictum *bonum diffusivum sui est*',[122] Christ's Cross is indeed the fulfilment of the natural law. McAleer is certainly right, too, to refuse to conceive of God's eternal law apart from God's self-giving wisdom and love revealed preeminently by Christ on the Cross. In so far as human beings participate by reason in God's eternal law, such participation belongs to the (primarily receptive, secondarily active) dynamism of the imitation of God, instantiated in the practice of *imitatio Christi*, whereby human beings become more and more fully the image of God that, as created, we are. As participation in the eternal law, the natural law is the imprint of the pattern of divine *ecstasis*, divine wisdom and love as revealed in Christ. In McAleer's words, 'The natural law of the body... is directed toward an increasing ecstasy in imitation of God's own nature (*divinus amor facit extasim inquantum scilicet facit appetitum hominis tendere in res amatas* [ST II–II, q. 175, a. 2]).'[123]

I do not, however, think that from McAleer's understanding of natural law need follow either an inability to account fully for the supernatural character of charity, or the view that Christ's Cross is somehow inscribed in the metaphysical order. The *ecstasis* that McAleer rightly emphasizes can have various levels; natural law's *ecstasis* differs in its mode from the ecstatic charity that attains communion with the Trinity. The *ecstasis* taught interiorly by natural law can be distinct from the *ecstasis* of charity, and yet the former can be taken up and fulfilled in the latter. To distinguish between the two is not to suggest an opposition between them: both the natural ecstatic dynamisms and the supernatural act of charity are participations in the one eternal law, whose depths are, as McAleer sees, revealed by the divine law of the grace of the Holy Spirit. Metaphysically, in

---

[121] Ibid., 73.   [122] Ibid., 75.   [123] Ibid., 74–5.

order to affirm the ecstatic character of being, one need not say that all being possesses, as being, *intrinsic communion with* (as opposed to participation in) the Trinity—as would seem to be suggested by the idea that the Cross is intrinsic to the metaphysical order. Nor, in my opinion, should one employ Christ's Cross to demonstrate that being qua being is relational or that creation and redemption (as acts of ecstatic goodness) are necessary to divine being as good. God's ecstatic acts of creation and redemption are free, not metaphysically necessary. Certainly God is 'ecstatic' in his Trinitarian relations, but 'being' describes what is one and utterly simple in God. Yet, none of this is to deny that God's *ecstasis*, as Trinitarian Creator, is written into the fabric of creation and of our rational participation in God's wise plan for human fulfilment. We are called by natural law to participate in this pattern of *ecstasis* in order to attain the fulfilment we desire. On the Cross, the Son of God invites us into an infinitely more intense pattern of *ecstasis* by which we may fulfil, and transcend, our natures in coming to share in the Trinitarian ecstatic communion of wisdom and love.

McAleer has thus relieved 'natural law' of the dull rationalism that distances some accounts of natural law from the theocentric patterns and practices of Scripture. In this way McAleer assists greatly in reclaiming natural law for the 'God of Abraham, Isaac, and Jacob', the God who in history requires ecstatic self-diffusion—Abraham's journeyings, the near-sacrifice of Isaac, Jacob's limp. Like Pinckaers, McAleer has shown how 'biblical' natural law doctrine finds, rather than constitutes, 'ecstatic' norms in nature.

CONCLUDING REFLECTIONS

In presenting his account of natural law, Rhonheimer states, 'Indeed, reason has a relationship to the natural inclinations—because they are *natural*—that mirrors that of the relationship between form and matter. Together they form a complex unity. . . . The naturalness of good, as it is formulated in the natural law, cannot, however, be reduced to the simple naturalness of the individual natural inclinations and their goods, ends, and acts. Such a reduction would be equivalent to reducing the *genus moris* of an act to its *genus naturae*.'[124] He draws out the implications of this point earlier in his article:

the human good is not simply an object 'given' to intellectual acts. The very nature of the intellect—emanating as it does from the spiritual soul which is a substantial form and thus the life principle of its corporeality—means that what is really good for man is, in a certain sense, constituted and formulated only in the intellectual acts themselves. The human and moral good is essentially a *bonum rationis*: a good of reason, for reason, and formulated by reason. Only within the horizon of this good, as it appears before the intellectual acts of the soul, does 'human nature' reveal itself in its normative significance. As a result, and even if at first sight this may seem paradoxical, knowledge of the human good *precedes* the right understanding of human nature. This cannot reveal its normative character before all that is natural in man has been interpreted in the light of that good that is the object of the acts of the intellect—and (as we will see later) not of the speculative intellect but of the practical intellect, from which the natural law emanates.[125]

In contrast, Pinckaers's account of the 'good' in terms of happiness, and of the integration of the natural inclinations, challenges Rhonheimer's claim that the human good is 'constituted and formulated only in the intellectual acts themselves'. Practical reason does not need to 'constitute' or 'establish' the teleological ordering of the human good, because it is already there in our created nature, moving our natural inclinations. The motive power of the end, as manifested in the hierarchical ordering of ends in our natural inclinations, establishes our freedom. The natural inclinations do not need to be excluded from normative significance, as Rhonheimer does, because the natural inclinations are in McAleer's phrase 'ecstatic'.

Indeed, McAleer's focus on *ecstasis* as the key to natural law's participated pattern enables him to achieve what Rhonheimer seeks to achieve as regards the demonstration of natural law's role in the active working out of our salvation. Lacking the entry-point of the ecstatic character of the good, Rhonheimer has trouble holding together the various inclinations of the hylomorphic human person. Thus, for instance, Rhonheimer remarks that 'at the level of their mere

[124] Rhonheimer, 'The Cognitive Structure of the Natural Law and the Truth of Subjectivity', 28.
[125] Ibid., 6–7.

naturalness, does following the tendency to conserve oneself or the sexual inclination also mean following the good and end due to man? How can we know what is not only *specific* to these inclinations according to their particular nature but also due to the person, that is to say, at the moment of following these inclinations, good for man *as man*?'[126] He is concerned that the 'person', what is 'good for man *as man*', and these natural inclinations' 'particular nature' may differ.[127] Or as he says in more detail with regard to the natural inclination for procreation—cited above but worth citing again:

Grasped by reason as a human good and made the content of a practical judgement, the object of this inclination is more than an inclination found in pure nature.... This natural inclination, grasped by reason and pursued in the order of reason—at the personal level—becomes love between two people, love with the requirement of exclusiveness (uniqueness) and of indissoluble faithfulness between persons (i.e., it is not mere attraction between bodies!), persons who understand that they are united in the task of transmitting human life. Faithful and indissoluble marriage between two people of different sexes, united in the shared task of transmitting human life, is precisely the truth of sexuality; it is sexuality understood as the human good of marriage. Like all the other forms of friendship and virtue, this specific type of friendship, which is what marriage is, is not found 'in nature.' It is the property and norm of a moral order, to which man has access through the natural law as an *ordinatio rationis*. What, according to Ulpian, 'nature has taught all animals' is certainly a presupposition for human love as well, but it does not yet express adequately the natural moral order to which this love belongs. As a result, in the case of man, what 'nature has taught all animals' is not even sufficient to establish any dutifulness or normativeness. If the animal does what its nature, endowed with a richness of instincts, prescribes to it, it performs its function. Can the same be said of man?[128]

---

[126] Ibid., 20.   [127] Ibid., 21.

[128] Ibid., 32–3. However, as Russell Hittinger remarks, 'The ends of being, living, and knowing win our natural assent; as such, we do not need to deliberate and to issue a command in order to move toward these ends. Although interpreters have been vexed by the Ulpinian dictum at the outset of the *Institutes*, that the *ius naturale* is "what nature teaches all animals", there is a relatively simple and plausible way to construe the dictum. When the Roman governor goes to Asia Minor, he understands that the ordinances of Roman positive law are not needed to move the inhabitants to copulate, procreate, and educate the young' (Hittinger, 'Yves R. Simon on Law, Nature, and Practical Reason', in *Acquaintance with the Absolute*, ed. Anthony O. Simon (New York: Fordham University Press, 1998), 119). See also Benedict M. Guevin, OSB, 'Aquinas's Use of Ulpian and the Question of Physicalism Revisited', *The Thomist*

He goes on to argue that a ' "natural given fact," which is relevant in some aspects and presupposed for the formation of the natural law, is certain relations of fittingness', among which is the conjunction of male and female, but 'the normativeness of these "relations of fittingness" or *adequationes* and the very notion of due (*debitum*) come from practical reason, which alone is able to order these relations of fittingness towards the end of virtue, which is the good of the human person'.[129]

This work of humanization, for Rhonheimer, produces from the water of 'nature' the wine of 'human nature'. But the water, as Pinckaers and McAleer show clearly, is already wine; the point of unity is the movement of *ecstasis* toward the good that belongs to the natural inclinations, a movement perfected by (not constituted by) the virtues.[130] Their metaphysical work, following Aquinas, illumines the consistency of teleology, the attraction of the good, in God's creative artistry. Aquinas compares God to an artist who infuses intelligibility into every aspect of his works of art: 'All natural things were produced by the Divine art, and so may be called God's works

---

63 (1999): 613–28, responding in part to Michael Crowe, 'St. Thomas and Ulpian's Natural Law', in *St. Thomas Aquinas 1274–1974: Commemorative Studies*, ed. Armand A. Maurer, vol. 1 (Toronto: Pontifical Institute of Mediaeval Studies, 1974), 261–82.

[129] Rhonheimer, 'The Cognitive Structure of the Natural Law and the Truth of Subjectivity', 35.

[130] To use the metaphor offered by Steven Long. As Long observes, 'Natural law—which is nothing other than a rational participation in the eternal law—is the normativity of that *order* that is divinely impressed upon, defines, and permeates the rational nature. For the rational creature *passively* receives from God its being, nature, natural powers, order of powers to end, hierarchy of ends reposing from the *finis ultimus*, and even the actual application of its natural volitional power to act. Only in so far as these are passively received—including rational nature itself and the very motion whereby the rational agent freely determines itself—may reason then participate or receive this order *rationally* as providing reasons to act or not to act. If the creature is to be normatively governed toward its end, it must be subject to divine causality. Natural law moral doctrine grows in the fertile loam of causally rich metaphysics and theism. It could be no other way. Human reason does not turn the water of mere *inclinatio* into the wine of *lex*, but is subject to an order of law by the very being and order that it passively participates and which it is *ordered* to receive rationally and preceptively' (Steven A. Long, 'Natural Law or Autonomous Practical Reason: Problems for the New Natural Law Theory', in *St. Thomas Aquinas and the Natural Law Tradition: Contemporary Perspectives*, ed. John Goyette, Mark S. Latkovic, and Richard S. Myers (Washington, DC: Catholic University of America Press, 2004), 165–93, at 191).

of art. Now every artist intends to give his work the best disposition; not absolutely the best, but the best as regards the proposed end.'[131] As regards the human body, its 'proximate end ... is the rational soul and its operations'. He holds therefore that 'God fashioned the human body in that disposition which was best, as most suited to such a form and to such operations'.[132] This formality, as McAleer makes clear, is ultimately 'ecstatic'. Pinckaers brings out the depths of the divine inscription of the good in human beings, so that freedom *depends* not on self-constitution (even participated self-constitution), but on the ecstatic pull of the Good for which, as Scripture tells us, human beings are made.

Thus the 'relations of fittingness' that one finds inscribed in human bodies—such as the conjunction of male and female—belong to the divine art and possess an intrinsic ecstatic intelligibility. If the ultimate end of the person is rational self-giving love and wisdom, one might expect that the natural inclinations, including those to self-preservation and procreation, express an inner dynamic that befits human persons. Pinckaers shows how this is so by recalling for us the place of happiness, friendship, and fruitfulness in a proper account of the natural inclinations. The attraction of the good inscribes teleology at the very root of our being. And since our being is rational, this teleology or attraction to the good is the fount of freedom.[133] The natural law's status as a 'participation' in the eternal law here takes on its central importance: as Daniel Westberg puts it, 'It is in the concept of participation that Thomas brings together practical reason and virtue, the interior principles of action, with law, the exterior

---

[131] I, q. 91, a. 3.   [132] Ibid.

[133] For further discussion, see Steven Long, 'Natural Law or Autonomous Practical Reason: Problems for the New Natural Law Theory', 186. See also Robert Sokolowski, 'What Is Natural Law? Human Purposes and Natural Ends', *The Thomist* 68 (2004): 507–29. Sokolowski suggests that the ordering of ends only manifests itself to the speculative reason after virtuous action has displayed the contours of a good life: 'Once the good life is manifested in action, philosophy can clarify and consolidate what has been accomplished' (527). Yet before philosophical clarification and consolidation occur, there is the intellectual apprehension of the existence of ends that befit human nature, e.g. food, drink, shelter, procreation and the raising of children, life in society, truth, God. In apprehending the existence of these ends, prior to philosophical reflection, one apprehends them as hierarchically ordered.

principle of action. The intellect itself is described as a sharing in the divine light, by which we know and judge things.'[134] Human flesh is rational flesh: it owes its being the kind of flesh it is, to the rational soul created by God to know and love ecstatically. This is the insight, thoroughly biblical, that Pinckaers and McAleer express so well through their attention to the ecstatic character of the good.

---

[134] Daniel Westberg, 'The Relation of Law and Practical Reason in Aquinas', in *The Future of Thomism*, ed. Deal Hudson and Dennis Moran (Mishawaka, IN: American Maritain Association, 1992), 279–90, at 287. Westberg goes on to note, 'The concept of law can be combined with practical reason because they describe two different points of view—the agent's and God's ... The doctrine of law is a description of the exterior principle of action, the expression of God's providence directing actions to an end. Without a doctrine of creation and a wise and loving God who desires to share his being this perspective is hardly possible, which is why we do not find this in Aristotle (who had to use the commonly recognized wise person as the standard for practical wisdom). Prudence was described by St. Thomas as the perfection of practical reason, requiring the development of other moral virtues, but not a notion of law as obligation. Nevertheless Augustine's doctrine of law fit well with a Christian view of prudence, because the agent who understands the correct means and ends for his life and is able to order them properly is the one who by the Holy Spirit participates in both God's wisdom and charity' (290).

4

Natural Law and the Order of Charity

Building upon the biblical questions and insights raised in the first chapter, Chapters 2 and 3 have undertaken to expose the central issues regarding the development today of a philosophical and theological articulation of natural law. As we have seen, attempts to ground 'natural law' anthropocentrically, outside of the Creator God and his providential ordering, led to disjunctions between 'nature' and 'freedom', and as a result to the obscuring of the ecstatically inclined constitution of the body–soul human person. No one grasped this situation more acutely than Friedrich Nietzsche, who in response attempted to build an 'ecstasis' of self-assertion, the distorted and tragic mirror image of our true fulfilment. In response, Chapter 3 sought to offer an understanding of natural law and natural inclinations consistent with the biblical depiction of human fulfilment through body–soul *ecstasis*.

The goal of this final chapter is to clarify the inscription of natural law within the biblical worldview. Given the distinction between created natural capacities and these capacities as transformed by the grace of the Holy Spirit, how should one speak of 'natural law'? Is it helpful or even possible to speak of 'natural law' once God has revealed that the vocation of human nature is to transcend itself through 'supernatural' charity?

Indeed, one might ask further, what does love have to do with 'law'? It has become commonplace to consider love and law to be ineluctably in tension. The first section of this chapter therefore takes up the work of the legal scholar Paul Kahn as illustrative of this supposed tension between love and law. By way of challenging this supposed tension, the second section carefully examines how

Thomas Aquinas sets forth the relationships between the various kinds of 'law'. I hope to show that Aquinas's biblically informed theology of law, like his theocentric and teleological understanding of the human natural inclinations, manifests the ecstatic creativity, the union of love and law, open to the human person in the quest for human fulfilment in the divine good.[1] This chapter thus puts the capstone upon my account of a theocentric and teleological 'biblical' natural law.

LOVE AND LAW: IN CONFLICT?

Paul Kahn, an expert on American constitutional law, argues in the introduction to his *Law and Love: The Trials of King Lear* that a conflict between love and law is intrinsic to modern Western culture. According to Kahn, Western societies, while structured by law, contain within themselves a critique of law, a hope or dream for the establishment of a community that will no longer need the restrictions of law: 'Western culture understands the rule of law as its highest political ideal yet simultaneously imagines a community beyond law. In this imagined community, love is the measure of action.'[2] He illustrates this situation by a quotation from Grant Gilmore's *The Ages of American Law*: ' "In Heaven, there will be no law. . . . In Hell there will be nothing but law and due process will be meticulously observed." '[3] The antagonism of law and love as 'fundamental archetypes' of Western culture emerges, according to Kahn, from a split between the Jewish and the Pauline/Christian understanding of law, both of which have been taken into the structure of Western culture without being reconciled. He affirms, 'This double sense of triumph and tragedy in law situates us squarely within the Judeo-Christian tradition, which contains two profoundly different traditions of law's rule. Jews are a

[1] For charity as commanded in the Torah, see *Summa Theologiae* I–II, q. 100, a. 10. Aquinas quotes Deuteronomy 6:5, 'you shall love the Lord your God with all your heart, and with all your soul, and with all your might', and Leviticus 19:18, 'you shall love your neighbour as yourself'.

[2] Paul W. Kahn, *Law and Love: The Trials of King Lear* (New Haven, CT: Yale University Press, 2000), xi.

[3] Ibid. In fact, heaven belongs to the eternal law.

people of law, Christians of love.'[4] While recognizing the existence of both Christian canon law and the Jewish eschatological vision of *olam-ha-ba*, the 'world to come' which in some versions does not include the legal *mitzvot*, Kahn holds that the two traditions embody radically different understandings of law, positive (Jewish) and negative (Christian).[5]

Quoting Romans 7:4, 'My brethren, you have died to the law through the body of Christ', and Galatians 3:10, 'For all who rely on works of law are under a curse', Kahn proposes that for Christianity, 'Law's rule is the state peculiar to fallen man; it is of the flesh, not the spirit. The highest truth, and true freedom, exists beyond law. According to this Pauline tradition, law is not our salvation but our prison.'[6] Examining Western culture in general and the United States of America in particular, Kahn finds both a sadness that we cannot break free of law and a triumphant 'founding myth' about becoming a community of law through revolution. This latter 'myth' has its original roots, Kahn thinks, in the Jewish tradition, which took secular form in Hobbes's understanding of how people transform a 'state of nature' into a state of law. In the Jewish tradition, 'law's source was divine revelation, and maintenance of the law was constitutive of the historical life of the community. Law made the community a single, intergenerational project with a unique meaning. In the modern myth of law, the sovereign people have replaced the sovereign Lord, and revolution has replaced revelation.'[7] It is through law that modern persons have access to the triumphant self-creative power of the original (Hobbesian) revolution.

Yet, this self-creative power is, so long as we cannot have another revolution, always somewhat distant and thus experienced as limiting.[8] The triumphant sense of belonging to a community of law constituted by the sovereign people, then, goes together with a desire to move beyond law—not only so as to become fully historically self-creative, but also to become free to express, beyond the dictates of

[4] Ibid., xii.   [5] Ibid., especially Kahn's fn. 2.   [6] Ibid., xiii.
[7] Ibid., xii.
[8] For insight into this situation, see Pierre Manent, *The City of Man*, trans. Marc A. LePain (French 1994; Princeton: Princeton University Press, 1998), especially chapter 6, 'The End of Nature'.

law by which evil acts are punished, perfect love and mercy. Kahn expresses both of these themes as regards the complex desire to overcome law:

We are born into law's rule, not into a prepolitical state of nature. Occupied with law, we never realize the full potential of our nature. Law is appropriate for finite man, but it never overcomes our fallen state. Beyond law are love, grace, and mercy. If we could realize these elements of our nature, we would not need law. Conversely, just to the degree that we need law we confirm our fallen state. A well-ordered state is indeed better than a disordered state of nature. Nevertheless, it is only the pride of fallen man that would find in the creation of law an element of divinity.[9]

In Kahn's view, this tension is positive: Americans both respect law and are willing to critique it on the basis of a higher standard (as was done, for instance, regarding the Constitution's approbation of slavery). In a manner that is representative of modern Western culture, Americans both find in law salvation from the 'state of nature' in which evildoing would have free reign, and idealize certain figures in history who seem to stand above law and critique it on the basis of a higher norm.

Thus Kahn suggests that in our culture Socrates and Christ 'symbolize a freedom and self-authenticity outside of law. One is executed by Athens, the other by Rome. In the end, the law of democratic Athens is no less problematic than that of autocratic Rome.'[10] The lesson of Socrates and Christ, Kahn concludes, is that as regards love no political order is better than any other: 'this important distinction among forms of political order disappears from the perspective of love. No form of political order—legal or otherwise—is adequate to love's understanding.'[11] For Kahn, law and love are completely different perspectives from which to view the world: on the one hand, the order of law is clearly a comprehensive order, in which every aspect of life has its regulated place; while on the other hand the order of love, too, makes demands upon every aspect of human life. As Kahn remarks, 'each pushes as far as possible, and thus each pushes against the other. There is no reason to believe these tensions can be resolved in theory or practice.'[12] Love is the area of private

---

[9] Kahn, *Law and Love*, xiii–xiv.   [10] Ibid., xiv.   [11] Ibid., xvii.
[12] Ibid.

virtue, whereas law is the political order of the state; both, Kahn holds, are equally indispensable, and one should not be privileged hierarchically above the other. Rather, the tension should simply be maintained and explored—as Kahn does in his book through an interpretation of Shakespeare's *King Lear*. He affirms in conclusion, 'We cannot choose between law and love, because we are equally committed to both. The values that we hold are multiple and in conflict. This is not just Lear's tragedy, but ours as well.'[13] The conflictual, yet creative, polarity between law and love belongs to the tragic dimension that is, on this reading, at the heart of human existence.

AQUINAS ON LAW AND LOVE

Is there any way to get beyond 'Lear's tragedy'?[14] Yes: contrary to Kahn's reading of the passages in St Paul, Christian worship of the God of Israel does indeed provide a unified vision of love and law that unites reason and will. The ultimate end of human beings is not an unrealizable longing to break through the limitations imposed by reason's construction of a 'state of law' out of an original 'state of nature', but rather the *ecstasis* of the divine Trinitarian communion of charity. This *ecstasis* entails the human creature embracing his or her creatureliness, thereby living in accord with the self-giving dynamism of the order of created nature, which is healed, perfected, and elevated in the order of grace.[15] As Hans Urs von Balthasar puts it, 'To be a Child of the Father, then, holds primacy over

---

[13] Ibid., xix.

[14] Note the parallels between Kahn's account of 'Lear's tragedy' and the late medieval nominalism sketched by Pinckaers. On late-medieval nominalist accounts of freedom, see also Christopher Toner, 'Angelic Sin in Aquinas and the Genesis of Some Central Objections to Contemporary Virtue Ethics', *The Thomist* 69 (2005): 79–125.

[15] On this point see e.g. Jean-Marie Aubert, 'Nature de la relation entre "lex nova" et "lex naturalis" chez saint Thomas d'Aquin', in *Morale e diritto nella prospettiva tomistica*, ed. Pontificia Accademia Romana di San Tommaso d'Aquino (Vatican City: Libreria Editrice Vaticana, 1982), 34–8. See also Ulrich Kühn's *Via Caritatis. Theologie des Gesetzes bei Thomas von Aquin* (Göttingen: Vandenhoeck & Ruprecht, 1965); Aubert, *Loi de Dieu, lois des hommes* (Paris: Desclée, 1964).

the whole drama of salvation.'[16] While it might seem that Thomas Aquinas's account of natural, eternal, and divine law is too abstractly metaphysical a path to approach the Creator's ordering wisdom in history that culminates our adoptive sonship in the Son, I will suggest that in fact his account beautifully exhibits the various dimensions of this ordering wisdom.[17] To appreciate his approach requires attending to the diverse participations in God's ordering wisdom ('eternal law').

A Theocentric Order

The first task is to apprehend how natural law participates in the eternal law, which involves repeating some details from earlier chapters. As we have seen, Aquinas's integration of law and love begins with his affirmation of God's creative knowledge, which, as the normatively directive ordering of the cosmos, is known as 'eternal law'.[18]

---

[16] Hans Urs von Balthasar, *Unless You Become Like This Child*, trans. Erasmo Leiva-Merikakis (San Francisco: Ignatius Press, 1991), 64.

[17] Pamela M. Hall's *Narrative and the Natural Law: An Interpretation of Thomistic Ethics* (Notre Dame, IN: University of Notre Dame Press, 1994) possesses a number of affinities with my approach. Hall's concern is primarily to show that Aquinas's understanding of natural law is not ahistorical. I agree with Hall that natural law, as operative in human beings, is historically contextualized. Likewise, to think of natural law as a rulebook, with the legalistic extrinsicism this suggests, is to misunderstand the role of the natural inclinations. Yet, I would argue that Hall minimizes too much Aquinas's view that the primary precepts of the natural law are known by all and cannot be effaced, although they can be misapplied and obscured.

[18] For Aquinas's analogous understanding of the term 'law', see Ralph McInerny, *Aquinas on Human Action* (Washington, DC: Catholic University of America Press, 1992), 108–12. On Aquinas's understanding of eternal law, and the sources of this concept in ancient philosophy and (as we have observed in Chapter 4) in Augustine, see e.g. Domingo M. Basso, 'La Ley Eterna en la Teologia de Santo Tomás', *Teologia* 11 (1974): 33–63; Joseph Collins, OP, 'God's Eternal Law', *The Thomist* 23 (1960): 497–532. Collins emphasizes the distinction between the eternal law and divine providence, which he sketches in terms of 'regnative' and 'monastic' prudence. He appeals to *De veritate* q. 5, a. 1, which asks whether providence belongs solely to God's knowledge or also to God's will. In answering the sixth objection, Aquinas distinguishes between the eternal law and divine providence, although this distinction must not be taken as a separation: 'Properly speaking, God's providence is not the eternal law; it is something that follows upon the eternal law. The eternal law should be thought of as existing in God as those principles of action exist in us which we know naturally and upon which we base our deliberation and choice. These belong to

Aquinas's understanding of 'eternal law' relies upon apprehending God as uniquely the Creator. The act of creation, while a free act, does not differ from the Act who God is. God is not a composite of potency and act; in God's simple eternity he is sheer dynamic Act of being, the fullness of Act—otherwise he, too, would be a finite entity (Heidegger's 'onto-theology'). God's act of creation is a free act because while God knows all things to which his power might extend, and thus knows all the finite modes in which creatures might participate his being, he need not will that such creatures come to be. But in fact God lovingly and wisely wills that some creatures, ordered to the divine good, come to be: no finite good is necessary for the perfect Trinitarian communion of life and love within the Godhead. This is the ecstatic diffusion of the Good, God's free act of unfathomable charity that brings creatures into being.

Against the temptation to anthropomorphize God, to place him at a creaturely level and to attribute the limitations of creatures to him, Isaiah prophesies in the name of God: 'To whom then will you compare me, that I should be like him? says the Holy One. Lift up your eyes on high and see: who created these? He who brings out their host by number, calling them all by name; by the greatness of his might, and because he is strong in power not one is missing.... The Lord is the everlasting God, the Creator of the ends of the earth. He does not faint or grow weary, his understanding is unsearchable' (Isa. 40:25–6, 28). God instructs Moses to identify him to the people as 'I am' (Exod. 3:14), needing no other appellation but sheer to-be; he is 'perfect' (Mt 5:48), he alone is 'good' (Mark 10:18), he is all-knowing: ' "Are not five sparrows sold for two pennies? And not

---

prudence or providence. Consequently, the law of our intellect is related to prudence as an indemonstrable principle is related to a demonstration. Similarly, the eternal law in God is not His providence, but, as it were, a principle of His providence; for this reason one can, without any inconsistency, attribute an act of providence to the eternal law in the same way that he attributes every conclusion of a demonstration to self-evident principles' (English trans. Robert W. Mulligan, SJ, in St. Thomas Aquinas, *Truth*, vol. 1 (1954; Indianapolis, IN: Hackett, 1994), 205). It should also be clear that the 'eternal law' is not a supernatural dynamism that augments the 'natural law': this misunderstanding mars Diana Fritz Cates's *Choosing to Feel: Virtue, Friendship, and Compassion for Friends* (Notre Dame, IN: University of Notre Dame Press, 1997): see 16–17.

one of them is forgotten before God. Why, even the hairs of your head are numbered" ' (Luke 12:6–7). As St John teaches, 'God is light and in him is no darkness at all' (1 John 1:5); 'God is greater than our hearts, and he knows everything' (1 John 3:20); 'God is love' (1 John 4:8).

On this biblical basis Aquinas affirms metaphysically:

> Now God, by His wisdom, is the Creator of all things in relation to which He stands as the artificer to the products of his art, as stated in the First Part (Q. 14, A. 8). Moreover He governs all the acts and movements that are to be found in each single creature, as was also stated in the First Part (Q. 103, A. 5). Wherefore as the type of the Divine Wisdom, inasmuch as by It all things are created, has the character of art, exemplar or idea; so the type of Divine Wisdom, as moving all things to their due end, bears the character of law. Accordingly the eternal law is nothing else than the type of the Divine Wisdom, as directing all actions and movements.[19]

The entire cosmic order is suffused with the intelligibility of the divine Word, as created through the Word and by the Word.[20] Aquinas explains that 'as the knowledge of God is only cognitive as regards God, whereas as regards creatures, it is both cognitive and operative, so the Word of God is only expressive of what is in God the Father, but is both expressive and operative of creatures; and therefore it is said (Ps. xxxii.9): *He spake, and they were made*; because in the Word is implied the operative idea of what God makes'.[21] In knowing himself in the Word, God knows creatures, and this knowledge includes God's work of creation—a work that includes the entirety of the gift of being, inclusive of the attainment of creatures to their ultimate end of sharing in God's Trinitarian communion. As created through the Word, creatures express an intelligible ordering to the fulfilment of

---

[19] I–II, q. 93, a. 1. For discussion of 'eternal law' in Aquinas, see also J. Tonneau, OP, 'The Teaching of the Thomist Tract on Law', *The Thomist* 34 (1970): 13–83.

[20] Here Aquinas is in accord not only with Scripture but also, as one would expect, with the patristic tradition of theological reflection. Cf. Athanasius's *On the Incarnation*, trans. a Religious of CSMV (Crestwood, NY: St. Vladimir's Orthodox Theological Seminary, 1993), where Athanasius states that 'nothing in creation had erred from the path of God's purpose for it, save only man. Sun, moon, heaven, stars, water, air, none of these had swerved from their order, but, knowing the Word as their Maker and their King, remained as they were made' (§ 43, pp. 78–9).

[21] I, q. 34, a. 3; cf. I, q. 34, a. 3, ad 3. See Gilles Emery, OP, 'The Personal Mode of Trinitarian Action in Saint Thomas Aquinas', *The Thomist* 69 (2005): 31–77.

their being.[22] In God's own knowledge, this ordering is 'law'.[23] All creatures therefore manifest an intelligible order to the common good of the universe that has the character, in God's knowledge, of 'eternal law'.[24]

The union of law and love thus has a 'cosmic' reach: God's wisdom and love are absent nowhere. Some attention to God's providence may be helpful at this point. As Aquinas states, 'Two things belong to providence—namely, the type of the order of things foreordained towards an end; and the execution of this order, which is called government. As regards the first of these, God has immediate providence over everything, because He has in His intellect the types of everything, even the smallest; and whatsoever causes He assigns to certain effects, He gives them the power to produce those effects.'[25] In guiding all things to their ultimate end, he works through both necessary and free intermediary causes, and, most mysteriously, he permits defects.[26] It follows that 'all things partake somewhat of the eternal law, in so far as, namely, from its being imprinted on them, they derive their respective inclinations to their proper acts and ends'.[27] All creatures, including all non-rational things, are ordered by inclinations, proper acts, and ends to the end of the common good of the universe, God (the Creator and Redeemer).[28] However, while this participation of non-rational creatures in the ordering wisdom of

---

[22] See I, q. 45, aa. 6 and 7; I, q. 44, a. 1.

[23] For the analogous use of 'law', see e.g. Russell Hittinger, 'Natural Law as "Law" ', chapter 2 of his *The First Grace* (Wilmington, DE: ISI Books, 2003); idem, 'Yves R. Simon on Law, Nature, and Practical Reason', in *Acquaintance with the Absolute*, ed. Anthony O. Simon (New York: Fordham University Press, 1998), 101–27, at 123–7; Stephen L. Brock, 'The Legal Character of Natural Law According to St. Thomas Aquinas' (Ph.D. diss., University of Toronto, 1988).

[24] I–II, q. 91, a. 1.   [25] I, q. 22, a. 3.

[26] Cf. I, q. 22, a. 2, especially ad 2; I, q. 22, a. 4. Cf. Patrick Lee, 'The Goodness of Creation, Evil, and Christian Teaching', *The Thomist* 64 (2000): 239–69.

[27] I–II, q. 91, a. 2. For further discussion, see Romanus Cessario, *Introduction to Moral Theology*, 81–2. As regards the human person, the ontological imprint of the eternal law, apprehended by human reason as true and at the practical level as regarding operation or action, can be received as 'law' because human beings are rational. But the imprint involves the entire body–soul person.

[28] For further discussion, see Oliva Blanchette, *The Perfection of the Universe according to Aquinas: A Teleological Cosmology* (University Park, PA: Pennsylvania State University Press, 1992); cf. I–II, q. 91, a. 2, ad 3; I–II, q. 91, a. 4, obj. 3; I–II, q. 91, a. 2.

God is 'law-like', this ordering is not *received* by such creatures as law: because, as we have already observed in earlier chapters, law in this proper sense requires mind.[29] Thus although St Paul, for instance, speaks of a 'law in my members', this sense of 'law' is analogous and denotes that 'law is in all those things that are inclined to something by reason of some law: so that any inclination arising from a law, may be called a law, not essentially but by participation as it were'.[30]

A Participation in the Eternal Law

As we have seen in earlier chapters, natural law properly refers to *rational* creatures' participation according to a rational mode in this eternal law. What kind of participation is this? Recall that Aquinas holds that only the whole people or someone who governs the whole people can make a law, because a law is ordered to the common good. Private persons cannot make law. Yet, referring in the *Summa Theologiae* to Romans 2:14—'when the Gentiles, who have not the law, do by nature those things that are of the law... they are a law to themselves'—Aquinas affirms that law is nonetheless *in* private persons: 'a law is in a person not only as in one that rules, but also by participation as in one that is ruled. In the latter way each one is a law to himself, in so far as he shares the direction that he receives from one who rules him.'[31] Each human being, then, receives direction *and* shares directive authority. The 'participation' here involves 'one that is ruled', and so this emphasizes being ruled by another. Yet the person who is being ruled is also able to be 'a law to himself'. Let us ask again: does this mean active self-rule, in which one establishes the law oneself, albeit through participation in another's rule? Or does it mean a more passive self-rule, consciously and intelligently receiving a law from 'outside' oneself that one does not constitute?

With regard to this question, Aquinas teaches that law can be in a human being in two ways. Law can be in a human ruler 'as in him that rules and measures'.[32] Natural law is not in human

---

[29] I–II, q. 90, a. 1.   [30] I–II, q. 90, a. 1, ad 1; cf. I–II, q. 91, a. 6.
[31] I–II, q. 90, a. 3, ad 1.   [32] I–II, q. 91, a. 2.

beings in this way. God, not human beings, rules and measures in natural law. As Aquinas states, 'The natural law is promulgated by the very fact that God instilled it into man's mind so as to be known by him naturally.'[33] Properly speaking, then, God promulgates natural law by creating human reason with its 'imprint' of the eternal law; human practical reason can be said to promulgate natural law only in a derivative and attenuated sense:[34] in so far as human reason is first ruled and measured by the governing wisdom of God, it can then serve well as the rule and measure of human action. Natural law is 'nothing else than an imprint on us of the Divine light'.[35] The difference between an anthropocentric and a theocentric account of natural law can be seen in Daniel Westberg's remark,

> Aquinas states that the fact that the human reason regulates the will, by which the will's goodness is measured, derives from the eternal law which is the divine reason. It is instructive that in explaining this and referring to Psalm 54.6 Thomas does not say that we have this light when we know the rules for human action, but that the light of this reason is in us to the extent that it shows to us good things, and regulates our will. When we know and desire the proper *fines* of human life, then we share in the light of the eternal law.[36]

The promulgation is God's work of imprinting upon the human person. As Aquinas observes regarding the promulgation of the eternal law: 'Promulgation is made by word of mouth or in writing; and in both ways the eternal law is promulgated: because both the Divine Word and the writing of the Book of Life are eternal. But the promulgation cannot be from eternity on the part of the

---

[33] I–II, q. 90, a. 4, ad 1. Aquinas affirms that 'no one can know the eternal law, as it is in itself, except the blessed who see God in His essence. But every rational creature knows it in its reflection, greater or less. For every knowledge of truth is a kind of reflection and participation of the eternal law, which is the unchangeable truth, as Augustine says (*De Vera Relig.* xxxi). Now all men know the truth to a certain extent, at least as to the common principles of the natural law' (I–II, q. 93, a. 2).

[34] Aquinas states, 'Human reason is not, of itself, the rule of things: but the principles impressed on it by nature, are general rules and measures of all things relating to human conduct, whereof the natural reason is the rule and measure, although it is not the measure of things that are from nature' (I–II, q. 91, a. 2, ad 3).

[35] I–II, q. 91, a. 2.

[36] Westberg, 'The Relation of Law and Practical Reason in Aquinas', 288.

creature that hears or reads.'[37] One way of 'hearing' the divine Word in the temporal order is through human reason. God bestows, or promulgates as law, the rational creature's 'share of the Eternal Reason, whereby it has a natural inclination to its proper act and end'.[38] As we remarked in the previous chapter, this rational participation is by no means separated from the natural inclinations of the human person.[39] This is true both because some of these natural inclinations are rational, and also because the inclinations that pertain to human bodiliness are *human*, since in the human composite the form (the human soul) aptly disposes the matter. It is not a case of a human soul *moving* a merely and separately animal body.[40]

Receptive and Active Rationality

Aquinas teaches, then, that natural law is in human beings by participation in the lawgiver's 'rule or measure', that is, by participation in the eternal law. As already indicated, this participation is both passive (or receptive) and active, with the active participation being founded upon the prior passive participation through the metaphysical constitution of powers, inclinations, and ends. With respect to human beings' passive participation in the eternal law, Aquinas appeals to a psalm:

Hence the Psalmist after saying (Ps. iv. 6): *Offer up the sacrifice of justice*, as though someone asked what the works of justice are, adds: *Many say, Who showeth us good things?* in answer to which question he says: *The light of Thy countenance, O Lord, is signed upon us*: thus implying that the light of natural

---

[37] I–II, q. 91, a. 1, ad 2.   [38] I–II, q. 91, a. 2.

[39] As Cessario notes, 'Natural law inclinations set in motion the active use of human reasoning powers...' (*Introduction to Moral Theology*, 93).

[40] Cf. the overviews provided in Benedict M. Ashley, OP, *Theologies of the Body: Humanist and Christian* (Boston, MA: Pope John XXIII Center, 1985). See also Ashley's account of natural law in terms of the hierarchically ordered 'basic needs' required for human flourishing: Ashley, 'The Anthropological Foundations of the Natural Law: A Thomistic Engagement with Modern Science', in *St. Thomas Aquinas and the Natural Law Tradition: Contemporary Perspectives*, ed. John Goyette, Mark S. Latkovic, and Richard S. Myers (Washington, DC: Catholic University of America Press, 2004), 3–16.

reason, whereby we discern what is good and what is evil, which is the function of the natural law, is nothing else than an imprint on us of the Divine light.[41]

The participatory character of natural law flows metaphysically from the fact that human reason is the 'imprint' of the divine Word. Natural law, Aquinas states, is *not* 'something different from the eternal law.'[42] As he observes, 'All law proceeds from the reason and will of the lawgiver; the Divine and natural laws from the reasonable will of God; the human law from the will of man, regulated by reason.'[43] We see here ever more deeply the radical theocentricity of Aquinas's account of natural law, made possible by his understanding of the non-competitive relationship between God and creatures, a relationship in which creatures are finite created modes of participating in the Creator God.[44]

With respect to human beings' active participation, since God's law is received in the rational creature according to a rational mode, human practical reason apprehends the natural law, beginning with the first self-evident principle or precept of the natural law, 'good is to be done and pursued, and evil is to be avoided'. As Aquinas states, 'All other precepts of the natural law are based upon this: so that whatever the practical reason naturally apprehends as man's good (or evil) belongs to the precepts of the natural law as something to be done or avoided.'[45] Because the first principles of natural law are self-evident,

---

[41] I–II, q. 91, a. 2. This text serves also as the ground for divine illumination theories of knowledge flowing from Augustine. Aquinas differs from his Franciscan contemporaries in this regard by holding that the imprint remains on the ontological level, not on the epistemological level. See Steven P. Marrone, *The Light of Thy Countenance: Science and Knowledge of God in the Thirteenth Century* (Leiden: Brill, 2000).

[42] I–II, q. 91, a. 2, ad 1.

[43] I–II, q. 97, a. 3. That this passive participation in the eternal law has not received sufficient attention recently (with notable exceptions) is in large part due to the work of scholars who read Aquinas's treatise on law, as Ralph McInerny puts it, 'in such a way that its dependence on what has gone before [the earlier questions of the *Summa Theologiae*] is overlooked or misunderstood. Seeing it in conjunction with the preceding, one is struck by the backward references, the link-ups, the continuity of the discussion with its prologue' (McInerny, *Aquinas on Human Action*, 109).

[44] See e.g. the essays in David B. Burrell, CSC, *Faith and Freedom: An Interfaith Perspective* (Oxford: Blackwell, 2004).

[45] I–II, q. 94, a. 2.

Aquinas can say that every human being knows the eternal law to some degree, because 'every knowledge of truth is a kind of reflection and participation of the eternal law', and all human beings 'know the truth to a certain extent, at least as to the common principles of the natural law'.[46]

In addition, because the apprehension of the good to be pursued requires speculative apprehension of the good as existing, human practical reason cannot here be separated from speculative reason.[47] We cannot do without the full range of human knowing. Given that law is 'a rule and measure of acts'[48] and 'a dictate

---

[46] I–II, q. 93, a. 2.

[47] Steven Long makes this point in response to the 'new natural law theory' of Germain Grisez and John Finnis: 'While the speculative intellect is ordered simply to the consideration of truth, *practical* knowledge adds a *further orientation toward operation.* Inasmuch as the practical intellect knows truth "just as the speculative" but is distinct from the speculative only in "directing the known truth to operation", it would appear that the notion of a truth with no speculative content whatsoever is alien to the thought of Aquinas: a contradiction in terms ... The new natural-law theorists confuse the truth that certain propositions by their nature bear essentially upon action—and hence are practical—with the distinct character of the knowing that is *presupposed by* such propositions *in order that they may be able to bear upon action.* That a certain proposition refers essentially to operation depends on prior *adequatio* regarding the nature of the end. The speculative considered precisively and formally is simply the knowing of an object apart from any accident of desire it may spark. The known object may accidentally (from the vantage of speculation) spark desire, and in doing so cause a new and rationally distinct practical engagement with the object. In this practical engagement the object is sought no longer simply for the sake of knowing it but as the terminus of desire and operation. Nonetheless at root this practical knowing is speculatively adequated' because 'rationally to desire a good is already to have been speculatively adequated to its truth. Thus the practical employment of the intelligence requires a prior speculative apprehension of the object. *This priority of speculative adequatio governs intellectual knowledge as such: speculative adequation is not something that can be temporarily left behind, only to be reconnected to later*' (Steven A. Long, 'Natural Law or Autonomous Practical Reason: Problems for the New Natural Law Theory', 169–71). Long adds that '*the chief point* is rather that at the font of practical knowing necessarily lies the adequation of the intellect to the real that is presupposed by truth as such and hence also by practical knowing. This is a prior speculative knowledge of the end that (owing to our appetitive and volitional natures) ignites our desire and the ensuing essentially practical deliberations. *Whereas purely speculative knowledge of practical objects is possible, practical reason is necessarily indebted to speculative reason in the adequation of mind to the good that is necessary if there is to be right appetite of the end*' (173).

[48] I–II, q. 90, a. 1.

of practical reason',[49] law, as the measure for action, is *practical*, ordered to action. Law properly regards 'the relationship to universal happiness'[50]—the common good, ultimately God himself. On these very grounds, however, the practical reason's knowing of the natural law would not be possible without the basic operation of speculative reason. This is so because practical reasoning cannot get going without the speculative apprehension of the human person's ends *qua* existing ends. From this speculative knowledge of existing ends, of the human teleological ordering that draws and attracts the will, appetition arises as the necessary root of *practical* reasoning or reasoning ordered to action.

In short, even though practical reasoning is distinct from, and in this sense not derived from, speculative reasoning, ontologically the former derives from the latter. The speculative knowledge of 'being' and 'true' is prior to and essential for the knowledge of 'good': an ordered teleology makes possible right reason's *practical* apprehension of the ends that elicit particular human actions. For instance, the preservation of one's life is desired and known operatively not only in itself but also for other higher ends, such as virtue, wisdom, and communion with God.[51] Thus in apprehending the existence of goods or ends perfective of the human person—including self-preservation, preservation of the species through procreation and education, life in society, and to know truth—human reason must apprehend the good or end within an ordered hierarchy in order to know the good or end in a practical way. Our rational pursuit of goods follows upon our apprehension of their degree of being.

---

[49] I–II, q. 91, a. 3; cf. I–II, q. 92, a. 2: 'a law is a dictate of reason, commanding something'.

[50] I–II, q. 90, a. 2.

[51] The practical reason does not need to humanize or bestow intelligibility upon a set of 'purely natural' bodily inclinations, because the entire *humanum* is ordered hierarchically toward the end of the human person, union with God. Aquinas makes clear that there is no tension between human nature as regards that 'which is common to man and other animals' and human nature as regards 'that which is proper to man', i.e. human reason (I–II, q. 94, a. 3, ad 2). If a particular act is truly 'against nature', understood as bodily nature, it is also against reason, because the soul is the form of the body and the body manifests the divine creative intelligibility in which the soul participates. For biblical warrants for this position, one might see the study of St Paul's theology of the body by Karl Olav Sandnes, *Belly and Body in the Pauline Epistles* (Cambridge: Cambridge University Press, 2002).

The first aspect of rationality is therefore fundamentally receptive rather than active; reason discerns rather than constitutes a God-given hierarchical and teleological ordering of the human person. Reason ordered to action knows (receptively rather than constitutively) the principles of natural law because of reason's participation in this God-given teleological ordering of the human person. These self-evident principles of the natural law serve in the practical reasoning the same purpose as that served by universal propositions (such as the whole is greater than the part) in the speculative reason.[52] The principles of natural law are foundational for any conclusion of practical reasoning: 'Accordingly the first direction of our acts to their end must be in virtue of the natural law.'[53] Applying and extending the precepts of natural law in particular cases of deliberation about action, however, requires the virtues, above all prudence.[54]

Order or Disorder?

As a wise ordering, natural law is not *arbitrary*, not mere power, but serves the work of love. Without wisdom, human beings cannot achieve actions that manifest love, but rather can only exercise power. Yet, Aquinas does not deny the tension that persists, in this life, between our understanding of 'law' and our desire for perfect love. It is clear to Aquinas that human sin has obscured the light of reason in human beings. This darkening of reason distorts human participation in the eternal law with respect to the ordering of human action to the common good, since the darkening of reason by sin makes it difficult for human beings to apply the principles of natural law and to formulate just human laws.[55] Here there is indeed a tension between 'law' and the aspirations of love. So is Kahn right after all?

We might ask in this regard: Is it meaningful to speak of an ordered 'eternal law' after sin? If sinful human beings freely rebel against God's law, have they not overturned the order of God's eternal law, won a measure of autonomy, and placed 'law' forever in opposition to

---

[52] I–II, q. 90, a. 1, ad 2; cf. I–II, q. 94, a. 2.   [53] I–II, q. 91, a. 2, ad 2.
[54] Cf. I–II, q. 94, a. 3.   [55] See I–II, q. 93, a. 3, ad 2.

divine love? Obviously, as Aquinas says, 'the good are perfectly subject to the eternal law, as always acting according to it'.[56] But rational creatures who, participating in God's eternal law (the 'natural law'), freely reject God's ordering of human actions to the common good, and impose a different ordering of human acts, seem to have escaped from God's ordering and to have succeeded in constituting their own ordering. Is this tension, in its apparent separation of 'law' and 'love', permanent?

Aquinas observes that the constitution of a rebellious ordering involves two levels: a darkening of the person's knowing of the eternal law coincides with a darkening, though not an elimination, of the person's natural inclination 'to that which is in harmony with the eternal law'.[57] Human beings are teleologically constituted to pursue good rather than evil, an inclination that coincides with the soul's capacity for knowledge. This inclination cannot be destroyed, but it can be darkened.[58] In non-rational animals disorder could only involve a darkening of the inclination to pursue good rather than evil. In the human person, given the distinction between knowledge and inclination, the disorder is twofold, although the two aspects go together due to the hylomorphic participation of the body in the soul.

This twofold disorder, however, does not dissolve human beings' subjection to the eternal law. Rather than granting that sinners experience 'autonomy', Aquinas remarks upon the sad punishment that sinners experience in and through their sins. As he states, 'the wicked are subject to the eternal law, imperfectly as to their actions, indeed, since both their knowledge of good, and their inclination thereto, are imperfect; but this imperfection on the part of action is supplied on the part of passion, in so far as they suffer what the eternal law decrees concerning them, according as they fail to act in harmony with that law'.[59] In rebelling against God's wisdom and rejecting his goodness, sinners are ordered to God by his justice. This penalty of sin is already

---

[56] I–II, q. 93, a. 6.

[57] I–II, q. 93, a. 6. On this darkening, see Cessario, *Introduction to Moral Theology*, 98–9. See also Russell Hittinger's presentation of John Paul II's discussion of natural law in *Veritatis Splendor* in Hittinger, *The First Grace*, 32.

[58] I–II, q. 93, a. 6, ad 2.   [59] I–II, q. 93, a. 6.

intrinsic to the sin, because in forfeiting one's own fulfilment, one suffers.[60]

In this view, then, love too is not a 'lawless' reality. Love requires fulfilling the law of justice toward God and one's neighbour. For its part 'law', in its deepest sense, is nothing less than love: to follow God's law is to love. In God's eternal law, therefore, disorder is already caught up within the *order* of love, and is experienced as a privation within that order.

Were we to stop here, however, we would not yet have reached the full manifestation of God's 'law' of love. We have merely arrived again, with somewhat more understanding, at the question with which we began this chapter: how does the *natural* law relate to *supernatural* charity? Now that we have firmly established the theocentric and receptive character of 'natural law', the next step in identifying the relationship between law and love is to enquire into the Pauline biblical passages that, as Kahn observes, appear to rule out any relationship at all.

Aquinas on Galatians 5:18 and Romans 8:14

Does not St Paul say that those who truly love, go beyond the limits of 'law'? Kahn quotes Romans 7:4, 'My brethren, you have died to the law through the body of Christ', and Galatians 3:10, 'For all who rely on works of law are under a curse.' Aquinas takes a very similar text, Galatians 5:18: 'If you are led by the spirit you are not under the law'.[61] He observes that Paul affirms in Romans 8:14 that the just, those who have become adopted sons in the Son, are led by the Holy Spirit; and thus it seems that the just are not 'under the law'. Is there in fact a biblical disjunction between law and love, the former Jewish and the latter Christian, a disjunction which would necessarily refute Aquinas's attempt to exhibit the unity of law and love?

---

[60] The eternal law thus includes the penalty of damnation (see ibid., ad 3), although why God, who is infinite wisdom and goodness, permits some rational creatures to reject their proper end is known only by the blessed in heaven who contemplate God's wise and good eternal law.

[61] I–II, q. 93, a. 6, obj. 1.

Aquinas interprets Galatians 5:18 through the lens of Romans 8:14, and he offers two interpretations. The first way in particular speaks to Kahn's understanding of law as primarily something that constrains and restricts human beings. Human beings as sinners inevitably at times experience 'law', even wise law, as something to fear and despise. Law plays this seemingly oppressive role when we, in our hearts, are rebels against the law. What impact then does love have upon this experience of law? Drawing upon Romans 8:14, Aquinas states, 'In this way the spiritual man is not under the law, because he fulfills the law willingly, through charity.'[62] Since God is love, God's eternal law for the right ordering of our actions toward the common good is fulfilled when we love God and, in God, love one another. Far from there being an ultimate tension between love and law, love fulfils the law. Paul in fact says exactly this: 'love is the fulfilling of the law' (Rom. 13:10). God's law, in its directives for just behaviour toward God and neighbour, mandates *ecstasis*, self-giving love. Aquinas explains elsewhere that 'the chief intention of the Divine law is to establish man in friendship with God. Now since likeness is the reason of love ... there cannot possibly be any friendship of man to God, Who is supremely good, unless man become good.'[63] Just as God is supremely self-diffusive Good, so also human beings must become 'ecstatic' or self-giving: we must give ourselves to God, and receive all from him, with a childlike dependence and trust. In this way, the virtue of charity enables human beings to fulfil the law's 'chief intention'.

If friendship with God is divine law's 'chief intention', however, why doesn't God command love in the Decalogue? Aquinas argues that the 'very dictate of natural reason' makes 'so evident as to need no promulgation' the precepts of love of neighbour and love of God.[64] We do not need to be *commanded* to know that the greatest Good, God, is most lovable, and that our fellow human beings, as God's creatures, should be loved. Having said this, Aquinas also recognizes that the Torah does command the love of God and neighbour, although not in the Decalogue.[65] Without love, one can fulfil in a limited sense individual precepts of the law; for instance, one can honour one's parents out of duty rather than love. But since it belongs

[62] I–II, q. 93, a. 6, ad 1.   [63] I–II, q. 99, a. 2.
[64] I–II, q. 100, a. 11.   [65] I–II, q. 100, a. 10.

to the natural law that human beings love God above all else and the neighbour in God, without love one cannot fulfil the natural law. Furthermore, without the grace of the Holy Spirit, human beings after original sin lack even this naturally ordered love of God. In the supernatural order that God has freely given in Christ and the Holy Spirit, charity enables human beings not only to love God but to attain true *friendship* with God as adopted sons and daughters in the Son.

Having resolved the problem raised by Galatians 5:18 in this manner, Aquinas offers a second possible interpretation. He affirms that when the Holy Spirit transforms our will so as to enable us to fulfil God's law willingly, our good actions are not constituted by our natural will aided by the Holy Spirit. Rather, the Holy Spirit truly transforms the will so as to make it capable of supernatural action whose object, in 'ecstatic' charity, is none other than the triune God himself. The graced will differs from the merely natural will, in that the person is now able to attain to communion with the Trinity. Our good actions are thus owed to the Holy Spirit; we ultimately have not ourselves to thank, but God. In this theocentric vein Aquinas points out that Galatians 5:18 'can be understood as meaning that the works of a man, who is led by the Holy Spirit, are the works of the Holy Spirit rather than his own. Therefore, since the Holy Spirit is not under the law ... it follows that such works, in so far as they are of the Holy Spirit, are not under the law.'[66] Put another way, God is not 'under' the eternal law; God is the eternal law.[67]

Even if St Paul sees no disjunction between love and law, however, we cannot yet move forward; we must ask whether 'law' really possesses a significant place in Christian ethics. It would seem clear that 'law' is linked more with the Old Testament, to be displaced by grace and faith in the New. Yet Aquinas suggests otherwise. He insists that we can speak of a unified 'divine law' that comprises Torah and Gospel, and he also speaks of the Gospel itself, not only the Torah, as a 'law'. Since this claim with respect to the

[66] I–II, q. 93, a. 6, ad 1. For further discussion of Aquinas on the Old Law, see also e.g. Ulrich Kühn, *Via Caritatis*, 163–91; J. P. M. van der Ploeg, OP, 'Le traité de saint Thomas de la loi ancienne', in *Lex et Libertas*, ed. Leo Elders, SVD, and K. Hedwig (Vatican City: Libreria Editrice Vaticana, 1987), 185–99.
[67] See I–II, q. 93, a. 4.

unity of 'divine law' has crucial implications for his integration of love and law, let us examine how he relates the Old Testament to the New.

One Divine 'Law'

In the divine law of the Torah, Aquinas suggests, three elements appear. First, one finds general moral precepts (the Decalogue) about right relationship with God and with neighbour; these precepts express right reason about how to relate justly to God and neighbour, and thus belong to the natural law as conclusions drawn from the first principles of the natural law.[68] Second, one finds specific laws about how Israel, in her particular time and place, is to relate justly to God in worship. These laws, which Aquinas terms 'ceremonial', are not universal but rather pertain to how Israel should instantiate, in her particular time and place, the moral law about right relationship with God. Third, one finds specific 'judicial' laws about political, economic, legal, and social relationships in Israel. Like the 'ceremonial' laws, these laws are not universal but pertain to how Israel should instantiate the moral law about right relationship between human beings (neighbours).

In Aquinas's view, then, the Torah is a pattern of divine wisdom, ordered to charity and intended to guide a particular nation, the Jewish people.[69] He explains that the Torah inculcates virtue because God's intention, expressed in Leviticus 19:2, is 'You shall be holy, for I the Lord your God am holy.'[70] In setting forth the pattern of right reason in moral action, and establishing laws for concretely instantiating this pattern in the daily worship of God and the human interactions of the people of Israel, the Torah, Aquinas says, is 'good' and in accord with reason.[71] In making this point Aquinas is agreeing with St Paul, whom Aquinas quotes: 'The Apostle says (Rom. vii. 12): *Wherefore the law indeed is holy, and the commandment holy, and just, and good*.'[72]

---

[68] See I–II, q. 100, aa. 1, 3.
[69] Cf. I–II, q. 100, a. 3, ad 1; cf. q. 100, a. 10; q. 99, a. 1. [70] I–II, q. 99, a. 2.
[71] I–II, q. 98, a. 1. [72] Ibid., *sed contra*.

If so, however, why does Paul (followed by Aquinas) refuse to grant that human beings can become righteous solely by following the Torah, the law that God gave Israel? If the law is God's gift and is good, why is something else needed for human righteousness, and is this 'something else' a rejection of restrictive 'law' in favour of ecstatic 'love'?

Drawing upon Pseudo-Dionysius, Aquinas observes that 'the good has various degrees'.[73] The Torah reveals God's wise plan for human action, but as the prophets make clear, the Torah itself is not the ultimate fulfilment of this plan. For Aquinas the 'divine law' is a unity composed of the Torah and the Gospel of Jesus Christ, from whom flows the grace of the Holy Spirit. Divine law is a unity because it reveals the *one* ultimate end, 'ecstatic' Trinitarian communion as children of God. The Torah instructs human beings about human action ordered to the end of dwelling with God, but it can only imperfectly lead human beings to this end. Therefore the Torah is a good but 'imperfect' law, because it cannot fully lead human beings to the ultimate end:

the end of Divine law is to bring man to that end which is everlasting happiness; which end is hindered by any sin, not only of external, but also of internal action. Consequently that which suffices for the perfection of human law, viz., the prohibition and punishment of sin, does not suffice for the perfection of the Divine law: but it is requisite that it should make man altogether fit to partake of everlasting happiness. Now this cannot be done save by the grace of the Holy Spirit, whereby *charity*, which fulfilleth the law ... *is spread abroad in our hearts* (Rom. v. 5): since *the grace of God is life everlasting* (*ibid.* vi. 23). But the Old Law could not confer this grace, for this was reserved to Christ; because, as it is written (Jo. i. 17), the law was given *by Moses, grace and truth came by Jesus Christ.* Consequently the Old Law was good indeed, but imperfect, according to Heb. vii. 19: *The law brought nothing to perfection.*[74]

As we have seen, for Aquinas '[l]aw is a rule and measure of acts, whereby man is induced to act or is restrained from acting',[75] and the goal of law is the common good because 'the first principle in

---

[73] I–II, q. 98, a. 1.

[74] Ibid. Cf. the reflections of Jean Gribomont, OSB, 'Le lien des deux testaments, selon la théologie de S. Thomas', *Ephemerides theologiae Lovanienses* 22 (1946): 70–89.

[75] I–II, q. 90, a. 1.

practical matters, which are the object of the practical reason, is the last end: and the last end of human life is bliss or happiness'.[76] As a good but imperfect body of law, the Torah needs something else to attain its own end.

What is needed, Aquinas teaches, is itself a 'law', though not a written law or one that can be understood as disjoined or isolated from the Torah.[77] Rather, the attainment of the end of the one divine law—the deepest possible participation, on earth, in God's eternal law—comes about through the fulfilment of the Torah. In accord with his theology of history, Aquinas envisions continuity and fulfilment, not a linear negation, even while some elements of the Torah are taken up and transformed within the fulfilment.[78] The 'end' of the one divine law is revealed fully only in the Torah's fulfilment. Aquinas explains, 'Man cannot fulfil all the precepts of the law, unless he fulfil the precept of charity, which is impossible without charity. Consequently it is not possible, as Pelagius maintained, for man to fulfil the law without grace.'[79] In the Torah's fulfilment, the four conditions of a perfect law are met: the 'law' of the grace of the Holy Spirit is the 'ordinance' of the divine Word who promulgates it; the ultimate common good (deification) of humankind is attained; human acts are internally directed 'according to the order of righteousness'; and obedience to the law is ensured.[80]

The Torah's fulfilment—the 'New Law' or the 'law of the New Testament'—is accomplished by Jesus Christ as Israel's true prophet, priest, and king. Citing Matthew 5:17–18, Aquinas observes that 'the

---

[76] I–II, q. 90, a. 2.

[77] Cf., for much of what follows, my *Christ's Fulfillment of Torah and Temple*. On the grounds that they have the same end and the same faith, Aquinas rejects the idea that the New Law and the Torah are 'diverse'. He points out that 'they both have the same end, namely, man's subjection to God; and there is but one God of the New and of the Old Testament, according to Rom. iii. 30: *It is one God that justifieth circumcision by faith, and uncircumcision through faith*' (I–II, q. 107, a. 1). As he affirms, 'The unity of faith under both Testaments witnesses to the unity of end' (ibid., ad 1). Rather than being diverse laws, they belong in distinct ways—as imperfect and perfect—to the same law.

[78] I–II, q. 91, a. 5.   [79] I–II, q. 100, a. 10, ad 3.

[80] I–II, q. 91, a. 5. For further discussion, see Laurent Sentis's excellent 'La lumière dont nous faisons usage. La règle de la raison et la loi divine selon Thomas d'Aquin', *Revue des sciences philosophiques et théologiques* 79 (1995): 49–69; Jean Tonneau, OP, 'The Teaching of the Thomist Tract on Law'.

end of every law is to make men righteous and virtuous' and that
the New Law accomplishes this, thereby fulfilling the end of the
Torah, 'by justifying men through the power of Christ's Passion'.[81]
He quotes Romans 8:3–4 in this regard: 'What the Law could not
do ... God sending His own Son in the likeness of sinful flesh ... hath
condemned sin in the flesh, that the justification of the Law might be
fulfilled in us.'[82] Human beings must participate, however, in what
Christ has accomplished. The fulfilment of the Torah in us, Aquinas
holds, comes about through 'the grace of the Holy Spirit, which is
given through faith in Christ. Consequently the New Law is chiefly the
grace itself of the Holy Spirit, which is given to those who believe in
Christ.'[83] The grace of the Holy Spirit enables the self-giving charity,
the radical *ecstasis*, that fulfils the law. Aquinas calls this grace of the
Holy Spirit the 'New Law'.

It might seem, however, that thus to call 'grace' a 'law' is again
to confuse the character of law with the character of love. Drawing
upon Augustine, Aquinas cites St Paul in this regard: '*Where is ... thy
boasting? It is excluded. By what law? Of works? No, but by the law of
faith* [Rom 3:27]: for he calls the grace itself of faith a *law*. And still
more clearly it is written (Rom. viii. 2): *The law of the spirit of life,
in Christ Jesus, hath delivered me from the law of sin and of death*.'[84]
Ultimately the source is Jeremiah 31:33, 'But this is the covenant
which I will make with the house of Israel after those days, says the
Lord: I will put my law within them, and I will write it upon their
hearts; and I will be their God, and they shall be my people.' On that
day, according to Jeremiah, each Israelite will know the Lord and will
receive the forgiveness of sins from the Creator (Jer. 31:34).[85] Aquinas
thus speaks with biblical warrant of the Torah's fulfilment as a 'New
Law', as 'in the first place a law that is written on our hearts',[86] the

---

[81] I–II, q. 107, a. 2.   [82] Ibid.   [83] I–II, q. 106, a. 1.   [84] Ibid.

[85] Like Bonaventure, Aquinas argues against those such as Joachim of Fiore who
suppose that the Holy Spirit was not fully given to the apostolic Church and therefore
imagine that the New Law will be displaced before the end of the world. Certainly
the heavenly beatific vision will fulfil the New Law just as the New Law fulfilled the
Torah, and indeed infinitely more so. Before the heavenly beatific vision, however, the
New Law is perfect, because by the New Law we already enjoy a foretaste of heavenly
communion. See I–II, q. 106, a. 4, ad 2.

[86] I–II, q. 106, a. 1. See also Galatians 6:2, 'Bear one another's burdens, and in
this way you will fulfil the law of Christ'; cf. Graham Stanton, 'What Is the Law of

law of the grace of the Holy Spirit who, uniting us in faith to Christ, conforms us to right reason and enables us to fulfil the moral law in charity whereby we attain our ultimate end. Certainly the New Law also contains written teachings that are requisite to the life of grace, but Aquinas points out that these teachings, while necessary, could not in themselves serve as an efficacious 'rule and measure of acts'. He emphasizes on the contrary that 'the letter, even of the Gospel would kill, unless there were the inward presence of the healing grace of faith'.[87] The New Law enables *ecstasis* and thus likens human beings, in Christ and by the Holy Spirit, to the Trinity. As Paul says, 'When we cry, "Abba! Father!" it is the Spirit himself bearing witness with our spirit that we are children of God, and if children, then heirs, heirs of God and fellow heirs with Christ, provided we suffer with him in order that we may also be glorified with him.... [T]he creation itself will be set free from its bondage to decay and obtain the glorious liberty of the children of God' (Rom. 8:15–17, 21).

Does Aquinas's account of divine law mean that before the coming of Christ, all human beings, including those in Israel who knew the Torah, did not possess the grace of the Holy Spirit? Does charitable *ecstasis* appear on the scene only at Pentecost? Appealing to his doctrine of 'implicit' faith, Aquinas consistently answers no. He insists that persons of all times and places have belonged, through faith in God's providential and saving will, to the New Law of grace.[88] Thus a strictly 'linear' account of human history, where the temporal separation of the Old Law and the New Law is absolute and insurmountable, will not do. Yet neither should one downplay the aspect of fulfilment in Christ and his Spirit (Pentecost), as if this fulfilment did not, despite the ongoing apparent reign of sin, unleash

---

Christ?' *Ex Auditu* 17 (2001): 47–59. Among the Fathers, Stanton treats Justin Martyr, who sees Christ as the 'new lawgiver'. Stanton also attends to the statue of Christ as lawgiver in the thirteenth-century Chartres Cathedral. Stanton notes, 'Luther, Zwingli and Calvin wrote extensively on the Sermon on the Mount as "the law of Christ" ' (50). For Luther, ' "The Law of Christ is the law of love" ' (54). Stanton summarizes his own viewpoint: 'What is the law of Christ? *In Gal 6:2 it is the law of Moses redefined by Christ, with the "love commandment" and "carrying the burdens of others" as its essence; it is fulfilled by Christ in his own self-giving love*' (56).

[87] I–II, q. 106, a. 2.

[88] See I–II, q. 106, a. 1, ad 3; I–II, q. 106, a. 3, ad 2; I–II, q. 107, a. 1, ad 2; and elsewhere.

in the world great faith, hope, and love, mediated sacramentally by the Church as Christ's Mystical Body, the People of God with Christ as her King.

All is reconfigured around Christ, the Messiah of Israel. This reconfiguring is not a negation but a consummation of Israel's sacrificial and communal identity, which continues to participate in its divine fulfilment. In Christ, we see law and love perfectly united.

Natural Law after the Revelation of Divine Law

It might appear that we have reached our conclusion, and in a sense we have; but our answer risks going too far and making irrelevant the very discussion of natural law that has been at the centre of this book. The theology of history sketched above might seem to elevate the divine law to such a degree that our question—whether love and law are in tension—has now been answered simply by changing the subject away from 'natural law' and 'eternal law'. Indeed given the concrete historical gift of divine law, why should Christian ethics continue to discuss natural law and eternal law?[89] Put succinctly, as Graham McAleer helps us to see, natural law and eternal law express the *ecstasis* inscribed in the created order, which is superabundantly fulfilled by grace. Natural law is not done away with by grace, as if God no longer draws us to himself by means of the created order. The divine law—the Torah and its fulfilment by the Gospel—should not be set in opposition to the eternal law, as if the eternal law were God's 'natural' plan and the divine law God's 'supernatural' plan.

---

[89]   Appealing to 'story' (as does Richard B. Hays, who as we saw is also influenced by Barth), Stanley Hauerwas writes, 'Do I mean to defend a Christian ethic that stresses redemption and grace as in essential discontinuity with creation and nature? Decidedly no! God has never been other than a saving God. That is as true of God as creator as it is of God as redeemer. By emphasizing the narrative character of our knowledge of God I mean to remind us that we do not know what it means to call God creator or redeemer apart from the story of his activity with Israel and Jesus. The language of creation and redemption, nature and grace, is a secondary theological language, that is sometimes mistaken for the story itself. "Creation" and "redemption" should be taken for what they are namely ways of helping us tell and hear the story rightly' (Hauerwas, *The Peaceable Kingdom: A Primer in Christian Ethics* (Notre Dame, IN: University of Notre Dame Press, 1983): 62–3). The question perhaps is how metaphysics and 'story' relate to each other. What is meant by 'the story itself'?

Indeed, for Aquinas the eternal law ultimately has a certain 'primacy', since the divine law is ordained for the achievement of the Trinity's eternal wise ordering (the eternal law). Aquinas's insistence that God's Trinitarian life, not the economy of salvation, be at the centre is one more instance of his profound theocentrism. Yet the divine law has its own 'primacy' in the sense that it alone, in history, reveals the glorious depths of the eternal law. As God's eternal knowledge of his governance of creatures to their ultimate end, the eternal law is promulgated in the begetting of the divine Word. The eternal law is God's wisdom as regards creatures, and this wisdom is not different from God's creative Word.[90] Thus the divine law is that 'whereby man shares more perfectly in the eternal law'.[91] The eternal law itself, in other words, includes the elements of the revealed divine law: God, in his knowledge of his plan for the governance of his creatures to their common good (ecstatic Trinitarian communion as children of God), knows from eternity the mystery of Christ and the sending of the Holy Spirit.

Similarly, the divine law includes the natural law. Aquinas affirms that the Torah and the Gospel contain 'whatever belongs to the natural law'.[92] Admittedly, this affirmation might seem problematic. If the natural law is our participation by our natural powers in God's eternal law for human fulfilment, would not the revealed Christological ultimate end cancel out any meaningful participation that our natural powers could have enjoyed, now that human fulfilment is seen to be *supernatural*? The answer is no because God's revealed ordering still has *God* as the human 'end', even though now supernatural *friendship* with God. This radicalizing of the 'end' does not do away with natural teleology, but rather intensifies it and makes it all the more relevant.

This point undergirds Aquinas's understanding of the place of the natural law within divine law. Aquinas states, 'The Old Law showed forth the precepts of the natural law, and added certain precepts of its

---

[90] See I–II, q. 93, a. 1, especially ad 2.   [91] I–II, q. 91, a. 4, ad 1.

[92] I–II, q. 94, a. 5. Aquinas thus sees no reason to approach natural law doctrine solely through philosophical resources. On this point see e.g. Philippe Delhaye, 'La "loi nouvelle" dans l'enseignement de s. Thomas', in *San Tommaso e la filosofia del diritto oggi*, ed. Pontificia Accademia Romana di San Tommaso d'Aquino (Vatican City: Libreria Editrice Vaticana, 1975), 73–103, at 88–9.

own. Accordingly, as to those precepts of the natural law contained in the Old Law, all were bound to observe the Old Law; not because they belonged to the Old Law, but because they belonged to the natural law.'[93] He affirms that, in various ways, all the 'moral precepts' of the Torah, when properly understood, belong to the natural law.[94] These moral precepts were binding not only upon the Jews to whom they had been revealed, but also upon all human beings, because these moral precepts of the natural law belong inextricably to the 'ecstatic' pattern of human fulfilment.

The Torah contains precepts of the natural law not only in the Decalogue, but also elsewhere. The general principles of the natural law, 'as, for instance, that one should do evil to no man, and other similar principles' such as the duty to love God and to love neighbour, are not directly found in the Decalogue but are found elsewhere in the Torah (and the Gospel).[95] Regarding these general principles Aquinas notes, however, that they are in a certain sense present in the Decalogue 'as principles in their proximate conclusions'.[96] The Decalogue also directly contains precepts of the natural law: 'there are certain things which the natural reason of every man, of its own accord and at once, judges to be done or not to be done: e.g., *Honor thy father and thy mother*, and, *Thou shalt not kill, Thou shalt not steal*: and these belong to the law of nature absolutely.'[97] In addition the Decalogue contains precepts of the natural law that, as requiring more reasoning to apprehend the injustice involved, expose human beings' need for divine teaching. Among these Aquinas cites 'Thou shalt not make to thyself a graven thing, nor the likeness of anything; thou shalt not take the name of the Lord thy God in vain.'[98]

The coming of Christ does not abrogate these precepts of the natural law. While the precepts now have their meaning within the revealed ordination of human beings to Trinitarian communion, and thus can be said to be transformed since they now engage a supernatural end, the content of the precepts remains the same. Why so? Would not the radical *ecstasis* of Trinitarian communion call for a new understanding of basic moral precepts? The answer is that

---

[93] I–II, q. 98, a. 5.   [94] I–II, q. 100, a. 1.
[95] See I–II, q. 100, a. 3, especially ad 1.   [96] I–II, q. 100, a. 3.
[97] I–II, q. 100, a. 1.   [98] Ibid.

human beings, precisely in order to be 'ecstatic' or self-giving rather than self-aggrandizing, must not deliberately kill the innocent, steal, commit adultery, lie, worship idols, and so forth.[99] These actions, as human reason knows through its natural receptive participation in God's wise ordering, do not conduce to human perfection: they are selfish actions that incline the person inward, rather than ecstatic actions that open the person to spiritual communion. The revelation of our ultimate end—the end that animates the whole divine law as the intention of the Lawgiver—does not make superfluous human participation in the eternal law by means of the natural capacities of reason. Aquinas remarks, 'For just as grace presupposes nature, so must the Divine law presuppose the natural law.'[100]

Not Natural Law Alone

But at this stage the opposite question arises: If 'ecstasis' is already grounded in natural law, would Christian moral reflection in fact consistently need to advert to 'divine law' or to hold that natural law rests upon a doctrine of eternal law?[101] I have suggested in previous chapters that lacking an orderer of all things who himself is radically

---

[99] The difference between 'natural law doctrine' and 'natural law' is here again evident. The precepts of natural law are recognized as true by many who would reject natural law doctrine. Here I agree with the critique of Stephen Macedo's *Liberal Virtues* (Oxford: Clarendon Press, 1990) offered by Robert P. George and Christopher Wolfe, 'Natural Law and Public Reason', in *Natural Law and Public Reason*, ed. Robert P. George and Christopher Wolfe (Washington, DC: Georgetown University Press, 2000), 51–74.

[100] I–II, q. 99, a. 2, ad 1.

[101] Thus John Finnis thinks it possible to present a full-scale account of natural law without reference to God's eternal law: see Finnis, *Natural Law and Natural Rights* (Oxford: Oxford University Press, 1980), Part II. Finnis's approach makes the doctrine of the eternal law tangential to the doctrine of the natural law except in so far as one might wish to probe toward the 'creative uncaused causality' (402) that may, and in Finnis's view does, lie behind natural law. Finnis assumes, in short, that one can begin with the human practical reasoner and arrive at the elements of natural law doctrine, whereas Aquinas's theocentric natural law doctrine moves in the other direction, beginning from the Creator God's providence (as the 'end' that draws the human being). This does not mean that Finnis considers the questions of God's existence and providence to be unimportant, although he does think that what can be known of God by natural reason cannot firmly establish natural law doctrine, which remains grounded for Finnis upon human subjectivity (405).

not among the ordered things—that is to say the Creator God's existence and providence—even very sophisticated contemporary efforts to describe natural 'law' (without a Lawgiver) cannot escape the charge of constructing and imposing preferences. But could not natural law doctrine sidestep this problem by proposing that there are certain precepts that, whether or not a Lawgiver exists, clearly belong to the pursuit of fundamental human goods, such as the command not to murder other people?

We should ask again, therefore, whether 'eternal law' and 'divine law' are necessary for natural law doctrine, or whether natural law doctrine can and should bracket these realities. Against fideism, Aquinas repeatedly affirms that 'the first general precepts of the natural law are self-evident to a subject having natural reason, and need no promulgation'.[102] He also observes that 'the precepts of the decalogue [as proximate conclusions from the self-evident principles] are such as the mind of man is ready to grasp at once'.[103] In a significant sense, then, Aquinas is optimistic about human reason's ability to perceive the divine ordering of human action toward human fulfilment. His optimism, however, stems from his view that reason is a participation in God, rather than an autonomous zone.[104] Here, I think, he parts ways with natural law theorists who propose to bracket or exclude the eternal law.

In addition, Aquinas warns that while sin cannot obscure the general principles of the natural law, it may prevent one from knowing conclusions that belong to the natural law.[105] The general principles, while unobscured by sin, may not be of much help when it comes to their application in particular actions. Even a general principle of the natural law may be obscured as regards the particular action—though not in the abstract—'in so far as reason is hindered from applying the general principle to a particular point of practice, on account of concupiscence or some other passion'.[106] Recall that the Decalogue, for Aquinas, consists in proximate conclusions flowing from the general principles of the natural law. These conclusions

---

[102] I–II, q. 100, a. 4, ad 1.   [103] I–II, q. 100, a. 6.

[104] Cf. John Rist, *Real Ethics*, especially chapters 6 and 9, as well as his short book *On Inoculating Moral Philosophy against God* (Milwaukee, WI: Marquette University Press, 2000).

[105] I–II, q. 94, a. 4.   [106] I–II, q. 94, a. 6.

belonging to the natural law God wills to *reveal* to Israel because sin had obscured them in human communities. Here Aquinas relies upon Romans 1 (with its debt to Wisdom of Solomon 13–19, as well as to Isaiah and the Psalms). The sins listed in Romans 1 suggest the importance of divine law for natural law doctrine.[107] And indeed, with regard to the natural law precepts of the Decalogue, Aquinas teaches that 'the natural law can be blotted out from the human heart, either by evil persuasions, just as in speculative matters errors occur in respect of necessary conclusions; or by vicious customs and corrupt habits, as among some men, theft, and even unnatural vices, as the Apostle states (Rom. i), were not esteemed sinful'.[108]

Bracketing the eternal and divine law does not work, then. Viewed from the negative side, it fails because of the difficulty in knowing natural law adequately. Although Cicero, without the assistance of biblical revelation, posited a God who inscribes a purposeful ordering into all things and gained a rich understanding of natural law, biblical revelation makes his account far more plausible, since otherwise disorder and death pose questions that his orderly vision is unable to answer. Viewed from the positive side, biblical revelation not only illumines the mind and will by removing the blinders of sin, but also shows that the 'ecstatic' pattern of natural law has been, from the beginning, taken up into the infinitely higher pattern of charity that is the Trinitarian communion: 'to all who received him, who believed in his name, he gave power to become children of God; who were born, not of blood nor of the will of the flesh nor of the will of man, but of God. And the Word became flesh and dwelt among us, full of grace and truth; we have beheld his glory, glory as of the only Son from the Father' (John 1:12–14).[109]

---

[107] Cf. my 'Knowing What Is "Natural": Reflections on Romans 1–2', forthcoming in *Logos*.

[108] I–II, q. 94, a. 6. See also I–II, q. 91, a. 4: 'on account of the uncertainty of human judgment, especially on contingent and particular matters, different people form different judgments on human acts; whence also different and contrary laws result. In order, therefore, that man may know without any doubt what he ought to do and what he ought to avoid, it was necessary for man to be directed in his proper acts by a law given by God, for it is certain that such a law cannot err.'

[109] This 'ecstatic' pattern of natural law, it should be noted, teaches us how to love created goods in God without clinging to created goods. Our love for created goods (including human persons) must be *ecstatically* ordered, so that their fulfilment, like ours, is found in their participation in the common good (God). Pamela Hall writes, 'The commonplace of the Christian spiritual tradition that the impermanence and

CONCLUDING REFLECTIONS

Paul Kahn seeks 'to explore the element of tragedy within our beliefs about the rule of law'.[110] As he puts it, this Western tragedy stems from what he takes to be the reality that '[n]o form of political order—legal or otherwise—is adequate to love's understanding'.[111] Love demands, he says, 'an ultimate transcendence of finitude',[112] and this demand cannot be met on earth. As noted above, Kahn assumes that the conflict between love and law in modern Western culture has, at its root, St Paul's rejection of Jewish law and the consequent intellectual development of Christian beliefs.

I have argued that no such polarity is intrinsic to Christian thought. Far from there being a tragic conflict between love and law, the two are one in a theology attuned to the Creator who loves us into existence and leads us to himself by his wisdom and love. In John's prologue to his Gospel we read, 'In the beginning was the Word, and the Word was with God, and the Word was God. He was in the beginning with God; all things were made through him, and without him was not anything made that was made. In him was life, and the life was the light of men' (John 1:1–4). It is this Word whose 'glory' is the divine self-giving wisdom and love, the divine action to make us his children and friends, intimate sharers in the Trinitarian life. This divine glory is, as manifested by the Son, God's wise plan to bring human creatures to himself; his eternal law for creatures is revealed to be perfect love. Natural law describes the reality that the natural powers of human being participate in this eternal law, that is, bear its imprint.

This natural law is not the same as our graced participation in God's own knowledge through faith, since graced participation goes beyond the power of human nature in itself. Yet neither does natural law stand opposed to the ordering of grace. On the contrary, the wise plan revealed by biblical revelation elevates and intensifies

fragility of natural goods constitutes a kind of pedagogy, teaching adherence to the eternal God, may not be the only lesson to be learned; loving God as last end need not entail a diminution of our love for goods and persons in this life' (Hall, *Narrative and the Natural Law*, 113). This is true but, given the condition of sin, the detachment required for true love may seem to be a 'diminution'.

110 Kahn, *Law and Love*, xv.   111 Ibid., xvii.   112 Ibid., xix.

the movement toward which the natural law already calls us, the movement of ecstasis, of self-giving love. Natural law, in its very structure, carries us outside ourselves: as Romanus Cessario puts it, 'The end draws.'[113] Rooted in metaphysical receptivity, natural law is our ordering to the human good, human flourishing, that we cannot give ourselves. Biblical revelation both provides the context for natural law as such (the theology of creation and providence), and reveals that natural law belongs within a greater pattern of self-giving communion or opening of oneself to another person, namely the order of grace. The Torah, with its divinely revealed precepts of the natural law, is fulfilled by the radical love of Christ. Illumined by the Bible, natural law appears as belonging to the pattern of our participation in the wisdom of divine love. We may speak of 'biblical' natural law precisely because law and love go hand in hand.

In this sense, Kahn is right to say that '[n]o form of political order—legal or otherwise—is adequate to love's understanding' and that love demands 'an ultimate transcendence of finitude'. But the natural law teaches us not that love therefore requires an overcoming of political order and law, but instead that true political 'order' and 'law' are God's gift. 'Order' and 'law' are not, in their deepest sense, realities that we constitute for ourselves. Rather, our efforts to constitute political order and law are grounded upon our prior reception, inscribed in our created natures, of an ordering of goods and inclinations that constitutes a 'law' for our happiness. This ordering flows from God and is his mode of drawing us, by means

---

[113] Romanus Cessario, OP, 'Aquinas on Christian Salvation', in *Aquinas on Doctrine*, ed. Thomas G. Weinandy, OFM Cap., Daniel A. Keating, and John P. Yocum (New York: T. & T. Clark, 2004), 117–37, at 118. Cessario explains, 'In the setting of the *Tertia Pars*, end refers back to the human creature and its perfection. In this scheme, which owes as much to Plato as to Aristotle, the divine goodness comprises more than an expression of generosity. Divine goodness points to the density of the divine being that precedes and undergirds all manifestations of God's goodness. To put it differently, the phrase "*bonitas divina*" becomes Aquinas' shorthand for the whole interplay of God–man relations as he conceives of it. "*Bonitas divina*" summarizes Aquinas' meditation on a central text of the New Testament: "For God so loved the world that he gave his only Son, that whoever believes in him should not perish but have eternal life" (John 3:16). This "giving" of God's goodness supposes the human person's free choosing even as it constitutes the condition for the possibility of free action' (118).

of our own created nature, to our ultimate end in him. Eternal law, in other words, is the starting point for a true appreciation of natural law. God is moving us toward an end—and were we not to recognize this, but were instead to seek to ground 'law' in our own (rational or bodily) motions, our desire for an unrestricted love would indeed require us to rebel against the dynamism of law, whose enduring validity we could in no way ground: even if today the fundamental goods of human life seemed to require a particular 'law', why should it be the same tomorrow, and what ensures its truth today? Lacking trust in the Creator God's providence for us, we would indeed have to reject, as Nietzsche does, our very creaturely finitude.

Is it possible to trust in the Creator God's providential care, given the violent fragmentation that characterizes human lives and deaths? Can we, as Jesus requires, 'turn and become like children' (Mt 18:3)? Were we to engage natural law solely philosophically, I do not think that it could sufficiently lay claim in this fallen world to our minds and hearts. Divine law—the revelation of the fullness of the creature–Creator relationship in the Old and New Testaments—makes it possible for human beings to follow out God's original gift, and to arrive fully at the 'political order' (Kahn) that God, in his wisdom, wills for us, none other than

the holy city, new Jerusalem, coming down out of heaven from God, prepared as a bride adorned for her husband; and I heard a great voice from the throne saying, 'Behold, the dwelling of God is with men. He will dwell with them, and they shall be his people, and God himself will be with them; he will wipe away every tear from their eyes, and death shall be no more, neither shall there be mourning nor crying nor pain any more, for the former things have passed away. (Rev. 21:2–4)[114]

Divine law is required for this end, not merely natural law on its own. This for two reasons. First, sin, not finitude per se, has destroyed all hopes of attaining a political order on earth that fully inscribes the pattern of ecstatic love, even though the political pursuit of such an ordering assists human societies in better manifesting love's precepts. Second, the divine Trinity has called us, by the grace of the Holy Spirit

---

[114] Cf. R. C. Petry, 'The Social Character of Heavenly Beatitude According to the Thought of St. Thomas Aquinas', *The Thomist* 7 (1944): 65–79.

bestowed upon us through Jesus Christ (who is 'the righteousness of God' (Rom. 3:22)), to a share in Christ's Body. Indeed, God has revealed that this has been his purpose from the beginning; natural law has, from the beginning, been taken up into this supernatural mode of God's moving us toward our end. Because of the fragmentation caused by sin and the Trinitarian communion that is our end, therefore, our appreciation of natural law doctrine is upheld not only by beginning with the eternal law, but also by placing the whole in light of divine law—ultimately the grace of the Holy Spirit flowing from Jesus Christ's sacrificial Cross and glorious Resurrection—revealed in Scripture and proclaimed as Good News in the Church, built up in love as Christ's Body.

Thus already, even in this world, our actions are related to the transcendent 'political' order, or the fullest possible 'law' of love, that is the Trinitarian communion made visible (to the eyes of faith) in the Church. The liberative 'political order' and perfect 'law' of love do not wait for heaven. On the contrary, they are already here, if only in a foretaste. Bracketing the divine law fails just as bracketing the eternal law does: from the beginning, and even now, the created gift of the natural law can only be appreciated and effectively followed from within the graced gift of love. The pattern of *ecstasis*, made manifest in the natural law and elevated by grace into personal communion with the Trinity, unifies law and love.

As Jesus teaches, then, 'Whoever humbles himself like this child, he is the greatest in the kingdom of heaven' (Mt 18:4).

Conclusion

Through exegesis of biblical texts and through philosophical and theological discussion, the chapters of this book have defended a theocentric, teleological natural law whose lineaments are revealed in the Decalogue and which conforms to the graced life's pattern of *ecstasis*. All human beings know natural law experientially, clouded though this knowledge is by human fallenness, and so philosophers (paradigmatically Cicero) have been able to develop natural law doctrine without the aid of biblical revelation. Yet I have argued that biblical revelation enriches the intelligibility and persuasiveness of natural law doctrine, and especially that a rejection of biblical faith inclines one toward rejection of any fruitful sense of 'natural law'. This is so because of the Bible's witness to creation and providence. As we have seen, the tradition of natural law reflection that, when further joined to Stoic and Aristotelian ideas, emerged from this biblical teaching has characteristic emphases. From a theocentric perspective attuned to human creatureliness, natural law doctrine highlights the teleological attraction of the good, and thereby makes clear that human fulfilment is found in going outside oneself rather than in self-seeking actions.

The significance of this tradition of natural law doctrine should be clear. Robert George observes that '[a]s Alasdair MacIntyre has shown, traditions supply background understandings in the absence of which important achievements of practical intelligence—practical insights—are scarcely possible. In other words, traditions can be, and sound traditions always are, bearers or carriers of the resources of practical rationality—that is, of reasonableness in the moral sphere.'[1]

---

[1] Robert P. George, 'What's Sex Got to Do with It? Marriage, Morality, and Rationality', *American Journal of Jurisprudence* 49 (2004): 63–85, at 68. MacIntyre's view has at times been misinterpreted as historicist relativism with respect to human rationality: see for instance Martin McKeever, CSSR, 'God's Justice? Right Reason? Justice and Rationality in Catholic Social Teaching in the Light of Alasdair MacIntyre's Conception of Traditions of Enquiry', *Studia Moralia* 43 (2005): 297–317. McKeever argues that 'justice and rationality are conceived of in correlative terms and as inherently tied to given institutional structures' (297). When such structures pass away,

This 'biblical' tradition of natural law reflection runs counter to the anthropocentric accounts that have been prevalent in the modern period. Matthew L. Lamb has articulated this divergence in terms of three differences between modern philosophy on the one hand and Jewish and Christian perspectives on the other:

The first is that reality is ultimately conflictual (Machiavelli, Hobbes, Locke, Hume, Marx); the second is that knowledge is power, discovering laws in order to impose conventional order upon monadized phenomena (Hobbes, Bacon, Leibniz, Franklin, Freud); and the third is the social correlative of the first two, namely, that social and cultural institutions are structures of legitimate domination whereby monadic individuals more or less agree to the forms of legitimate coercion (legal force and fear) required to establish and maintain the conventional orders of enlightened society (Hobbes, Hume, Smith, Marx, Weber). Within this context, freedom is freedom to pursue one's own individual self-interest. Freedom is basically value-neutral, for any supra-individual norm is taken as no more than conventional, and so imposed either by dictate or by consensus. There are only, then, procedural norms—no substantive norms—for what is good. Hence the distinction between legality and morality is a distinction without a difference. In a word, there is the instrumentalization of nature, life, and society.[2]

The 'instrumentalization' of nature that Lamb describes, in which human power and human construction are at the centre, contrasts with the theocentric and teleological vision of created nature, including human nature, that we find in Genesis, the Wisdom literature, the Gospel of John, the Letter to the Romans, and elsewhere in Scripture.[3]

---

so do the particular forms of 'justice and rationality'. A 'tradition' then comprises a set of 'interacting rationalities'—each of which is 'historical, conflictual, dialectical, and open' (316)—from the different time periods in which the tradition has been active. For an effort to guard against such misunderstanding, see Alasdair MacIntyre, 'Moral Relativism, Truth and Justification', in *Moral Truth and Moral Tradition: Essays in Honor of Peter Geach and Elizabeth Anscombe*, ed. Luke Gormally (Portland, OR: Four Courts Press, 1994), 6–24.

[2] Matthew L. Lamb, 'Inculturation and Western Culture: The Dialogical Experience between Gospel and Culture', *Communio* 21 (1994): 124–44, at 141.

[3] A different position is taken by John Milbank. Having shown that modernity and postmodernity involve the 'blurring of the distinction between nature and culture' (Milbank, 'The Gospel of Affinity', in *The Strange New World of the Gospel: Re-Evangelizing in the Postmodern World*, ed. Carl E. Braaten and Robert W. Jenson (Grand Rapids, MI: Eerdmans, 2002), 1) so that, after Nietzsche, 'people no longer seem to find any need to identify a human essence—no longer is human

Let us recall this sapiential biblical worldview. In Wisdom of Solomon, God's love is connected with human ordering of life in accord with wisdom: 'in every generation she [wisdom] passes into holy souls and makes them friends of God, and prophets; for God loves nothing so much as the man who lives with wisdom' (Wisd. 7:27–8). God loves wisdom (8:3), and human beings should love wisdom (8:2). It is wisdom who fashions and orders the entire universe

---

auto-creation operating within essential parameters' (2) and the 'humanum' seems infinitely plastic, Milbank (with some nuances) celebrates this situation: 'Postmodernism, I have said, is the obliteration of boundaries. And Christianity is the religion of the obliteration of boundaries... I suggest, more cautiously, that Christianity itself invented a discourse and tradition of living beyond the law—and that the West is still thinking and living through this idea' (9). He proposes that 'the Christian going beyond-the-law nonetheless preserves and elevates the law' (11). As he explains it, Christianity becomes a religion of Kantian practical reasoning in a Hegelian mode: 'Religious people tend, instinctively, to feel uneasy in the face of a general collapse of all that was once regarded as natural. They are tempted to fall back on an insistence that God has made the human species and all others as they should be, and that either nature, or God's positive law, has given clear and firm guidance for the conduct of human sexual relations and reproduction. The trouble with this approach, though, is that an open-ended transformation of the natural world has always been regarded by Christian theology as proper to our *humanum*, and even as intrinsic to the redemption of humanity and the cosmos, looking towards the *eschaton*. Already, throughout history, we have drastically altered both nature and our bodies, and questions of right and wrong here have never been decidable *merely* in terms of what has been pre-given by divine design. Certainly, that must be ceaselessly attended to, but questions of right and wrong in those instances more ultimately require a discernment of teleology, and a ceaseless discrimation of what is good in itself... When it comes to contemporary practical examples, we need to continue to exercise this power of discernment. For example, surrogate father- or motherhood is not wrong because it violates the pre-given process of reproduction. Rather, we have to ask very complex questions about what such procedures will do to human identity—and whether the different identities that may thereby emerge are richer or weaker identities, more viable or else more unstable and threatened. Ultimately, we have to ask whether the co-belonging of sex and procreation alone sustains human beings as more than commodities, because they are thereby the outcome of personal encounters at once both accidental and yet chosen, in a fashion that is irreplaceable, and essential to an ontological grammar that we should continue to elect. (I believe the answer is yes.) But such reflections involve not a refusal of choice, nor a mere postmodern resignation to choice, but a kind of higher-level "choice about choice." At present, of course, we woefully lack cultural practices that might mediate our intersubjective metachoices' (11–12). It seems to me that many elements are missing in Milbank's account, among others the order of creation as that order manifests itself without the anthropocentric fluidity that Milbank appears here to assume.

(7:22, 8:1). Wisdom is praised in almost divine terms as uniting all things for good:

For in her [wisdom] there is a spirit that is intelligent, holy, unique, manifold, subtle, mobile, clear, unpolluted, distinct, invulnerable, loving the good, keen, irresistible, beneficent, humane, steadfast, sure, free from anxiety, all-powerful, overseeing all, and penetrating through all spirits that are intelligent and pure and most subtle. For wisdom is more mobile than any motion; because of her pureness she pervades and penetrates all things. For she is a breath of the power of God, and a pure emanation of the glory of the Almighty; therefore nothing defiled gains entrance into her. For she is a reflection of eternal light, a spotless mirror of the working of God, and an image of his goodness. (7:22–6)

Love and wisdom here go together, and the fashioning and ordering of all things by the loving spirit of wisdom causes the universe to have an intelligible order. God gives wisdom to human beings (8:21) so that they can understand this intelligible order that God, through wisdom, has inscribed in the universe (including in the nature and powers of free, rational creatures). Wisdom enables human beings to act virtuously and to do God's will. We read, 'Who has learned thy counsel, unless thou hast given wisdom and sent thy holy Spirit from on high? And thus the paths of those on earth were set right, and men were taught what pleases thee, and were saved by wisdom' (9:17–18). Even if human beings suffer persecution on earth for their love of wisdom, furthermore, God will not allow the wicked to triumph over the wise. Their deaths for righteousness' sake, though tragic when measured by human standards, are precious in God's eyes, and God will give them the reward of eternal life while punishing the wicked (3:1–10). God's wisdom spans heaven and earth, God and human beings, and accomplishes God's justice among those who seek to thwart God's people: 'thy all-powerful word leaped from heaven, from the royal throne, into the midst of the land that was doomed, a stern warrior carrying the sharp sword of thy authentic command, and stood and filled all things with death, and touched heaven while standing on the earth' (18:15–16).

Similarly the book of Sirach teaches that God's wisdom infuses all things: 'The Lord himself created wisdom; he saw her and apportioned her, he poured her out upon all his works' (Sir. 1:9). This outpouring of wisdom upon God's works provides the universe with its own wisdom or order. This is clearly the case, according to Sirach, with the stars (16:27–8). It is also the case with human beings, though in a more complex way. God gives human beings the knowledge of good and evil (17:7), and he also gives to Israel the law that leads human beings to true wisdom (15:1). Sharing in wisdom involves not only the special gift of the law, but also the work of human reason (14:20–2). Thus although wisdom has spread herself through the whole universe and has (to a degree) found a place in every nation, God gave to wisdom the city of Jerusalem as her special dwelling place (24:3–12). Sirach thereby connects wisdom with the Torah. As Sirach states, 'All this is the book of the covenant of the Most High God, the law which Moses commanded us as an inheritance for the congregations of Jacob. It fills men with wisdom' (24:23–5). Yet Sirach is also aware that the wisdom that God bestows upon all his works is known by many who do not have the benefit of the Torah.

The book of Proverbs, too, includes numerous passages in praise of personified wisdom. Wisdom is God's first creation, and assists in the formation of everything else (Prov. 8:22–31). Wisdom is accessible to those who love her: 'I love those who love me, and those who seek me diligently find me' (8:17). To know wisdom requires, as in Sirach, not so much intelligence as 'fear of the Lord' (1:7; 9:10). Instruction in wisdom enables human beings to know how to do good and avoid evil, and to know how to govern others for their good (8:12–21). God's wisdom imbues both the cosmos and human life: 'The Lord by wisdom founded the earth; by understanding he established the heavens; by his knowledge the deeps broke forth, and the clouds drop down the dew. My son, keep sound wisdom and discretion; let them not escape from your sight, and they will be life for your soul and adornment for your neck' (3:19–22). Everything bespeaks God's wisdom, and yet human beings must seek it in order to know it (2:1–11).

Discussing the figure of wisdom in the Wisdom literature, the Old Testament scholar Leo Perdue compares Sirach's 'word theology, especially in terms of Wisdom as the life-giving and ordering principle of creation and as the commandments that give direction to life'[4] to the personification of wisdom as a lovable and loving woman, beloved of God, in Proverbs and the Wisdom of Solomon. As he summarizes the figure of wisdom: 'Divine Wisdom, the lover of God, becomes, through God's charity, the lover of the wise, making God and God's creation and providence open at least to limited understanding.'[5] Not only the inanimate created order exhibits God's wisdom, but so also does the realm of free human action. Both are governed by God's wisdom or providence. Thus the entire creation, non-rational and rational, manifests in its intelligible order God's governing wisdom. To the degree that human beings

---

[4] Leo G. Perdue, *Wisdom and Creation: The Theology of Wisdom Literature* (Nashville, TN: Abingdon Press, 1994), 251. Perdue's work contrasts with that of John J. Collins, among others, who criticizes any 'tendency to "baptize" wisdom as an offshoot of the historical faith of Israel' (Collins, 'The Biblical Precedent for Natural Theology', in *Encounters with Biblical Theology* (Minneapolis, MN: Fortress, 2005), 91–104, at 97). Against Gerhard von Rad's *Wisdom in Israel*, Collins holds that the wisdom books 'make no reference to a knowledge of Yahweh other than what is developed within the principles of wisdom itself. There is nothing to suggest that wisdom is in any sense an offshoot of the religion of Israel. Rather, the knowledge and fear of Yahweh that plays a crucial role in the wisdom books is grounded in the religious experience of the wise throughout the Near East for centuries before Israel was born. The religious character of wisdom must not be confused with the influence of the history and institutions of Israel. Even when the sages speak of Yahweh, they speak of him in language derived from universal human experience. The knowledge of Yahweh is not equated with special revelation, but with a dimension of common experience. Accordingly the religious character of wisdom must be appreciated in universal experiential categories' (97). This observation includes Sirach and the Wisdom of Solomon despite their efforts to draw in the history of Israel (102). Thus discussing the moral 'order' that is emphasized by the wisdom literature (with 'affinities', Collins notes, 'with other Near Eastern conceptions, especially the Egyptian notion of Maat' (99)), Collins observes, 'The term "order" is not found in the vocabulary of wisdom but is nevertheless appropriate for the experience of the world expressed in the linking of Act and Consequence and in personified Wisdom. This experience is religious, but, once again, it is the religious dimension of common human experience. It does not claim legitimation by reference to any special revelation or to the history of Israel' (101). Whereas Collins celebrates this movement toward 'universal experiential categories', other scholars, such as H. D. Preuss and G. E. Wright, have identified the same movement and criticized the wisdom literature on this basis, as Collins points out in a further essay in his volume, 'Proverbial Wisdom and the Yahwist Vision', 105–16. It seems to me that Perdue is correct to emphasize the place of the Torah's doctrine of creation in Israel's wisdom literature, and that this remains the essential point even if one detects, with Collins and others, the influence of Middle Platonism (see Collins, 'Natural Theology and Biblical Tradition: The Case of Hellenistic Judaism', in the same volume, 117–26).

[5] Perdue, *Wisdom and Creation*, 251.

seek wisdom, they come to share more and more deeply in God's providence.

Ben Witherington III has emphasized the significance of the Wisdom literature for the Christologies of the Gospels,[6] and his interpretation of the Prologue to the Gospel of John, John 1:1–14, is particularly valuable in this regard. Witherington makes clear that the Prologue describes the Word as divine, not merely created or semi-divine. The coming of the divine Word to the world parallels God's sending of the Torah to Israel, but here the place of the Torah is taken by Christ.[7] Witherington observes that quite probably the key influence on the early Christological hymns, among which he numbers John 1:1–14, 'is the earlier Jewish reflection on the career of personified Wisdom, who is said in Proverbs 8 to be involved in the work of creation, who is said in Sirach 24 to have come and dwelt in the midst of God's people, and who is said in *1 Enoch* 42 to have been rejected by those people and so returned to dwell in heaven with God.'[8] Noting that the Wisdom literature's reflection on the figure of wisdom often takes the form of a theology of creation, Witherington points out that it is not surprising then that the early Christological hymns devote significant space to the Word's role in creation. Now that the Creator has become the Redeemer, wisdom and love can be seen to be fully united.

The Gospel of John's Prologue thus goes beyond, in three primary ways, the personification of 'wisdom' in the Wisdom literature. First, the Word is not, as 'wisdom' is in the Wisdom literature, the firstborn creature whose being, and work of ordering, belongs strictly to the side of the created order. Rather, as Witherington says, 'The key phrase *kai theos en ho logos* [John 1:1] does not mean "the Word was a god," but rather "the Word was God." Notice it does not say "the Word was *the* God" for this then would mean the Word was all there was to the Godhead.'[9] Second, the divine Word, like personified 'wisdom', is present in the creative ordering; but the divine Word is clearly the

---

[6] See in particular Witherington's *Jesus the Sage: The Pilgrimage of Wisdom* (Minneapolis, MN: Fortress Press, 1994), which traces in detail the impact of the Wisdom literature upon the books of the New Testament.

[7] Ben Witherington III, *John's Wisdom: A Commentary on the Fourth Gospel* (Louisville, KY: Westminster John Knox Press, 1995), 49.

[8] Ibid., 51.   [9] Ibid., 53.

Creator. His creative ordering is the gift of 'life' and 'light' (John 1:4–5). Witherington notes that this 'light' metaphorically describes 'revelation or enlightenment that comes from God': the light is wisdom. Third, 'the Word became flesh and lived among us' (John 1:14). As the evangelist John goes on to teach, the incarnate Word, Jesus Christ, suffered and died for our sins so as to give us the gift of eternal life in communion with the Father, Son, and Holy Spirit.

The wisdom in God's created order, a wisdom that reflects God himself, is therefore no dry or abstract formula. Rather, God's wisdom for the created order, as revealed in the incarnate Word, is sheer self-giving or sacrificial love. Not only are creatures created so as to give themselves to God, but indeed God himself is preeminently revealed as radically self-giving Love. The wisdom inscribed in the created order—a wisdom that, as promulgated by God in the created order so as to lead creatures to their good, is a 'law'—is not opposed to love. On the contrary, the command to radical love is at the very core of law. Christ's sacrificial love takes up the self-giving law of love inscribed in the fabric of the created order, and draws this wisdom of the created order into the supernatural realm of the Trinitarian Wisdom and Love. Put more technically, divine grace builds upon and perfects nature, in a way that exhibits the openness of creation to grace and the full penetration of creation by grace. Christ himself, the Word incarnate, reveals the ultimate 'law' by which God orders his creation to its end—the end of union with God in new creation. As Witherington points out, Christ replaces 'Torah as God's Logos'[10] (cf. John 1:17); the wisdom inscribed in the created order, a wisdom associated in Sirach with the Torah, is now fully revealed and fulfilled in Christ, the incarnate Word who fulfils and transforms the Torah.[11]

The Bible thus connects the wisdom inscribed in the created order, the Torah, and the 'life' and 'light' of the creative Word whose incarnate suffering, death, and resurrection manifest and accomplish

---

[10] Ibid.

[11] For further theological reflection upon the theme of fulfilment, see my *Christ's Fulfillment of Torah and Temple: Salvation according to Thomas Aquinas* (Notre Dame, IN: University of Notre Dame Press, 2002). I discuss the theme again in chapter 2 of my *Sacrifice and Community: Jewish Offering and Christian Eucharist* (Oxford: Blackwell, 2005).

divine justice and charity.[12] In seeking to explore how God orders his creatures to their end (the new creation), then, theologians must find ways to do justice to the links between the created order, the Torah, and the Word. If true 'law' is 'an ordinance of reason for the common good, made by him who has care of the community, and promulgated',[13] then the intelligible wisdom that, as we have seen from the Wisdom literature, God inscribes and makes manifest in the created 'order' so as to lead creation, including rational creatures, to the ultimate end is, in a real sense, 'law'. Yet such law cannot be separated from God's covenantal love as manifested in Israel's Torah and in Christ Jesus, since the very way that God plans ultimately to draw his wayward creatures to their end of Trinitarian communion is through the giving of the Torah and of the divine Word. Just as God's law cannot be separated from his love, neither can his love be separated from law.

Natural law makes sense within this biblically revealed framework. It is not that natural law, as such, depends upon revelation: to imply this would be to deny the workings of the very 'nature' that natural law doctrine defends.[14] Rather, it is that outside of the framework of revelation, and particularly when one has deliberately rejected the biblical framework, it becomes difficult to conceive of an ordering in human beings that is not ultimately a human construction—a convention rather than an ordering, arbitrary power rather than wisdom. David Hart has noted that this biblical vision preserves and elevates the best aspects of pagan thought:

Catholic Christianity—East and West—did not abandon antiquity's vision of a world alive in every part, charged with vital intellect; it saw the motive force at the heart of creation not as an unreasoning engine of material causality, but as an ecstasy of spiritual intelligence and desire. The entire cosmos, it was

---

[12] This is true not merely of the Catholic Bible, which includes Wisdom of Solomon and Sirach, but of the Protestant Bible as well, because as Witherington and others have shown the influence of Wisdom of Solomon and Sirach is found throughout the New Testament.

[13] *Summa Theologiae* I-II, q. 90, a. 4.

[14] The cautionary tale found in Ralph McInerny's *Praeambula Fidei: Thomism and the God of the Philosophers* (Washington, DC: Catholic University of America Press, 2006) is instructive here.

possible to believe, was drawn ever onward by the yearning of all things for the goodness of God. It was possible to believe, indeed, that the principle of all physical and spiritual motion was, in Dante's phrase, 'the love that moves the sun and other stars.'[15]

In Hart's view, and in mine, this biblical vision remains compelling and persuasive. By contrast the modern anthropocentric view, as Hart describes it, seems implausible and terrible: 'What had never yet arisen in imagination was "nature" in the modern sense: a closed causal continuum, conceived (by theists) as the intricate artifice of a God whose transcendence is a kind of absence, or (by atheists) as a purely fortuitous event concerning which the absence of any God is the only "transcendent" truth.'[16]

'Biblical' natural law, in short, defends a theocentric and teleological story of the world. The biblical story depicts the existence of a teleological ordering, given by God, in human moral life. The final word is not death: God's love orders all. Without such hope for a meaningful 'ultimate end' to human existence, as Matthew Lamb notes, even the primary natural law precepts become difficult to sustain, as 'disgust with this life' produces approval of 'the practices of death such as abortion and euthanasia'.[17] Reclaiming natural law within its biblical context—creation and redemption, love and law—thus holds out hope for the human creature by affirming, once again, the central aspect of natural law, namely its participation in God's eternal law by which God draws us to himself. After the anthropocentric reconfigurations of modernity and postmodernity, such natural law doctrine expresses an appreciation for human freedom (Kant, Rousseau) and for the working out in history of the transcendent destiny of human beings (Hegel, Nietzsche). At the same time, it avoids the self-cleaving tendency in anthropocentric natural law doctrine and instead recognizes human fulfilment as achieved through imitation of the divine *ecstasis*.

One might ask in conclusion: Could natural law thus understood have any place in pluralist cultures, in light of the widespread rejection of God and teleology? If natural law doctrine should be

---

[15] David Bentley Hart, *The Doors of the Sea: Where Was God in the Tsunami?* (Grand Rapids, MI: Eerdmans, 2005), 48–9.

[16] Ibid., 49.   [17] Lamb, 'Inculturation and Western Culture', 144.

theocentric and teleological, and if it follows that biblical revelation is not an embarrassment but a profound aid to philosophical reflection on natural law, could such natural law doctrine gain a hearing? Because human beings are creatures who need God and are fulfilled by particular kinds of actions, such natural law doctrine will over the long term be far more plausible than any alternative. Yet, it will not be so without bold Christian witness in leading sacrificial lives, lives of ecstatic love. Filled with hope for life with God and relying upon God's strength and mercy, let us recall, both as a conclusion and as a starting-point, Jesus' instruction to his disciples about the path of true human flourishing:

'With men this is impossible, but with God all things are possible.' Then Peter said in reply, 'Lo, we have left everything and followed you. What then shall we have?' Jesus said to them, 'Truly, I say to you, in the new world, when the Son of man shall sit on his glorious throne, you who have followed me will also sit on twelve thrones, judging the twelve tribes of Israel. And every one who has left houses or brothers or sisters or father or mother or children or lands, for my name's sake, will receive a hundredfold, and inherit eternal life. But many that are first will be last, and the last first. (Mt 19:26–30)

Works Cited

Adams, Marilyn McCord. 'Ockham on Will, Nature, and Morality', in *The Cambridge Companion to Ockham*, edited by Paul Vincent Spade, Cambridge: Cambridge University Press, 1999, 245–72.

Aertsen, Jan. 'Aquinas and the Human Desire for Knowledge', *American Catholic Philosophical Quarterly* 79 (2005): 411–30.

—— 'Natural Law in the Light of the Doctrine of the Transcendentals', in *Lex et Libertas*, edited by Leo Elders, SVD, and K. Hedwig, Vatican City: Libreria Editrice Vaticana, 1987, 99–112.

—— *Nature and Creature: Thomas Aquinas's Way of Thought*, New York: E. J. Brill, 1988.

Aquinas, Thomas. *On Human Nature*, edited by Thomas S. Hibbs, Indianapolis, IN: Hackett, 1999.

—— *Scriptum super Sententiis*.

—— *Summa Theologiae*.

—— *Truth* [*Quaestiones Disputatae de Veritate*], translated by Robert W. Mulligan, SJ, vol. 1 (1954) Indianapolis, IN: Hackett, 1994.

Ariew, Roger, and Marjorie Green, editors. *Descartes and His Contemporaries: Meditations, Objections, and Replies*, Chicago: University of Chicago Press, 1995.

Arkes, Hadley. *First Things: An Inquiry into the First Principles of Morals and Justice*, Princeton: Princeton University Press, 1986.

—— 'That "Nature Herself Has Placed in Our Ears a Power of Judging": Some Reflections on the "Naturalism" of Cicero', in *Natural Law Theory: Contemporary Essays*, edited by Robert P. George, Oxford: Oxford University Press, 1992, 245–77.

Arnhart, Larry. *Darwinian Natural Right: The Biological Ethics of Human Nature*, Albany, NY: State University of New York Press, 1998.

Ashley, Benedict M., OP. 'The Anthropological Foundations of the Natural Law: A Thomistic Engagement with Modern Science', in *St. Thomas Aquinas and the Natural Law Tradition: Contemporary Perspectives*, edited by John Goyette, Mark S. Latkovic, and Richard S. Myers, Washington, DC: Catholic University of America Press, 2004, 3–16.

—— *Theologies of the Body: Humanist and Christian*, Boston, MA: The Pope John XXIII Center, 1985.

Athanasius. *On the Incarnation*, translated by a religious of CSMV, Crestwood, NY: St Vladimir's Orthodox Theological Seminary, 1993.

Aubert, Jean-Marie. *Le droit romain dans l'oeuvre de saint Thomas*, Paris: J. Vrin, 1955.

—— *Loi de Dieu, lois des hommes*, Paris: Desclée, 1964.

—— 'Nature de la relation entre "lex nova" et "lex naturalis" chez saint Thomas d'Aquin', in *Morale e diritto nella prospettiva tomistica*, ed. Pontificia Accademia Romana di San Tommaso d'Aquino, Vatican City: Libreria Editrice Vaticana, 1982, 34–8.

Augustine of Hippo. *Of True Religion*, translated by J. H. S. Burleigh, Chicago: Henry Regnery, 1959.

—— *On Free Choice of the Will*, translated by Thomas Williams, Indianapolis, IN: Hackett, 1993.

Austgen, Robert J. *Natural Motivation in the Pauline Epistles*, 2nd edn., Notre Dame, IN: University of Notre Dame Press, 1969.

Barr, James. *Biblical Faith and Natural Theology*, Oxford: Clarendon Press, 1993.

Barton, John. *Ethics and the Old Testament*, Harrisburg, PA: Trinity Press International, 1998.

—— 'Virtue in the Bible', *Studies in Christian Ethics* 12 (1999): 12–22.

Basso, Domingo M. 'La Ley Eterna en la Teologia de Santo Tomás', *Teologia* 11 (1974): 33–63.

Bayer, Oswald. 'Self-Creation? On the Dignity of Human Beings', *Modern Theology* 20 (2004): 275–90.

Beiser, Frederick C., editor. *The Cambridge Companion to Hegel*, Cambridge: Cambridge University Press, 1993.

Benedict XVI, Pope. *Deus Caritas Est*, 2005.

Biggar, Nigel. 'Barth's Trinitarian Ethic', in *The Cambridge Companion to Karl Barth*, edited by John Webster, Cambridge: Cambridge University Press, 2000.

Black, Rufus. *Christian Moral Realism: Natural Law, Narrative, Virtue, and the Gospel*, Oxford: Oxford University Press, 2000.

Blanchette, Oliva. *The Perfection of the Universe According to Aquinas: A Teleological Cosmology*, University Park, PA: Pennsylvania State University Press, 1992.

Bobbio, Norberto. *Thomas Hobbes and the Natural Law Tradition*, translated by Daniela Gobetti, Chicago: University of Chicago Press, 1993.

Bockmuehl, Markus. *Jewish Law in Gentile Churches: Halakhah and the Beginning of Christian Public Ethics*, Edinburgh: T. & T. Clark, 2000.

Boersma, Hans. 'On the Rejection of Boundaries: Radical Orthodoxy's Appropriation of St. Augustine', *Pro Ecclesia* 15 (2006): 418–47.

Bonino, Serge-Thomas, OP. ' "Nature et grace" dans l'encyclique *Deus caritas est*', *Revue Thomiste* 105 (2005): 531–49.

Bourke, Vernon J. 'The Background of Aquinas' Synderesis Principle', in *Graceful Reason: Essays in Ancient and Medieval Philosophy*, edited by Lloyd P. Gerson, Toronto: Pontifical Institute of Mediaeval Studies, 1983, 345–60.

—— 'Is Thomas Aquinas a Natural Law Ethicist?' *The Monist* 58 (1974): 52–66.

Bowles, John. *Leviathan: Hobbes and His Critics*, London: Jonathan Cape, 1951.

Boyd, Craig A. 'Participation Metaphysics, the *Imago Dei*, and the Natural Law in Aquinas' Ethics', *New Blackfriars* 88 (2007): 274–87.

Braaten, Carl E. 'Response', in *A Preserving Grace: Protestants, Catholics, and Natural Law*, edited by Michael Cromartie, Grand Rapids, MI: Eerdmans, 1997, 31–40.

Braaten, Carl E., and Robert W. Jenson, editors. *The Strange New World of the Gospel: Re-Evangelizing in the Postmodern World*, Grand Rapids, MI: Eerdmans, 2002.

Braaten, Carl E., and Christopher R. Seitz, editors. *I Am the Lord Your God: Christian Reflections on the Ten Commandments*, Grand Rapids, MI: Eerdmans, 2005.

Brock, Stephen L. 'The Legal Character of Natural Law According to St. Thomas Aquinas', Ph.D. dissertation, University of Toronto, 1988.

—— 'Natural Inclination and the Intelligibility of the Good in Thomistic Natural Law', *Vera Lex* 6 (2005): 57–78.

—— Review of *Natural Law and Practical Reason: A Thomist View of Moral Autonomy* by Martin Rhonheimer, *The Thomist* 66 (2002): 311–15.

Brown, Oscar J. *Natural Rectitude and Divine Law in Aquinas: An Approach to an Integral Interpretation of the Thomistic Doctrine of Law*, Toronto: Pontifical Institute of Mediaeval Studies, 1981.

Buber, Martin. *On the Bible: Eighteen Studies*, edited by Nahum N. Glatzer, New York: Syracuse University Press, 2000.

Bucar, Elizabeth M., and Barbra Barnett, editors. *Does Human Rights Need God?* Grand Rapids, MI: Eerdmans, 2005.

Buckle, Stephen. *Natural Law and the Theory of Property: Grotius to Hume*, Oxford: Oxford University Press, 1991.

Buckley, Michael, SJ. *At the Origins of Modern Atheism*, New Haven: Yale University Press, 1987.

—— *Denying and Disclosing God: The Ambiguous Progress of Modern Atheism*, New Haven: Yale University Press, 2004.

Burrell, David B., CSC. 'Creation, Metaphysics, and Ethics', *Faith and Philosophy* 18 (2001): 204–21.

Burrell, David B., CSC. *Faith and Freedom: An Interfaith Perspective*, Oxford: Blackwell, 2004.

Butler, Sara. 'Women's Ordination and the Development of Doctrine', *The Thomist* 61 (1997): 501–24.

Carroll, M. Daniel. 'Seeking the Virtues Among the Prophets: The Book of Amos as a Test Case', *Ex Auditu* 17 (2001): 77–96.

Cates, Diana Fritz. *Choosing to Feel: Virtue, Friendship, and Compassion for Friends*, Notre Dame, IN: University of Notre Dame Press, 1997.

Cessario, Romanus, OP. 'Aquinas on Christian Salvation', in *Aquinas on Doctrine*, edited by Thomas G. Weinandy, OFM Cap., Daniel A. Keating, and John P. Yocum, New York: T. & T. Clark, 2004, 117–37.

—— *Introduction to Moral Theology*, Washington, DC: Catholic University of America Press, 2001.

Chappell, Vere, editor. *The Cambridge Companion to Locke*, Cambridge: Cambridge University Press, 1994.

Chroust, Anton-Hermann. 'Hugo Grotius and the Scholastic Natural Law Tradition', *New Scholasticism* 17 (1943): 101–33.

—— 'The Philosophy of Law from St. Augustine to St. Thomas Aquinas', *New Scholasticism* 20 (1946): 26–71.

Cicero. *The Nature of the Gods*, translated by Horace C. P. McGregor, New York: Penguin, 1972.

—— *On Duties*, translated by Walter Miller, Loeb Classical Library, Cambridge, MA: Harvard University Press, 1913.

Collins, John J. *Encounters with Biblical Theology*, Minneapolis, MN: Fortress Press, 2005.

Collins, Joseph, OP. 'God's Eternal Law', *The Thomist* 23 (1960): 497–532.

Cranston, Maurice, and Richard Peters, editors. *Hobbes and Rousseau*, Garden City, NY: Anchor Books, 1972.

Cromartie, Michael, editor. *A Preserving Grace: Protestants, Catholics, and Natural Law*, Grand Rapids, MI: Eerdmans, 1997.

Crowe, Michael. 'St. Thomas and Ulpian's Natural Law', in *St. Thomas Aquinas 1274–1974: Commemorative Studies*, edited by Armand A. Maurer, vol. 1, Toronto: Pontifical Institute of Mediaeval Studies, 1974, 261–82.

Curran, Charles E. 'Natural Law in Moral Theology', in *Readings in Moral Theology*, vol. 7: *Natural Law and Theology*, edited by Charles E. Curran and Richard A. McCormick, SJ, New York: Paulist Press, 1991, 247–95.

Curran, Charles E., and Richard A. McCormick, SJ, editors. *Readings in Moral Theology*, vol. 7: *Natural Law and Theology*, New York: Paulist Press, 1991.

Dauphinais, Michael. 'Loving the Lord Your God: The *Imago Dei* in Saint Thomas Aquinas', *The Thomist* 63 (1999): 241–67.

Delhaye, Philippe. 'La "loi nouvelle" dans l'enseignement de s. Thomas', in *San Tommaso e la filosofia del diritto oggi*, edited by the Pontificia Accademia Romana di San Tommaso d'Aquino, Vatican City: Libreria Editrice Vaticana, 1975, 73–103.

Descartes, René. *Discourse on Method* and the *Meditations*, translated by F. E. Sutcliffe. New York: Penguin, 1968.

Di Blasi, Fulvio, editor. *God and the Natural Law: A Rereading of Thomas Aquinas*, translated by David Thunder, South Bend, IN: St Augustine's Press, 2006.

Dodd, C. H. *New Testament Studies*, Manchester: Manchester University Press, 1953.

Douglas, Mary. *Leviticus as Literature*, Oxford: Oxford University Press, 1999.

—— *Purity and Danger: An Analysis of Concepts of Pollution and Taboo*, New York: Penguin, 1970.

Dunkle, Brian L., SJ. 'A Development in Origen's View of the Natural Law', *Pro Ecclesia* 13 (2004): 337–51.

Dupré, Louis. *The Enlightenment and the Intellectual Foundations of Modern Culture*, New Haven: Yale University Press, 2004.

—— *Passage to Modernity: An Essay in the Hermeneutics of Nature and Culture*, New Haven: Yale University Press, 1993.

Elders, Leo, SVD, and K. Hedwig, editors. *Lex et Libertas*, Vatican City: Libreria Editrice Vaticana, 1987.

Emery, Gilles, OP. 'L'unité de l'homme, âme et corps, chez S. Thomas d'Aquin', *Nova et Vetera* (French) 75 (2000): 53–76.

—— 'The Personal Mode of Trinitarian Action in Saint Thomas Aquinas', *The Thomist* 69 (2005): 31–77.

Filmer, Robert. *Patriarcha and Other Writings*, edited by J. P. Sommerville, Cambridge: Cambridge University Press, 1991.

Finnis, John. *Aquinas: Moral, Political, and Legal Theory*, Oxford: Oxford University Press, 1998.

—— *'Historical Consciousness' and Theological Foundations*, Toronto: Pontifical Institute of Mediaeval Studies, 1992.

—— *Natural Law and Natural Rights*, Oxford: Clarendon Press, 1980.

Flannery, Kevin, SJ. *Acts Amid Precepts: The Aristotelian Logical Structure of Thomas Aquinas' Moral Theory*, Washington, DC: Catholic University of America Press, 2001.

—— 'Five Republics', in *Human Nature in Its Wholeness: A Roman Catholic Perspective*, edited by Daniel N. Robinson, Gladys M. Sweeney, and

Richard Gill, LC, Washington, DC: Catholic University of America Press, 2006, 34–56.

Flippen, Douglas. 'Natural Law and Natural Inclinations', *New Scholasticism* 5 (1986): 284–316.

Fortin, Ernest. *The Birth of Philosophic Christianity: Studies in Early Christian and Medieval Thought*, edited by J. Brian Benestad, Lanham, MD: Rowman & Littlefield, 1996.

—— *Human Rights, Virtue, and the Common Good: Untimely Meditations on Religion and Politics*, edited by J. Brian Benestad, Lanham, MD: Rowman & Littlefield, 1996.

Fuchs, Josef. *Natural Law: A Theological Investigation*, translated by H. Reckter and J. Dowling, New York: Sheed & Ward, 1965.

George, Robert P. 'Kelsen and Aquinas on the Natural Law Doctrine', in *St. Thomas Aquinas and the Natural Law Tradition: Contemporary Perspectives*, edited by John Goyette, Mark S. Latkovic, and Richard S. Myers, Washington, DC: Catholic University of America Press, 2004, 237–59.

—— 'Natural Law and Human Nature', in *Natural Law Theory: Contemporary Essays*, edited by Robert P. George, Oxford: Clarendon Press, 1992, 31–41.

—— 'Natural Law and Positive Law', in *The Autonomy of Law: Essays on Legal Positivism*, edited by Robert P. George, Oxford: Clarendon Press, 1996, 321–34.

—— 'What's Sex Got to Do with It? Marriage, Morality, and Rationality', *American Journal of Jurisprudence* 49 (2004): 63–85.

George, Robert P., editor. *The Autonomy of Law: Essays on Legal Positivism*, Oxford: Clarendon Press, 1996.

George, Robert P., editor. *Natural Law Theory: Contemporary Essays*, Oxford: Oxford University Press, 1992.

George, Robert P., and Christopher Wolfe, editors. *Natural Law and Public Reason*, Washington, DC: Georgetown University Press, 2000.

Gerson, Lloyd P., editor. *Graceful Reason: Essays in Ancient and Medieval Philosophy*, Toronto: Pontifical Institute of Mediaeval Studies, 1983.

Gillespie, Michael Allen. *Nihilism before Nietzsche*, Chicago: University of Chicago Press, 1995.

Gormally, Luke. 'Marriage and the Prophylactic Use of Condoms', *National Catholic Bioethics Quarterly* 5 (2005): 735–49.

Gormally, Luke, editor. *Moral Truth and Moral Tradition: Essays in Honor of Peter Geach and Elizabeth Anscombe*, Portland, OR: Four Courts Press, 1994.

Goyette, John, Mark S. Latkovic, and Richard S. Myers, editors. *St. Thomas Aquinas and the Natural Law Tradition: Contemporary Perspectives*, Washington, DC: Catholic University of America Press, 2004.

Grabill, Stephen J. *Rediscovering the Natural Law in Reformed Theological Ethics*, Grand Rapids, MI: Eerdmans, 2006.

Gribomont, Jean, OSB. 'Le lien des deux testaments, selon la théologie de S. Thomas', *Ephemerides theologiae Lovanienses* 22 (1946): 70–89.

Grisez, Germain. 'The First Principle of Practical Reason: A Commentary on the *Summa Theologiae*, 1–2, Question 94, Article 2', *Natural Law Forum* 10 (1965): 168–201.

—— 'Natural Law and Natural Inclinations: Some Comments and Clarifications', *New Scholasticism* 6 (1987): 307–20.

Grotius, Hugo. *De iure belli ac pacis*, English edition: *On the Law of War and Peace*, translated by Francis W. Kelsey. Oxford: Oxford University Press, 1925.

Guevin, Benedict M., OSB. 'Aquinas's Use of Ulpian and the Question of Physicalism Revisited', *The Thomist* 63 (1999): 613–28.

—— 'On the Use of Condoms to Prevent Acquired Immune Deficiency Syndrome: Argument of Martin Rhonheimer', *National Catholic Bioethics Quarterly* 5 (2005): 40–8.

Guroian, Vigen. 'Human Rights and Modern Western Faith: An Orthodox Christian Assessment', in *Does Human Rights Need God?* edited by Elizabeth M. Bucar and Barbra Barnett, Grand Rapids, MI: Eerdmans, 2005, 41–7.

—— *Incarnate Love: Essays in Orthodox Ethics*, Notre Dame, IN: University of Notre Dame Press, 1987.

Haakonssen, Knud. *Natural Law and Moral Philosophy: From Grotius to the Scottish Enlightenment*, Cambridge: Cambridge University Press, 1996.

Hall, Pamela M. *Narrative and the Natural Law: An Interpretation of Thomistic Ethics*, Notre Dame, IN: University of Notre Dame Press, 1994.

—— 'The Old Law and the New Law (Ia IIae, qq. 98–108)', in *The Ethics of Aquinas*, edited by Stephen J. Pope, Washington, DC: Georgetown University Press, 2002, 194–206.

Harak, G. Simon, SJ. *Virtuous Passions: The Formation of Christian Character*, New York: Paulist Press, 1993.

Harrison, Ross. *Hobbes, Locke, and Confusion's Masterpiece*, Cambridge: Cambridge University Press, 2003.

Hart, David Bentley. *The Beauty of the Infinite*, Grand Rapids, MI: Eerdmans, 2003.

Hart, David Bentley. *The Doors of the Sea: Where Was God in the Tsunami?* Grand Rapids, MI: Eerdmans, 2005.

Hauerwas, Stanley. 'Abortion Theologically Understood', in *Virtues and Practices in the Christian Tradition: Christian Ethics after MacIntyre*, edited by Nancy Murphy, Brad J. Kallenberg, and Mark Thiessen Nation (1997) Notre Dame, IN: University of Notre Dame Press, 2003, 221–38.

—— 'Christian Ethics in Jewish Terms: A Response to David Novak', *Modern Theology* 16 (2000): 293–9.

—— *The Peaceable Kingdom: A Primer in Christian Ethics*, Notre Dame, IN: University of Notre Dame Press, 1983.

Hays, Richard B. 'The Future of *Christian* Biblical Scholarship', *Nova et Vetera* 4 (2006): 95–120.

—— *The Moral Vision of the New Testament: A Contemporary Introduction to New Testament Ethics*, San Francisco: HarperSanFrancisco, 1996.

Hegel, G. W. F. *Phenomenology of Spirit*, translated by A. V. Miller (1807) Oxford: Oxford University Press, 1977.

Hibbs, Thomas. Introduction to *On Human Nature* by Thomas Aquinas, edited by Thomas S. Hibbs, Indianapolis, IN: Hackett, 1999, vii–xxi.

—— *Virtue's Splendor*, New York: Fordham University Press, 2001.

Hittinger, Russell. *The First Grace: Rediscovering the Natural Law in a Post-Christian World*, Wilmington, DE: ISI Books, 2003.

—— 'Introduction to Modern Catholicism', in *The Teachings of Modern Christianity*, vol. 1: *On Law, Politics, and Human Nature*, edited by John Witte, Jr., and Frank S. Alexander, New York: Columbia University Press, 2006.

—— 'Natural Law and Catholic Moral Theology', in *A Preserving Grace: Protestants, Catholics, and Natural Law*, edited by Michael Cromartie, Grand Rapids, MI: Eerdmans, 1997, 1–30.

—— 'Natural Law and Virtue: Theories at Cross Purposes', in *Natural Law Theory: Contemporary Essays*, edited by Robert P. George, Oxford: Oxford University Press, 1992, 42–70.

—— 'Pope Leo XIII (1810–1903)', in *The Teachings of Modern Christianity*, vol. 1: *On Law, Politics, and Human Nature*, edited by John Witte, Jr., and Frank Alexander, New York: Columbia University Press, 2006, 39–74.

—— 'Theology and Natural Law Theory', *Communio* 17 (1990): 402–8.

—— 'Yves R. Simon on Law, Nature, and Practical Reason', in *Acquaintance with the Absolute*, edited by Anthony O. Simon, New York: Fordham University Press, 1998, 101–27.

Hobbes, Thomas. *Leviathan*, edited by Edwin Curley, Indianapolis, IN: Hackett, 1994.

Hook, Sidney, editor. *Law and Philosophy: A Symposium*, New York: New York University Press, 1964.

Horsley, Richard A. 'The Law of Nature in Philo and Cicero', *Harvard Theological Review* 71 (1978): 35–59.

Hudson, Deal, and Dennis Moran, editors. *The Future of Thomism*, Mishawaka, IN: American Maritain Association, 1992.

Hume, David. *A Treatise of Human Nature*, edited by Ernest C. Mossner (1739), New York: Penguin, 1985.

Hütter, Reinhard. '*Desiderium Naturale Visionis Dei—Est autem duplex hominis beatitude sive felicitas*: Some Observations about Lawrence Feingold's and John Milbank's Recent Interventions in the Debate over the Natural Desire to See God', *Nova et Vetera* 5 (2007): 81–131.

Hütter, Reinhard, and T. Dieter, editors. *Ecumenical Ventures in Ethics: Protestants Engage Pope John Paul II's Moral Encyclicals*, Grand Rapids, MI: Eerdmans, 1998.

Ingham, Nicholas, OP. 'The Rectitude of Inclination', *The Thomist* 60 (1996): 417–37.

John Paul II, Pope. *Memory and Identity: Conversations at the Dawn of a Millennium*, New York: Rizzoli, 2005.

—— *Theology of the Body*, translated by Michael Waldstein, Boston: Pauline Books and Media, 2006.

—— *Veritatis Splendor*, 1993.

Kahn, Paul W. *Law and Love: The Trials of King Lear*, New Haven: Yale University Press, 2000.

Kant, Immanuel. *Grounding for the Metaphysics of Morals*, translated by James W. Ellington, 3rd edn. (1785), Indianapolis, IN: Hackett, 1993.

Kass, Leon. *The Hungry Soul: Eating and the Perfecting of Our Nature*, Chicago: University of Chicago Press, 1999.

Kerr, Fergus, OP. *After Aquinas: Versions of Thomism*, Oxford: Blackwell, 2002.

Kerr, Fergus, OP, editor. *Contemplating Aquinas: On the Varieties of Interpretation*, London: SCM Press, 2003.

Keyt, David, and Fred D. Miller, Jr., editors. *A Companion to Aristotle's Politics*, Oxford: Blackwell, 1991.

King, Peter. 'Ockham's Ethical Theory', in *The Cambridge Companion to Ockham*, edited by Paul Vincent Spade, Cambridge: Cambridge University Press, 1999, 227–44.

Koenig, Harry C., editor. *Principles for Peace: Selections from Papal Documents, Leo XIII to Pius XII*, Washington, DC: National Catholic Welfare Conference, 1943.

Kühn, Ulrich. *Via Caritatis. Theologie des Gesetzes bei Thomas von Aquin*, Göttingen: Vandenhoeck & Ruprecht, 1965.

Lamb, Matthew L. 'Inculturation and Western Culture: The Dialogical Experience between Gospel and Culture', *Communio* 21 (1994): 124–44.

—— 'Nature Is Normative for Culture', *Nova et Vetera* 3 (2005): 153–62.

Lawler, Peter Augustine. 'Natural Law and the American Regime: Murray's *We Hold These Truths*', *Communio* 9 (1982): 368–88.

Lee, Patrick. 'The Goodness of Creation, Evil, and Christian Teaching', *The Thomist* 64 (2000): 239–69.

Leo XIII, Pope. *Libertas Praestantissimum*, in *The Great Encyclical Letters of Pope Leo XIII (1878–1903)* (1903), Rockford, IL: Tan Books, 1995, 227–44.

Levenson, Jon. *Sinai and Zion: An Entry into the Jewish Bible*, San Francisco: Harper & Row, 1985.

Levering, Matthew. *Christ's Fulfillment of Torah and Temple: Salvation According to Thomas Aquinas*, Notre Dame, IN: University of Notre Dame Press, 2002.

—— 'God and Natural Law: Reflections on Genesis 22', forthcoming in *Modern Theology*.

—— 'Knowing What Is "Natural": Reflections on Romans 1–2', forthcoming in *Logos*.

—— *Sacrifice and Community: Jewish Offering and Christian Eucharist*, Oxford: Blackwell, 2005.

Lewis, C. S. *The Abolition of Man: How Education Develops Man's Sense of Morality*, New York: Macmillan, 1955.

Lisska, Anthony J. *Aquinas's Theory of Natural Law: An Analytic Reconstruction*, Oxford: Clarendon Press, 1996.

Locke, John. *Two Treatises of Government*, edited by Mark Goldie (1689) London: J. M. Dent, 1993.

Long, Steven A. 'Natural Law or Autonomous Practical Reason: Problems for the New Natural Law Theory', in *St. Thomas Aquinas and the Natural Law Tradition*, edited by John Goyette, Mark S. Latkovic, and Richard S. Myers, Washington, DC: Catholic University of America Press, 2004, 165–93.

—— 'On the Loss, and Recovery, of Nature as a Theonomic Principle: Reflections on the Nature/Grace Controversy', *Nova et Vetera* 5 (2007): 133–83.

—— 'On the Possibility of a Purely Natural End for Man', *The Thomist* 64 (2000): 211–37.

—— Review of *Heart of the World, Center of the Church*, by David L. Schindler, *Crisis* (June 1997).

—— 'St. Thomas Aquinas through the Analytic Looking-Glass', *The Thomist* 65 (2001): 259–300.

—— *The Teleological Grammar of the Moral Act*, Naples, FL: Sapientia Press, 2007.

Löwith, Karl. *From Hegel to Nietzsche: The Revolution in Nineteenth-Century Thought*, translated by David E. Green. New York: Columbia University Press, 1991.

MacIntyre, Alasdair. *Dependent Rational Animals: Why Human Beings Need the Virtues*, Chicago: Open Court, 1999.

—— 'Moral Relativism, Truth and Justification', in *Moral Truth and Moral Tradition: Essays in Honor of Peter Geach and Elizabeth Anscombe*, edited by Luke Gormally, Portland, OR: Four Courts Press, 1994, 6–24.

—— *Three Rival Versions of Moral Enquiry: Encyclopedia, Genealogy, and Tradition*, Notre Dame, IN: University of Notre Dame Press, 1990.

—— *Whose Justice? Which Rationality?* Notre Dame, IN: University of Notre Dame Press, 1988.

Manent, Pierre. *The City of Man*, translated by Marc A. LePain, Princeton: Princeton University Press, 1998.

Marion, Jean-Luc. 'The Place of the *Objections* in the Development of Cartesian Metaphysics', in *Descartes and His Contemporaries: Meditations, Objections, and Replies*, edited by Roger Ariew and Marjorie Green, Chicago: University of Chicago Press, 1995, 7–20.

Maritain, Jacques. *The Rights of Man and Natural Law*, translated by Doris C. Anson. New York: Gordian Press, 1971.

Marrone, Steven P. *The Light of Thy Countenance: Science and Knowledge of God in the Thirteenth Century*, Leiden: Brill, 2000.

Martens, John W. *One God, One Law: Philo of Alexandria on the Mosaic and Greco-Roman Law*, Leiden: Brill, 2003.

Matera, Frank J. *New Testament Ethics: The Legacies of Jesus and Paul*, Louisville, KY: Westminster John Knox Press, 1996.

Maurer, Armand A., editor. *St. Thomas Aquinas 1274–1974: Commemorative Studies*, vol. 1, Toronto: Pontifical Institute of Mediaeval Studies, 1974.

McAleer, G. J. *Ecstatic Morality and Sexual Politics: A Catholic and Antitotalitarian Theory of the Body*, New York: Fordham University Press, 2005.

McInerny, Daniel. *The Difficult Good: A Thomistic Approach to Moral Conflict and Human Happiness*, New York: Fordham University Press, 2006.

McInerny, Ralph. *Aquinas on Human Action*, Washington, DC: Catholic University of America Press, 1992.

—— 'Foreword', in Fulvio Di Blasi, *God and the Natural Law: A Rereading of Thomas Aquinas*, translated by David Thunder, South Bend, IN: St Augustine's Press, 2006.

—— *Implicit Moral Knowledge*, edited by Fulvio Di Blasi, Rubbettino: Soveria Mannelli, 2006.

McInerny, Ralph. *Praeambula Fidei: Thomism and the God of the Philosophers*, Washington, DC: Catholic University of America Press, 2006.

—— 'Thomistic Natural Law and Aristotelian Philosophy', in *St. Thomas Aquinas and the Natural Law Tradition: Contemporary Perspectives*, edited by John Goyette, Mark S. Latkovic, and Richard S. Myers, Washington, DC: Catholic University of America Press, 2004, 25–39.

McKeever, Martin, CSSR. 'God's Justice? Right Reason? Justice and Rationality in Catholic Social Teaching in the Light of Alasdair MacIntyre's Conception of Traditions of Enquiry', *Studia Moralia* 43 (2005): 297–317.

Michalson, Gordon E., Jr. *Kant and the Problem of God*, Oxford: Blackwell, 1999.

Milbank, John. 'The Gospel of Affinity', in *The Strange New World of the Gospel: Re-Evangelizing in the Postmodern World*, edited by Carl E. Braaten and Robert W. Jenson, Grand Rapids, MI: Eerdmans, 2002, 1–20.

—— *The Suspended Middle: Henri de Lubac and the Debate concerning the Supernatural*, Grand Rapids, MI: Eerdmans, 2005.

Miller, Fred D., Jr. 'Aristotle on Natural Law and Justice', in *A Companion to Aristotle's Politics*, edited by David Keyt and Fred D. Miller, Jr., Oxford: Blackwell, 1991, 279–306.

Mintz, Samuel I. *The Hunting of Leviathan*, Cambridge: Cambridge University Press, 1962.

Mirus, Christopher V. 'Aristotle's *Agathon*', *Review of Metaphysics* 57 (2004): 515–36.

Murphy, Nancy, Brad J. Kallenberg, and Mark Thiessen Nation, editors, *Virtues and Practices in the Christian Tradition: Christian Ethics after MacIntyre* (1997), Notre Dame, IN: University of Notre Dame Press, 2003.

Murray, John Courtney, SJ. 'The Problem of Mr. Rawls's Problem', in *Law and Philosophy: A Symposium*, edited by Sidney Hook, New York: New York University Press, 1964, 29–34.

—— *We Hold These Truths: Catholic Reflections on the American Proposition* (1960), Lanham, MA: Sheed & Ward, 1988.

Nietzsche, Friedrich. *On the Advantage and Disadvantage of History for Life*, translated by Peter Preuss (1874), Indianapolis, IN: Hackett, 1980.

Novak, David. *The Election of Israel: The Idea of the Chosen People*, Cambridge: Cambridge University Press, 1995.

—— *Jewish–Christian Dialogue: A Jewish Justification*, Oxford: Oxford University Press, 1989.

—— 'Maimonides and Aquinas on Natural Law', in *St. Thomas Aquinas and the Natural Law Tradition*, edited by John Goyette, Mark S. Latkovic, and

Richard S. Myers, Washington, DC: Catholic University of America Press, 2004, 43–65.

—— *Natural Law in Judaism*, Cambridge: Cambridge University Press, 1998.

—— *Talking with Christians: Musings of a Jewish Theologian*, Grand Rapids, MI: Eerdmans, 2005.

O'Regan, Cyril. *Gnostic Return in Modernity*, Albany, NY: State University of New York Press, 2001.

—— *The Heterodox Hegel*, Albany, NY: State University of New York Press, 1994.

Osborne, Thomas M., Jr. *Love of Self and Love of God in Thirteenth-Century Ethics*, Notre Dame, IN: University of Notre Dame Press, 2005.

—— 'Ockham as a Divine-Command Theorist', *Religious Studies* 41 (2005): 1–22.

Ouellet, Marc. 'The Foundations of Ethics According to Hans Urs von Balthasar', *Communio* 17 (1990): 379–401.

Pangle, Thomas L. *Political Philosophy and the God of Abraham*, Baltimore, MD: Johns Hopkins University Press, 2003.

Parsons, Susan F. 'Concerning Natural Law: The Turn in American Aquinas Scholarship', in *Contemplating Aquinas: On the Varieties of Interpretation*, edited by Fergus Kerr, OP, London: SCM Press, 2003, 163–83.

Perdue, Leo G. *Wisdom and Creation: The Theology of Wisdom Literature*, Nashville, TN: Abingdon Press, 1994.

Petry, R. C. 'The Social Character of Heavenly Beatitude According to the Thought of St. Thomas Aquinas', *The Thomist* 7 (1944): 65–79.

Pinckaers, Servais, OP. *The Pinckaers Reader: Renewing Thomistic Moral Theology*, edited by John Berkman and Craig Steven Titus, Washington, DC: Catholic University of America Press, 2005.

—— *The Sources of Christian Ethics*, 3rd edn., translated by Mary Thomas Noble, OP (1985), Washington, DC: Catholic University of America Press, 1995.

Pius XI, Pope. *Mit Brennender Sorge*, in *Principles for Peace: Selections from Papal Documents, Leo XIII to Pius XII*, edited by Harry C. Koenig, Washington, DC: National Catholic Welfare Conference, 1943.

Pope, Stephen J., editor. *The Ethics of Aquinas*, Washington, DC: Georgetown University Press, 2002.

Popkin, Richard. *The History of Scepticism: From Savonarola to Bayle*, rev. edn., Oxford: Oxford University Press, 2003.

Porter, Jean. *Nature as Reason: A Thomistic Theory of the Natural Law*, Grand Rapids, MI: Eerdmans, 2005.

—— 'Reason, Nature, and the End of Human Life: A Consideration of John Finnis's *Aquinas*', *Journal of Religion* 80 (2000): 476–84.

Porter, Jean. Review of *Natural Law and Practical Reason* by Martin Rhonheimer, *Theological Studies* 62 (2001): 851–3.

Provan, Iain. ' "All These I Have Kept Since I Was a Boy" (Luke 18:21): Creation, Covenant, and the Commandments of God', *Ex Auditu* 17 (2001): 31–46.

Putnam, Hilary, *The Collapse of the Fact/Value Dichotomy and Other Essays*, Cambridge, MA: Harvard University Press, 2002.

Ratzinger, Joseph, and Marcello Pera. *Without Roots: The West, Relativism, Christianity, Islam*, translated by Michael F. Moore, New York: Basic Books, 2006.

Rawls, John. 'Legal Obligation and the Duty of Fair Play', in *Law and Philosophy: A Symposium*, edited by Sidney Hook, New York: New York University Press, 1964, 3–18.

Reimers, Adrian. 'Karol Wojtyla on the Natural Moral Order', *National Catholic Bioethics Quarterly* 4 (2004): 317–34.

Rhonheimer, Martin. 'The Cognitive Structure of the Natural Law and the Truth of Subjectivity', *The Thomist* 67 (2003): 1–44.

—— 'Contraception, Sexual Behavior, and Natural Law: Philosophical Foundation of the Norm of *Humanae Vitae*', *The Linacre Quarterly* 56 (1989): 20–57.

—— *Die Perspektive der Moral: Philosophische Grundlagen der Tugendethik*, Berlin: Akademie Verlag, 2001.

—— 'The Moral Significance of Pre-Rational Nature in Aquinas: A Reply to Jean Porter (and Stanley Hauerwas)', *American Journal of Jurisprudence* 48 (2003): 253–80.

—— *Natural Law and Practical Reason: A Thomist View of Moral Autonomy*, translated by Gerald Malsbary (German 1987), New York: Fordham University Press, 2000.

—— 'The Perspective of the Acting Person and the Nature of Practical Reason: The "Object of the Human Act" in Thomistic Anthropology of Action', *Nova et Vetera* 2 (2004): 461–516.

—— *La prospettiva della morale: Fondamenti dell'etica filosofica*, Rome: Armando, 1994.

—— *Praktische Vernunft und Vernünftigkeit der Praxis: Handlungstheorie bei Thomas von Aquin in ihrer Entstehung aus dem Problemkontext der Aristotelischen Ethik*, Berlin: Akademie Verlag, 1994.

—— 'The Truth about Condoms', *The Tablet* 258.8545 (10 July 2004): 10–11.

Ricken, Friedo. 'Naturrecht I: Altkirchliche, mittelalterliche und römisch-katholische Interpretationen', in *Theologische Realenzyklopädie*, Berlin: de Gruyter, 1977.

Rigali, Norbert J., SJ. 'Artificial Birth Control: An Impasse Revisited', *Theological Studies* 47 (1986): 681–90.

Rist, John. *Real Ethics: Rethinking the Foundations of Morality*, Cambridge: Cambridge University Press, 2002.

—— *On Inoculating Moral Philosophy against God*, Marquette: Marquette University Press, 2000.

Rommen, Heinrich A. *The Natural Law: A Study in Legal and Social History and Philosophy*, translated by Thomas R. Hanley, OSB (German 1936, 1947), Indianapolis, IN: Liberty Fund, 1998.

Rousseau, Jean-Jacques. *The Basic Political Writings*, translated and edited by Donald A. Cress, Indianapolis, IN: Hackett, 1987.

—— 'Discourse on the Origin of Inequality' (1754) in idem, *The Basic Political Writings*, translated and edited by Donald A. Cress. Indianapolis, IN: Hackett, 1987.

Sandnes, Karl Olav. *Belly and Body in the Pauline Epistles*, Cambridge: Cambridge University Press, 2002.

Schindler, David L. 'Charity, Justice, and the Church's Activity in the World', *Communio* 33 (2006): 346–67.

—— 'Christology and the *Imago Dei*: Interpreting *Gaudium et Spes*', *Communio* 23 (1996): 156–84.

—— 'Religion and Secularity in a Culture of Abstraction: On the Integrity of Space, Time, Matter, and Motion', in *The Strange New World of the Gospel: Re-Evangelizing in the Postmodern World*, edited by Carl E. Braaten and Robert W. Jenson, Grand Rapids, MI: Eerdmans, 2002.

—— 'Religious Freedom, Truth, and American Liberalism: Another Look at John Courtney Murray', *Communio* 21 (1994): 696–741.

—— 'The Significance of World and Culture for Moral Theology: *Veritatis Splendor* and the "Nuptial-Sacramental" Nature of the Body', *Communio* 31 (2004): 111–42.

Schneewind, Jerome B. *The Invention of Autonomy: A History of Modern Moral Philosophy*, Cambridge: Cambridge University Press, 1998.

—— 'Locke's Moral Philosophy', in *The Cambridge Companion to Locke*, edited by Vere Chappell, Cambridge: Cambridge University Press, 1994, 199–225.

Schockenhoff, Eberhard. *Natural Law and Human Dignity: Universal Ethics in an Historical World*, translated by Brian McNeil, Washington, DC: Catholic University of America Press, 2003.

Schreiner, Susan E. 'Calvin's Use of Natural Law', in *A Preserving Grace: Protestants, Catholics, and Natural Law*, edited by Michael Cromartie, Grand Rapids, MI: Eerdmans, 1997, 51–76.

Schumacher, Michele M., editor. *Women in Christ: Toward a New Feminism,* Grand Rapids, MI: Eerdmans, 2004.

Schürmann, Heinz, Joseph Cardinal Ratzinger, and Hans Urs von Balthasar. *Principles of Christian Morality*, translated by Graham Harrison (1975), San Francisco: Ignatius Press, 1986.

Scruton, Roger, Peter Singer, Christopher Janaway, and Michael Tanner. 'Hegel', in *German Philosophers: Kant, Hegel, Schopenhauer, Nietzsche*, Oxford: Oxford University Press, 1997.

Secada, Jorge. *Cartesian Metaphysics: The Late Scholastic Origins of Modern Philosophy*, Cambridge: Cambridge University Press, 2000.

Seitz, Christopher R. 'The Ten Commandments: Positive and Natural Law and the Covenants Old and New—Christian Use of the Decalogue and Moral Law', in *I Am the Lord Your God: Christian Reflections on the Ten Commandments*, edited by Carl E. Braaten and Christopher R. Seitz, Grand Rapids, MI: Eerdmans, 2005, 18–38.

Sentis, Laurent. 'La lumière dont nous faisons usage. La règle de la raison et la loi divine selon Thomas d'Aquin', *Revue des sciences philosophiques et théologiques* 79 (1995): 49–69.

Simon, Anthony O., editor. *Acquaintance with the Absolute*, New York: Fordham University Press, 1998.

Simon, Yves R. *The Tradition of Natural Law: A Philosopher's Reflections* (1965), New York: Fordham University Press, 1992.

Singer, Peter. 'Hegel', in Roger Scruton *et al.*, *German Philosophers: Kant, Hegel, Schopenhauer, Nietzsche*, Oxford: Oxford University Press, 1997, 147–50.

Smith, Janet E. 'The Morality of Condom Use by HIV-Infected Spouses', *The Thomist* 70 (2006): 27–69.

Sokolowski, Robert. 'What Is Natural Law? Human Purposes and Natural Ends', *The Thomist* 68 (2004): 507–29.

Spade, Paul Vincent, editor. *The Cambridge Companion to Ockham*, Cambridge: Cambridge University Press, 1999.

Stanton, Graham. 'What Is the Law of Christ?' *Ex Auditu* 17 (2001): 47–59.

Stout, Jeffrey. 'Truth, Natural Law, and Ethical Theory', in *Natural Law Theory: Contemporary Essays*, edited by Robert P. George, Oxford: Oxford University Press, 1992, 71–102.

Strauss, Leo. *An Introduction to Political Philosophy: Ten Essays by Leo Strauss*, edited by Hilail Gildin, Detroit: Wayne State University Press, 1989.

——*Natural Right and History*, Chicago: University of Chicago Press, 1953.

—— *The Political Philosophy of Thomas Hobbes: Its Basis and Genesis*, 2nd edn., Chicago: University of Chicago Press, 1952.

—— *Studies in Platonic Political Philosophy*, Chicago: University of Chicago Press, 1983.

Taylor, Charles. *Sources of the Self: The Making of Modern Identity*, Cambridge, MA: Harvard University Press, 1989.

Tierney, Brian. *The Idea of Natural Rights: Studies on Natural Rights, Natural Law, and Church Law 1150–1625* (1997), Grand Rapids, MI: Eerdmans, 2001.

—— 'Villey, Ockham and the Origin of Individual Rights', in *The Weightier Matters of the Law: Essays on Law and Religion*, edited by John Witte, Jr., and Frank S. Alexander, Atlanta, GA: Scholars Press, 1988, 1–31.

Toner, Christopher. 'Angelic Sin in Aquinas and the Genesis of Some Central Objections to Contemporary Virtue Ethics', *The Thomist* 69 (2005): 79–125.

Tonneau, J., OP. 'The Teaching of the Thomist Tract on Law', *The Thomist* 34 (1970): 13–83.

Torrell, Jean-Pierre, OP. 'Nature et grace chez Thomas d'Aquin', *Revue Thomiste* 101 (2001): 167–202.

—— *Saint Thomas Aquinas*, translated by Robert Royal, 2 vols., Washington, DC: Catholic University of America Press, 2003.

Tuck, Richard. *Natural Rights Theories: Their Origin and Development*, Cambridge: Cambridge University Press, 1979.

Twomey, D. Vincent. 'Moral Renewal Through Renewed Moral Reasoning', *Josephinum Journal of Theology* 10 (2003): 210–29.

Van der Ploeg, J. P. M., OP. 'Le traité de saint Thomas de la loi ancienne', in *Lex et Libertas*, edited by Leo Elders, SVD, and K. Hedwig, Vatican City: Libreria Editrice Vaticana, 1987, 185–99.

Veatch, Henry B. *Swimming Against the Current in Contemporary Philosophy*, Washington, DC: Catholic University of America Press, 1990.

Verhey, Allen. *Remembering Jesus: Christian Community, Scripture, and the Moral Life*, Grand Rapids, MI: Eerdmans, 2002.

Villey, Michel. *Le droit et les droits de l'homme*, Paris: Presses Universitaires de France, 1983.

—— *La formation de la pensée juridique moderne*, 4th edn., Paris: Montchrestien, 1975.

Vogel, Steven. *Against Nature: The Concept of Nature in Critical Theory*, Albany, NY: State University of New York Press, 1996.

Von Balthasar, Hans Urs. *The Christian State of Life*, translated by Sr. Mary Frances McCarthy, San Francisco: Ignatius Press, 1983.

—— *The Glory of the Lord: A Theological Aesthetics*, vol. 4: *The Realm of Metaphysics in Antiquity*, translated by Brian McNeil, CRV, Andrew Louth, John Saward, Rowan Williams, and Oliver Davies (1967) San Francisco: Ignatius Press, 1989.

—— 'Nine Propositions on Christian Ethics', in Heinz Schürmann, Joseph Cardinal Ratzinger, and Hans Urs von Balthasar, *Principles of Christian Morality*, translated by Graham Harrison (1975) San Francisco: Ignatius Press, 1986.

—— *Unless You Become Like This Child*, translated by Erasmo Leiva-Merikakis. San Francisco: Ignatius Press, 1991.

Von Hartmann, Eduard. *Philosophie des Unbewußten*, Berlin, 1869.

Waldstein, Michael. 'Dietrich von Hildebrand and St. Thomas Aquinas on Goodness and Happiness', *Nova et Vetera* 1 (2003): 403–64.

—— Introduction to Pope John Paul II, *Theology of the Body*, translated by Michael Waldstein, Boston: Pauline Books and Media, 2006.

Wannenwetsch, Bernd. 'Intrinsically Evil Acts; or: Why Euthanasia and Abortion Cannot Be Justified', in *Ecumenical Ventures in Ethics: Protestants Engage Pope John Paul II's Moral Encyclicals*, edited by Reinhard Hütter and Theodor Dieter, Grand Rapids, MI: Eerdmans, 1998, 185–215.

—— 'You Shall Not Kill—What Does It Take? Why We Need the Other Commandments if We Are to Abstain from Killing', in *I Am the Lord Your God: Christian Reflection on the Ten Commandments*, edited by Carl E. Braaten and Christopher R. Seitz, Grand Rapids, MI: Eerdmans, 2005, 148–74.

Webster, John, editor. *The Cambridge Companion to Karl Barth*, Cambridge: Cambridge University Press, 2000.

—— *Word and Church: Essays in Christian Dogmatics*, Edinburgh: T. & T. Clark, 2001.

Weinandy, Thomas G., OFM Cap., Daniel A. Keating, and John P. Yocum, editors. *Aquinas on Doctrine*, New York: T. & T. Clark, 2004.

Weinreb, Lloyd L. *Natural Law and Justice*, Cambridge, MA: Harvard University Press, 1987.

Welch, Lawrence J. 'Christ, the Moral Law, and the Teaching Authority of the Magisterium', *Irish Theological Quarterly* 64 (1999): 16–28.

—— 'Faith and Reason: The Unity of the Moral Law in Christ', *Irish Theological Quarterly* 66 (2001): 249–58.

Westberg, Daniel. 'The Reformed Tradition and Natural Law', in *A Preserving Grace: Protestants, Catholics, and Natural Law*, edited by Michael Cromartie, Grand Rapids, MI: Eerdmans, 1997, 103–17.

—— 'The Relation Between Positive and Natural Law in Aquinas', *Journal of Law and Religion* 11 (1994–5): 1–22.

—— 'The Relation of Law and Practical Reason in Aquinas', in *The Future of Thomism*, edited by Deal Hudson and Dennis Moran, Mishawaka, IN: American Maritain Association, 1992, 279–90.

—— *Right Practical Reason: Aristotle, Action, and Prudence in Aquinas*, Oxford: Clarendon Press, 1994.

Westphal, Kenneth. 'The Basic Context and Structure of Hegel's *Philosophy of Right*', in *The Cambridge Companion to Hegel*, edited by Frederick C. Beiser, Cambridge: Cambridge University Press, 1993.

Wheeler, Sondra. 'Creation, Community, Discipleship: Remembering Why We Care about Sex', *Ex Auditu* 17 (2001): 60–72.

Witherington, Ben, III. *Jesus the Sage: The Pilgrimage of Wisdom*, Minneapolis, MN: Fortress Press, 1994.

—— *John's Wisdom: A Commentary on the Fourth Gospel*, Louisville, KY: Westminster John Knox Press, 1995.

Witte, John, Jr., and Frank S. Alexander, editors. *The Teachings of Modern Christianity on Law, Politics, and Human Nature*, vol. 1, New York: Columbia University Press, 2006.

Witte, John, Jr., and Frank S. Alexander, editors. *The Weightier Matters of the Law: Essays on Law and Religion*, Atlanta, GA: Scholars Press, 1988.

Index